C000217254

VANISHING
ENGLAND

VANISHING ENGLAND

P H DITCHFIELD & FRED ROE

BRACKEN BOOKS

LONDON

PUBLISHER'S NOTE

Vanishing England was first published in 1910 and reflects the author's concerns for what he then saw as the decline in traditional English life and customs. Today, some eighty years later, much of what the author wrote about has already taken place. The publisher's intentions in reprinting this volume is to provide a window into the past and allow the reader to experience not only the glories of English cultural heritage, but also the concerns which were prevalent at that time.

This edition published in 1993 by Studio Editions Ltd
Princess House, 50 Eastcastle Street London WIN 7AP, England

Copyright © this edition Studio Editions 1993

ISBN 1 85891 048 X
Printed in Czechoslovakia

CONTENTS

The George Inn, Norton St. Philip, Somerset

LIST OF ILLUSTRATIONS

VANISHING ENGLAND

LIST OF ILLUSTRATIONS

VANISHING ENGLAND

VANISHING ENGLAND

CHAPTER I

INTRODUCTION

THIS book is intended not to raise fears but to record facts. We wish to describe with pen and pencil those features of England which are gradually disappearing, and to preserve the memory of them. It may be said that we have begun our quest too late; that so much has already vanished that it is hardly worth while to record what is left. Although much has gone, there is still, however, much remaining that is good, that reveals the artistic skill and taste of our forefathers, and recalls the wonders of old-time. It will be our endeavour to tell of the old country houses that Time has spared, the cottages that grace the village green, the stern grey walls that still guard some few of our towns, the old moot halls and public buildings. We shall see the old-time farmers and rustics gathering together at fair and market, their games and sports and merry-makings, and whatever relics of old English life have been left for an artist and scribe of the twentieth century to record.

Our age is an age of progress. *Altiora peto* is its motto. The spirit of progress is in the air, and lures its votaries on to higher flights. Sometimes they discover that they have been following a mere will-o'-the-wisp, that leads them into bog and quagmire whence no escape is possible. The England of a century, or even of half a century ago,

I

has vanished, and we find ourselves in the midst of a busy, bustling world that knows no rest or peace. Inventions tread upon each other's heels in one long vast bewildering procession. We look back at the peaceful reign of the pack-horse, the rumbling wagon, the advent of the merry coaching days, the "Lightning" and the "Quicksilver," the chaining of the rivers with locks and bars, the network of canals that spread over the whole country ; and then the first shriek of the railway engine startled the echoes of the countryside, a poor powerless thing that had to be pulled up the steep gradients by a chain attached to a big stationary engine at the summit. But it was the herald of the doom of the old-world England. Highways and coaching roads, canals and rivers, were abandoned and deserted. The old coachmen, once lords of the road, ended their days in the poorhouse, and steam, almighty steam, ruled everywhere.

Now the wayside inns wake up again with the bellow of the motor-car, which like a hideous monster rushes through the old-world villages, startling and killing old slow-footed rustics and scampering children, dogs and hens, and clouds of dust strive in very mercy to hide the view of the terrible rushing demon. In a few years' time the air will be conquered, and aeroplanes, balloons, flying-machines and air-ships, will drop down upon us from the skies and add a new terror to life.

> Not in vain the distance beacons.   Forward, forward let us range,
> Let the great world spin for ever down the ringing grooves of change.

Life is for ever changing, and doubtless everything is for the best in this best of possible worlds; but the antiquary may be forgiven for mourning over the destruction of many of the picturesque features of bygone times and revelling in the recollections of the past. The half-educated and the progressive—I attach no political meaning to the term—delight in their present environment, and care not to inquire too deeply into the origin of things ; the study of evolution and development is outside their sphere; but yet, as Dean Church once wisely said, "In our eagerness for improvement it concerns us to be on our guard against the temptation of thinking that we can have the fruit or the flower, and yet destroy the root. . . . It concerns us that we do not despise our birthright and cast away our heritage of gifts and of powers, which we may lose, but not recover."

Every day witnesses the destruction of some old link with the past life of the people of England. A stone here, a buttress there—it matters not; these are of no consequence to the innovator or the iconoclast. If it may be our privilege to prevent any further spoliation of the heritage of Englishmen, if we can awaken any respect or reverence for the work of our forefathers, the labours of both artist and author will not have been in vain. Our heritage has been sadly diminished, but it has not yet altogether disappeared, and it is our object to try to record some of those objects of interest which are so fast perishing and vanishing from our view, in order that the remembrance of all the treasures that our country possesses may not disappear with them.

The beauty of our English scenery has in many parts of the country entirely vanished, never to return. Coal-pits, blasting furnaces, factories, and railways have converted once smiling landscapes and pretty villages into an inferno of black smoke, hideous mounds of ashes, huge mills with lofty chimneys belching forth clouds of smoke that kills vegetation and covers the leaves of trees and plants with exhalations. I remember attending at Oxford a lecture delivered by the late Mr. Ruskin. He produced a charming drawing by Turner of a beautiful old bridge spanning a clear stream, the banks of which were clad with trees and foliage. The sun shone brightly, and the sky was blue, with fleeting clouds. "This is what you are doing with your scenery," said the lecturer, as he took his palette and brushes; he began to paint on the glass that covered the picture, and in a few minutes the scene was transformed. Instead of the beautiful bridge a hideous iron girder structure spanned the stream, which was no longer pellucid and clear, but black as the Styx ; instead of the trees arose a monstrous mill with a tall chimney vomiting black smoke that spread in heavy clouds, hiding the sun and the blue sky. "That it what you are doing with your scenery," concluded Mr. Ruskin —a true picture of the penalty we pay for trade, progress,

Rural Tenements, Capel, Surrey

and the pursuit of wealth. We are losing faith in the testimony of our poets and painters to the beauty of the English landscape which has inspired their art, and much of the charm of our scenery in many parts has vanished. We happily have some of it left still where factories are not, some interesting objects that artists love to paint. It is well that they should be recorded before they too pass away.

Old houses of both peer and peasant and their contents are sooner or later doomed to destruction. Historic mansions full of priceless treasures amassed by succeeding generations of old families fall a prey to relentless fire. Old panelled rooms and the ancient floor-timbers understand not the latest experiments in electric lighting, and yield themselves to the flames with scarce a struggle. Our forefathers were content with hangings to keep out the draughts and open fireplaces to keep them warm. They were a hardy race, and feared not a touch or breath of cold. Their degenerate sons must have an elaborate heating apparatus, which again distresses the old timbers of the house and fires their hearts of oak. Our forefathers, indeed, left behind them a terrible legacy of danger— that beam in the chimney, which has caused the destruction of many country houses. Perhaps it was not so great a source of danger in the days of the old wood fires. It is deadly enough when huge coal fires burn in the grates. It is a dangerous, subtle thing. For days, or even for a week or two, it will smoulder and smoulder; and then at last it will blaze up, and the old house with all its precious contents is wrecked.

The power of the purse of American millionaires also tends greatly to the vanishing of much that is English— the treasures of English art, rare pictures and books, and even of houses. Some nobleman or gentleman, through the extravagance of himself or his ancestors, or on account of the pressure of death duties, finds himself impoverished. Some of our great art dealers hear of his unhappy state, and knowing that he has some fine paintings—a Vandyke or a Romney—offer him twenty-five or thirty thousand pounds for a work of art. The temptation proves irresistible. The picture is sold, and soon finds its way into the gallery of a rich American, no one in England having the power or the good taste to purchase it. We spend our money in other ways. The following conversation was overheard at Christie's: "Here is a beautiful thing; you should buy it," said the speaker to

a newly fledged baronet. "I'm afraid I can't afford it,"
replied the baronet. "Not afford it?" replied his companion. "It will cost you infinitely less than a baronetcy
and do you infinitely more credit." The new baronet
seemed rather offended. At the great art sales rare folios

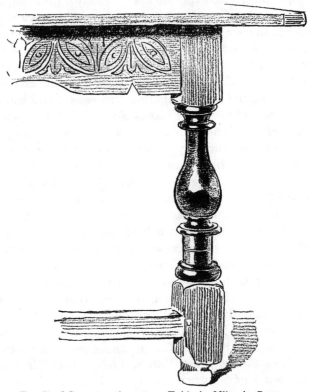

Detail of Seventeenth-century Table in Milton's Cottage,
Chalfont St. Giles

of Shakespeare, pictures, Sèvres, miniatures from English
houses are put up for auction, and of course find their
way to America. Sometimes our cousins from across the
Atlantic fail to secure their treasures. They have striven
very eagerly to buy Milton's cottage at Chalfont St.
Giles, for transportation to America ; but this effort
has happily been successfully resisted. The carved

table in the cottage was much sought after, and was
with difficulty retained against an offer of £150.   An
old window of fifteenth-century workmanship in an old
house at Shrewsbury was nearly exploited by an enterprising American for the sum of £250; and some
years ago an application was received by the Home
Secretary for permission to unearth the body of William
Penn, the founder of Pennsylvania, from its grave in the
burial-ground of Jordans, near Chalfont St. Giles, and
transport it to Philadelphia.   This action was successfully
opposed by the trustees of the burial-ground, but it was
considered expedient to watch the ground for some time
to guard against the possibility of any illicit attempts at
removal.

It was reported that an American purchaser had been
more successful at Ipswich, where in 1907 a Tudor house
and corner-post, it was said, had been secured by a London
firm for shipment to America.   We are glad to hear that
this report was incorrect, that the purchaser was an English
lord, who re-erected the house in his park.

Wanton destruction is another cause of the disappearance of old mansions.   Fashions change even in house-
building.   Many people prefer new lamps to old ones,
though the old ones alone can summon genii and recall
the glories of the past, the associations of centuries of
family life, and the stories of ancestral prowess.   Sometimes fashion decrees the downfall of old houses.   Such
a fashion raged at the beginning of the last century,
when every one wanted a brand-new house built after the
Palladian style ; and the old weather-beaten pile that had
sheltered the family for generations, and was of good
old English design with nothing foreign or strange about
it, was compelled to give place to a new-fangled dwelling-place which was neither beautiful nor comfortable.
Indeed, a great wit once advised the builder of one
of these mansions to hire a room on the other side of the
road and spend his days looking at his Palladian house,
but to be sure not to live there.

Many old houses have disappeared on account of the loyalty of their owners, who were unfortunate enough to reside within the regions harassed by the Civil War. This was especially the case in the county of Oxford. Still you may see avenues of venerable trees that lead to no house. The old mansion or manor-house has vanished. Many of them were put in a posture of defence. Earthworks and moats, if they did not exist before, were hastily constructed, and some of these houses were bravely defended by a competent and brave garrison, and were thorns in the sides of the Parliamentary army. Upon the triumph of the latter, revenge suffered not these nests of Malignants to live. Others were so battered and ruinous that they were only fit residences for owls and bats. Some loyal owners destroyed the remains of their homes lest they should afford shelter to the Parliamentary forces. David Walter set fire to his house at Godstow lest it should afford accommodation to the " Rebels." For the same reason Governor Legge burnt the new episcopal palace, which Bancroft had only finished ten years before at Cuddesdon. At the same time Thomas Gardiner burnt his manor-house in Cuddesdon village, and many other houses were so battered that they were left untenanted, and so fell to ruin.[1] Sir Bulstrode Whitelock describes how he slighted the works at Phillis Court, " causing the bulwarks and lines to be digged down, the grafts [i.e. moats] filled, the drawbridge to be pulled up, and all levelled. I sent away the great guns, the granadoes, fireworks, and ammunition, whereof there was good store in the fort. I procured pay for my soldiers, and many of them undertook the service in Ireland." This is doubtless typical of what went on in many other houses. The famous royal manor-house of Woodstock was left battered and deserted, and " haunted," as the readers of *Woodstock* will remember, by an " adroit and humorous royalist named Joe Collins," who frightened the commissioners away by

[1] *History of Oxfordshire*, by J. Meade Falkner.

his ghostly pranks. In 1651 the old house was gutted
and almost destroyed. The war wrought havoc with
the old houses, as it did with the lives and other
possessions of the conquered.

But we are concerned with times less remote, with the
vanishing of historic monuments, of noble specimens of
architecture, and of the humble dwellings of the poor, the

Seventeenth-century Trophy

picturesque cottages by the wayside, which form such
attractive features of the English landscape. We have
only to look at the west end of St. Albans Abbey Church,
which has been " Grimthorped " out of all recognition,
or at the over-restored Lincoln's Inn Chapel, to see
what evil can be done in the name of " Restoration," how
money can be lavishly spent to a thoroughly bad
purpose.

Property in private hands has suffered no less than

many of our public buildings, even when the owner is a lover of antiquity and does not wish to remove and to destroy the objects of interest on his estate. Estate agents are responsible for much destruction. Sir John Stirling Maxwell, Bart., F.S.A., a keen archæologist, tells how an agent on his estate transformed a fine old grim sixteenth-century fortified dwelling, a very perfect specimen of its class, into a house for himself, entirely altering the character of its appearance, adding a lofty oriel and spacious windows with a new door and staircase, while some of the old stones were made to adorn a rockery in the garden. When he was abroad the elaborately contrived entrance for the defence of a square fifteenth-century keep with four square towers at the corners, very curious and complete, were entirely obliterated by a zealous mason. In my own parish I awoke one day to find the old village pound entirely removed by order of an estate agent, and a very interesting stand near the village smithy for fastening oxen when they were shod disappeared one day, the village publican wanting the posts for his pig-sty. County councils sweep away old bridges because they are inconveniently narrow and steep for the tourists' motors, and deans and chapters are not always to be relied upon in regard to their theories of restoration, and squire and parson work sad havoc on the fabrics of old churches when they are doing their best to repair them. Too often they have decided to entirely demolish the old building, the most characteristic feature of the English landscape, with its square grey tower or shapely spire, a tower that is, perhaps, loopholed and battlemented, and tells of turbulent times when it afforded a secure asylum and stronghold when hostile bands were roving the countryside. Within, piscina, ambrey, and rood-loft tell of the ritual of former days. Some monuments of knights and dames proclaim the achievements of some great local family. But all this weighs for nothing in the eyes of the renovating squire and parson. They must have a grand, new, modern church with much architectural pretension and fine decora-

tions which can never have the charm which attaches to
the old building. It has no memories, this new structure.
It has nothing to connect it with the historic past. Besides,
they decree that it must not cost too much. The scheme
of decoration is stereotyped, the construction mechanical.
There is an entire absence of true feeling and of any real
inspiration of devotional art. The design is conventional,
the pattern uniform. The work is often scamped and
hurried, very different from the old method of building.
We note the contrast. The medieval builders were never
in a hurry to finish their work. The old fanes took
centuries to build; each generation doing its share,
chancel or nave, aisle or window, each trying to make the
church as perfect as the art of man could achieve. We
shall see how much of this sound and laborious work has
vanished, a prey to restoration and ignorant renovation.
We shall see the house-breaker at work in rural
hamlet and in country town. Vanishing London we
shall leave severely alone. Its story has been already
told in a large and comely volume by my friend Mr.
Philip Norman. Besides, is there anything that has not
vanished, having been doomed to destruction by the
march of progress, now that Crosby Hall has gone the
way of life in the Great City? A few old halls of the City
companies remain, but most of them have given way to
modern palaces; a few City churches, very few, that
escaped the Great Fire, and every now and again we hear
threatenings against the masterpieces of Wren, and
another City church has followed in the wake of all the
other London buildings on which the destroyer has laid
his hand. The site is so valuable; the modern world of
business presses out the life of these fine old edifices.
They have to make way for new-fangled erections built in
the modern French style with sprawling gigantic figures
with bare limbs hanging on the porticoes which seem to
wonder how they ever got there, and however they were
to keep themselves from falling. London is hopeless!
We can but delve its soil when opportunities occur in

order to find traces of Roman or medieval life. Churches, inns, halls, mansions, palaces, exchanges have vanished, or are quickly vanishing, and we cast off the dust of London streets from our feet and seek more hopeful places.

But even in the sleepy hollows of old England the pulse

Fred Roe

Old Shop, formerly standing in Cliffe
High Street, Lewes

beats faster than of yore, and we shall only just be in time to rescue from oblivion and the house-breaker some of our heritage. Old city walls that have defied the attacks of time and of Cromwell's Ironsides are often in danger from the wiseacres who preside on borough corporations. Town halls picturesque and beautiful in their old age have to make way for the creations of the local architect. Old shops have to be pulled down in order to provide a site for a universal emporium or a motor garage. Nor are buildings the only things that are passing away. The extensive use of motor-cars and highway vandalism are destroying the peculiar beauty of the English roadside. The swift-speeding cars create clouds of white dust which settles upon the hedges and trees, covering them with it and obscuring the wayside flowers and hiding all their attractiveness. Corn and grass are injured and destroyed by the dust clouds. The charm and poetry of the country walk are destroyed by motoring demons, and the wayside cottage-gardens, once the most attractive feature of the English landscape, are ruined. The elder England, too, is vanishing in the modes, habits, and manners of her people. Never was the truth of the old oft-quoted Latin proverb—*Tempora mutantur, et nos mutamur in illis* — so pathetically emphatic as it is to-day. The people are changing in their habits and modes of thought. They no longer take pleasure in the simple joys of their forefathers. Hence in our chronicle of Vanishing England we shall have to refer to some of those strange customs which date back to primeval ages, but which the railways, excursion trains, and the schoolmaster in a few years will render obsolete.

In recording the England that is vanishing the artist's pencil will play a more prominent part than the writer's pen. The graphic sketches that illustrate this book are far more valuable and helpful to the discernment of the things that remain than the most effective descriptions. We have tried together to gather up the fragments that remain that nothing be lost ; and though there may be much that we have not gathered, the examples herein given of some of the treasures that are left may be useful in creating a greater reverence for the work bequeathed to us by our forefathers, and in strengthening the hands of those who would preserve them. Happily we are still able to use the present participle, not the past. It is vanishing England, not vanished, of which we treat; and if we can succeed in promoting an affection for the relics of antiquity that time has spared, our labours will not have been in vain or the object of this book unattained.

Paradise Square, Banbury

CHAPTER II

THE DISAPPEARANCE OF ENGLAND

UNDER this alarming heading, "The Disappearance of England," the *Gaulois* recently published an article by M. Guy Dorval on the erosion of the English coasts. The writer refers to the predictions of certain British men of science that England will one day disappear altogether beneath the waves, and imagines that we British folk are seized by a popular panic. Our neighbours are trembling for the fate of the *entente cordiale*, which would speedily vanish with vanishing England; but they have been assured by some of their savants that the rate of erosion is only one kilometre in a thousand years, and that the danger of total extinction is somewhat remote. Professor Stanislas Meunier, however, declares that our "panic" is based on scientific facts. He tells us that the cliffs of Brighton are now one kilometre farther away from the French coast than in the days of Queen Elizabeth, and that those of Kent are six kilometres farther away than in the Roman period. He compares our island to a large piece of sugar in water, but we may rest assured that before we disappear beneath the waves the period which must elapse would be greater than the longest civilizations known in history. So we may hope to be able to sing "Rule Britannia" for many a long year.

Coast erosion is, however, a serious problem, and has caused the destruction of many a fair town and noble forest that now lie beneath the seas, and the crumbling cliffs on our eastern shore threaten to destroy many a village church and smiling pasture. Fishermen tell you that when storms rage and the waves swell they have heard the bells chiming in the towers long covered by the seas, and nigh the picturesque village of Bosham we were told of a stretch of sea that was called the Park. This as late as the days of Henry VIII was a favourite royal hunting forest, wherein stags and fawns and does disported themselves; now fish are the only prey that can be slain therein.

The Royal Commission on coast erosion relieves our minds somewhat by assuring us that although the sea gains upon the land in many places, the land gains upon the sea in others, and that the loss and gain are more or less balanced. As a matter of area this is true. Most of the land that has been rescued from the pitiless sea is below high-water mark, and is protected by artificial banks. This work of reclaiming land can, of course, only be accomplished in sheltered places, for example, in the great flat bordering the Wash, which flat is formed by the deposit of the rivers of the Fenland, and the seaward face of this region is gradually being pushed forward by the careful processes of enclosure. You can see the various old sea walls which have been constructed from Roman times onward. Some accretions of land have occurred where the sea piles up masses of shingle, unless foolish people cart away the shingle in such quantities that the waves again assert themselves. Sometimes sand silts up as at Southport in Lancashire, where there is the second longest pier in England, a mile in length, from the end of which it is said that on a clear day with a powerful telescope you may perchance see the sea, that a distinguished traveller accustomed to the deserts of Sahara once found it, and that the name Southport is altogether a misnomer, as it is in the north and there is no port at all.

But however much as an Englishman I might rejoice that the actual area of "our tight little island," which after all is not very tight, should not be diminishing, it would be a poor consolation to me, if I possessed land and houses on the coast of Norfolk which were fast slipping into the sea, to know that in the Fenland industrious farmers were adding to their acres. And day by day, year by year, this destruction is going on, and the gradual melting away of land. The attack is not always persistent. It is intermittent. Sometimes the progress of the sea seems to be stayed, and then a violent storm arises and falling cliffs and submerged houses proclaim the sway of the relentless waves. We find that the greatest loss has occurred on the east and southern coasts of our island. Great damage has been wrought all along the Yorkshire sea-board from Bridlington to Kilnsea, and the following districts have been the greatest sufferers : between Cromer and Happisburgh, Norfolk; between Pakefield and South-wold, Suffolk ; Hampton and Herne Bay, and then St. Margaret's Bay, near Dover ; the coast of Sussex, east of Brighton, and the Isle of Wight; the region of Bourne-mouth and Poole ; Lyme Bay, Dorset, and Bridgwater Bay, Somerset.

All along the coast from Yarmouth to Eastbourne, with a few exceptional parts, we find that the sea is gaining on the land by leaps and bounds. It is a coast that is most favourably constructed for coast erosion. There are no hard or firm rocks, no cliffs high enough to give rise to a respectable landslip ; the soil is composed of loose sand and gravels, loams and clays, nothing to resist the assaults of atmospheric action from above or the sea below. At Covehithe, on the Suffolk coast, there has been the greatest loss of land. In 1887 sixty feet was claimed by the sea, and in ten years (1878–87) the loss was at the rate of over eighteen feet a year. In 1895 another heavy loss occurred between Southwold and Covehithe and a new cove formed. Easton Bavent has entirely disappeared, and so have the once prosperous villages of Covehithe, Burgh-next-Walton, and Newton-by-Corton, and the same fate seems to be awaiting Pakefield, Southwold, and other coast-lying towns. Easton Bavent once had such a flourishing fishery that it paid an annual rent of 3110 herrings ; and millions of herrings must have been caught by the fishermen of disappeared Dunwich, which we shall

2

visit presently, as they paid annually "fish-fare" to the clergy of the town 15,377 herrings, besides 70,000 to the royal treasury.

The summer visitors to the pleasant watering-place Felixstowe, named after St. Felix, who converted the East Anglians to Christianity and was their first bishop, that being the place where the monks of the priory of St. Felix in Walton held their annual fair, seldom reflect that the old Saxon burgh was carried away as long ago as 1100 A.D. Hence Earl Bigot was compelled to retire inland and erect his famous castle at Walton. But the sea respected not the proud walls of the baron's stronghold; the strong masonry that girt the keep lies beneath the waves; a heap of stones, called by the rustics Stone Works, alone marks the site of this once powerful castle. Two centuries later the baron's marsh was destroyed by the sea, and eighty acres of land was lost, much to the regret of the monks, who were thus deprived of the rent and tithe corn.

The old chroniclers record many dread visitations of the relentless foe. Thus in 1237 we read: "The sea burst with high tides and tempests of winds, marsh countries near the sea were flooded, herds and flocks perished, and no small number of men were lost and drowned. The sea rose continually for two days and one night." Again in 1251: "On Christmas night there was a great thunder and lightning in Suffolk; the sea caused heavy floods." In much later times Defoe records: "Aldeburgh has two streets, each near a mile long, but its breadth, which was more considerable formerly, is not proportionable, and the sea has of late years swallowed up one whole street." It has still standing close to the shore its quaint picturesque town hall, erected in the fifteenth century. Southwold is now practically an island, bounded on the east by the sea, on the south-west by the Blyth River, on the north-west by Buss Creek. It is only joined to the mainland by a narrow neck of shingle that divides Buss Creek from the sea. I think that I should prefer to hold property

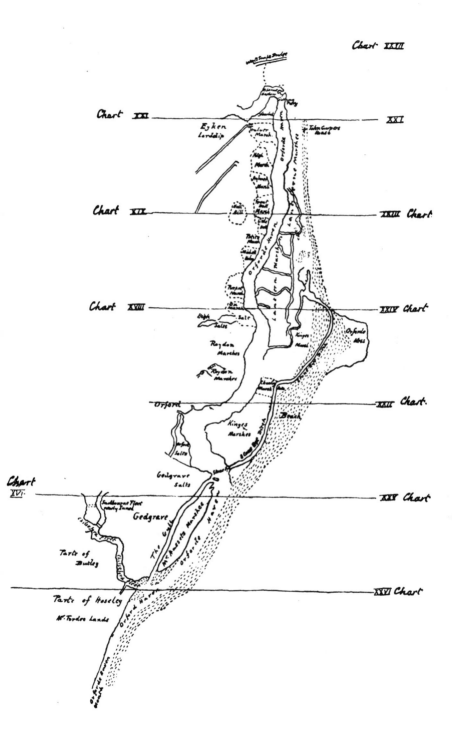

in a more secure region. You invest your savings in stock, and dividends decrease and your capital grows smaller, but you usually have something left. But when your land and houses vanish entirely beneath the waves, the chapter is ended and you have no further remedy except to sue Father Neptune, who has rather a wide beat and may be difficult to find when he is wanted to be served with a summons.

But the Suffolk coast does not show all loss. In the north much land has been gained in the region of Beccles, which was at one time close to the sea, and one of the finest spreads of shingle in England extends from Alde-burgh to Bawdry. This shingle has silted up many a Suffolk port, but it has proved a very effectual barrier against the inroads of the sea. Norden's map of the coast made in 1601[1] shows this wonderful mass of shingle, which has greatly increased since Norden's day. It has been growing in a southerly direction, until the Alde River had until recently an estuary ten miles in length. But in 1907 the sea asserted itself, and " burst through the stony barrier, making a passage for the exit of the river one mile further north, and leaving a vast stretch of shingle and two deserted river-channels as a protection to the Marshes of Hollesley from further inroads of the sea."[2] Formerly the River Alde flowed direct to the sea just south of the town of Aldeburgh. Perhaps some day it may be able to again force a passage near its ancient course or by Havergate Island. This alteration in the course of rivers is very remarkable, and may be observed at Christ Church, Hants.

It is pathetic to think of the historic churches, beautiful villages, and smiling pastures that have been swept away by the relentless sea. There are no less than twelve towns and villages in Yorkshire that have been thus buried, and five in Suffolk. Ravensburgh, in the former

---

[1] It is now in possession of Mr. Kenneth M. Clark, by whose permission the accompanying plan, reproduced from the *Memorials of Old Suffolk*, was made.

[2] *Memorials of Old Suffolk*, edited by V. B. Redstone, p. 226.

county, was once a flourishing seaport. Here landed
Henry IV in 1399, and Edward IV in 1471. It returned
two members to Parliament. An old picture of the place
shows the church, a large cross, and houses; but it has
vanished with the neighbouring villages of Redmare,
Tharlethorp, Frismarch, and Potterfleet, and "left not a
wrack behind." Leland mentions it in 1538, after which
time its place in history and on the map knows it no
more. The ancient church of Kilnsea lost half its fabric
in 1826, and the rest followed in 1831. Alborough Church
and the Castle of Grimston have entirely vanished.
Mapleton Church was formerly two miles from the
sea; it is now on a cliff with the sea at its feet,
awaiting the final attack of the all-devouring enemy.
Nearly a century ago Owthorne Church and churchyard were overwhelmed, and the shore was strewn
with ruins and shattered coffins. On the Tyneside the
destruction has been remarkable and rapid. In the
district of Saltworks there was a house built standing
on the cliff, but it was never finished, and fell a
prey to the waves. At Percy Square an inn and two
cottages have been destroyed. The edge of the cliff in
1827 was eighty feet seaward, and the banks of Percy
Square receded a hundred and eighty feet between the
years 1827 and 1892. Altogether four acres have disappeared. An old Roman building, locally known as
"Gingling Geordie's Hole," and large masses of the
Castle Cliff fell into the sea in the 'eighties. The remains
of the once flourishing town of Seaton, on the Durham
coast, can be discovered amid the sands at low tide. The
modern village has sunk inland, and cannot now
boast of an ancient chapel dedicated to St. Thomas of
Canterbury, which has been devoured by the waves.

Skegness, on the Lincolnshire coast, was a large and
important town; it boasted of a castle with strong fortifications and a church with a lofty spire; it now lies deep
beneath the devouring sea, which no guarding walls
could conquer. Far out at sea, beneath the waves, lies

old Cromer Church, and when storms rage its bells are
said to chime. The churchyard wherein was written the
pathetic ballad "The Garden of Sleep" is gradually
disappearing, and "the graves of the fair women that
sleep by the cliffs by the sea" have been outraged, and
their bodies scattered and devoured by the pitiless waves.

One of the greatest prizes of the sea is the ancient city
of Dunwich, which dates back to the Roman era. The
Domesday Survey shows that it was then a considerable
town having 236 burgesses. It was girt with strong
walls; it possessed an episcopal palace, the seat of the
East Anglian bishopric; it had (so Stow asserts) fifty-two
churches, a monastery, brazen gates, a town hall, hospitals, and the dignity of possessing a mint. Stow tells
of its departed glories, its royal and episcopal palaces,
the sumptuous mansion of the mayor, its numerous
churches and its windmills, its harbour crowded with ship-
ping, which sent forth forty vessels for the king's service
in the thirteenth century. Though Dunwich was an important place, Stow's description of it is rather exag-
gerated. It could never have had more than ten churches
and monasteries. Its "brazen gates" are mythical, though
it had its Lepers' Gate, South Gate, and others. It was
once a thriving city of wealthy merchants and industrious
fishermen. King John granted to it a charter. It suffered from the attacks of armed men as well as from the
ravages of the sea. Earl Bigot and the revolting barons
besieged it in the reign of Edward I. Its decay was
gradual. In 1342, in the parish of St. Nicholas, out of
three hundred houses only eighteen remained. Only
seven out of a hundred houses were standing in the parish
of St. Martin. St. Peter's parish was devastated and de-
populated. It had a small round church, like that at
Cambridge, called the Temple, once the property of the
Knights Templars, richly endowed with costly gifts. This
was a place of sanctuary, as were the other churches in
the city. With the destruction of the houses came also
the decay of the port which no ships could enter. Its

rival, Southwold, attracted the vessels of strangers. The markets and fairs were deserted. Silence and ruin reigned over the doomed town, and the ruined church of All Saints is all that remains of its former glories, save what the storms sometimes toss along the beach for the study and edification of antiquaries.

As we proceed down the coast we find that the sea is still gaining on the land. The old church at Walton-on-the-Naze was swept away, and is replaced by a new one. A flourishing town existed at Reculver, which dates back to the Romans. It was a prosperous place, and had a noble church, which in the sixteenth century was a mile from the sea. Steadily have the waves advanced, until a century ago the church fell into the sea, save two towers which have been preserved by means of elaborate sea-walls as a landmark for sailors.

The fickle sea has deserted some towns and destroyed their prosperity; it has receded all along the coast from Folkestone to the Sussex border, and left some of the famous Cinque Ports, some of which we shall visit again, Lymne, Romney, Hythe, Richborough, Stonor, Sandwich, and Sarre high and dry, with little or no access to the sea. Winchelsea has had a strange career. The old town lies beneath the waves, but a new Winchelsea arose, once a flourishing port, but now deserted and forlorn with the sea a mile away. Rye, too, has been forsaken. It was once an island; now the little Rother stream conveys small vessels to the sea, which looks very far away.

We cannot follow all the victories of the sea. We might examine the inroads made by the waves at Selsea. There stood the first cathedral of the district before Chichester was founded. The building is now beneath the sea, and since Saxon times half of the Selsea Bill has vanished. The village of Selsea rested securely in the centre of the peninsula, but only half a mile now separates it from the sea. Some land has been gained near this projecting headland by an industrious farmer. His farm surrounded a large cove with a narrow mouth through

which the sea poured.   If he could only dam up that
entrance, he thought he could rescue the bed of the cove
and add to his acres.   He bought an old ship and sank
it by the entrance and proceeded to drain.   But a tire-
some storm arose and drove the ship right across the
cove, and the sea poured in again.   By no means dis-

Disused Mooring-Post on bank of the Rother, Rye

couraged, he dammed up the entrance more effectually,
got rid of the water, increased his farm by many acres,
and the old ship makes an admirable cow-shed.
    The Isle of Wight in remote geological periods was
part of the mainland.   The Scilly Isles were once joined
with Cornwall, and were not severed until the fourteenth
century, when by a mighty storm and flood, 140 churches
and villages were destroyed and overwhelmed, and 190
square miles of land carried away.   Much land has been

lost in the Wirral district of Cheshire. Great forests
have been overwhelmed, as the skulls and bones of deer
and horse and fresh-water shell-fish have been frequently
discovered at low tide. Fifty years ago a distance of
half a mile separated Leasowes Castle from the sea ; now
its walls are washed by the waves. The Pennystone, off
the Lancashire coast by Blackpool, tells of a submerged
village and manor, about which cluster romantic legends.

Such is the sad record of the sea's destruction, for which
the industrious reclamation of land, the compensations
wrought by the accumulation of shingle and sand dunes
and the silting of estuaries can scarcely compensate us.
How does the sea work this? There are certain rock-
boring animals, such as the Pholas, which help to decay
the rocks. Each mollusc cuts a series of augur-holes
from two to four inches deep, and so assists in destroying
the bulwarks of England. Atmospheric action, the disintegration of soft rocks by frost and by the attack of the
sea below, all tend in the same direction. But the foolish
action of man in removing shingle, the natural protection
of our coasts, is also very mischievous. There is an instance of this in the Hall Sands and Bee Sands, Devon.
A company a few years ago obtained authority to dredge
both from the foreshore and sea-bed. The Commissioners
of Woods and Forests and the Board of Trade granted
this permission, the latter receiving a royalty of £50 and
the former £150. This occurred in 1896. Soon afterwards a heavy gale arose and caused an immense amount
of damage, the result entirely of this dredging. The company had to pay heavily, and the royalties were returned
to them. This is only one instance out of many which
might be quoted. We are an illogical nation, and our
regulations and authorities are weirdly confused. It appears that the foreshore is under the control of the Board
of Trade, and then a narrow strip of land is ruled over by
the Commissioners of Woods and Forests. Of course
these bodies do not agree ; different policies are pursued
by each, and the coast suffers. Large sums are some-

times spent in coast-defence works.   At Spurn no less
than £37,433 has been spent out of Parliamentary grants,
besides £14,227 out of the Mercantile Marine Fund.
Corporations or county authorities, finding their coasts
being worn away, resolve to protect it.   They obtain a
grant in aid from Parliament, spend vast sums, and often
find their work entirely thrown away, or proving itself
most disastrous to their neighbours.   If you protect one
part of the coast you destroy another.   Such is the rule of
the sea.   If you try to beat it back at one point it will
revenge itself on another.   If only you can cause shingle
to accumulate before your threatened town or homestead,
you know you can make the place safe and secure from
the waves.   But if you stop this flow of shingle you may
protect your own homes, but you deprive your neighbours of this safeguard against the ravages of the sea.   It
was so at Deal.   The good folks of Deal placed groynes
in order to stop the flow of shingle and protect the town.
They did their duty well ; they stopped the shingle and
made a good bulwark against the sea.   With what result ?
In a few years' time they caused the destruction of San-
down, which had been deprived of its natural protection.
Mr. W. Whitaker, F.R.S., who has walked along the
whole coast from Norfolk to Cornwall, besides visiting
other parts of our English shore, and whose contributions
to the Report of the Royal Commission on Coast Erosion
are so valuable, remembers when a boy the Castle of San-
down, which dated from the time of Henry VIII.   It was
then in a sound condition and was inhabited.   Now it is
destroyed, and the batteries farther north have gone too.
The same thing is going on at Dover.   The Admiralty
Pier causes the accumulation of shingle on its west side,
and prevents it from following its natural course in a north-
easterly direction.   Hence the base of the cliffs on the
other side of the pier and harbour is left bare and unpro-
tected ; this aids erosion, and not unfrequently do we hear
of the fall of the chalk cliffs.
    Isolated schemes for the prevention of coast erosion are

of little avail.   They can do no good, and only increase
the waste and destruction of land in neighbouring shores.
Stringent laws should be passed to prevent the taking
away of shingle from protecting beaches, and to prohibit
the ploughing of land near the edge of cliffs, which
greatly assists atmospheric destructive action from above.
The State has recently threatened the abandonment of the
coastguard service.   This would be a disastrous policy.
Though the primary object of coastguards, the prevention
of smuggling, has almost passed away, the old sailors
who act as guardians of our coast-line render valuable
services to the country.   They are most useful in looking
after the foreshore.   They save many lives from wrecked
vessels, and keep watch and ward to guard our shores, and
give timely notice of the advance of a hostile fleet, or of
that ever-present foe which, though it affords some protection for our island home from armed invasion, does
not fail to exact a heavy tithe from the land it guards,
and has destroyed so many once flourishing towns and
villages by its ceaseless attack.

CHAPTER III

OLD WALLED TOWNS

THE destruction of ancient buildings always causes grief and distress to those who love antiquity. It is much to be deplored, but in some cases is perhaps inevitable. Old-fashioned half-timbered shops with small diamond-paned windows are not the most convenient for the display of the elegant fashionable costumes effectively draped on modelled forms. Motor-cars cannot be displayed in antiquated old shops. Hence in modern up-to-date towns these old buildings are doomed, and have to give place to grand emporiums with large plate-glass windows and the refinements of luxurious display. We hope to visit presently some of the old towns and cities which happily retain their ancient beauties, where quaint houses with oversailing upper stories still exist, and with the artist's aid to describe many of their attractions.

Although much of the destruction is, as I have said, inevitable, a vast amount is simply the result of ignorance and wilful perversity. Ignorant persons get elected on town councils—worthy men doubtless, and able men of business, who can attend to and regulate the financial affairs of the town, look after its supply of gas and water, its drainage and tramways ; but they are absolutely ignorant of its history, its associations, of architectural beauty, of anything that is not modern and utilitarian. Unhappily, into the care of such men as these is often confided the custody of historic buildings and priceless treasures, of ruined abbey and ancient walls, of objects consecrated by the lapse of centuries and by the associations of hundreds of years of corporate life ; and it is not surprising that in many cases they betray their trust. They are not interested in such things. "Let bygones be bygones," they say. "We care not for old rubbish." Moreover, they frequently resent interference and instruction. Hence they destroy wholesale what should be preserved, and England is the poorer.

Not long ago the Edwardian wall of Berwick-on-Tweed was threatened with demolition at the hands of those who ought to be its guardians—the Corporation of the town. An official from the Office of Works, when he saw the be-grimed, neglected appearance of the two fragments of this wall near the Bell Tower, with a stagnant pool in the fosse, bestrewed with broken pitchers and rubbish, reported that the Elizabethan walls of the town which were under the direction of the War Department were in excellent condition, whereas the Edwardian masonry was utterly neglected. And why was this relic of the town's former greatness to be pulled down? Simply to clear the site for the erection of modern dwelling-houses. A very strong protest was made against this act of municipal barbarism by learned societies, the Society for the Preservation of Ancient Buildings, and others, and we hope that the hand of the destroyer has been stayed.

Most of the principal towns in England were protected by walls, and the citizens regarded it as a duty to build them and keep them in repair. When we look at some of these fortifications, their strength, their height, their thickness, we are struck by the fact that they were very great achievements, and that they must have been raised with immense labour and gigantic cost. In turbulent and war-like times they were absolutely necessary. Look at some of these triumphs of medieval engineering skill, so strong, so massive, able to defy the attacks of lance and arrow, ram or catapult, and to withstand ages of neglect and the storms of a tempestuous clime. Towers and bastions stood at intervals against the wall at convenient distances, in order that bowmen stationed in them could shoot down any who attempted to scale the wall with ladders anywhere within the distance between the towers. All along the wall there was a protected pathway for the defenders to stand, and machicolations through which boiling oil or

Old Houses built on the Town Wall, Rye

lead, or heated sand could be poured on the heads of the attacking force. The gateways were carefully constructed, flanked by defending towers with a portcullis, and a guard-room overhead with holes in the vaulted roof of the gateway for pouring down inconvenient substances upon the heads of the besiegers. There were several gates, the usual number being four ; but Coventry had twelve, Canterbury six, and Newcastle-on-Tyne seven, besides posterns.

Berwick-upon-Tweed, York, Chester, and Conway have maintained their walls in good condition. Berwick has three out of its four gates still standing. They are called Scotchgate, Shoregate, and Cowgate, and in the last two still remain the original massive wooden gates with their bolts and hinges. The remaining fourth gate, named Bridgate, has vanished. We have alluded to the neglect of the Edwardian wall and its threatened destruction. Conway has a wall a mile and a quarter in length, with twenty-one semicircular towers along its course and three great gateways besides posterns. Edward I built this wall in order to subjugate the Welsh, and also the walls round Carnarvon, some of which survive, and Beaumaris. The name of his master-mason has been preserved, one Henry le Elreton. The muniments of the Corporation of Alnwick prove that often great difficulties arose in the matter of wall-building. Its closeness to the Scottish border rendered a wall necessary. The town was frequently attacked and burnt. The inhabitants obtained a licence to build a wall in 1433, but they did not at once proceed with the work. In 1448 the Scots came and pillaged the town, and the poor burgesses were so robbed and despoiled that they could not afford to proceed with the wall and petitioned the King for aid. Then Letters Patent were issued for a collection to be made for the object, and at last, forty years after the licence was granted, Alnwick got its wall, and a very good wall it was—a mile in circumference, twenty feet in height and six in thickness ; "it had four gateways—Bondgate, Clayport, Pottergate, and Narrowgate. Only the first-named of these is standing. It is three stories in height. Over the central archway is a panel on which was carved the Brabant lion, now almost obliterated. On either side is a semi-octagonal tower. The masonry is composed of huge blocks to which time and weather have given dusky tints. On the front facing

the expected foes the openings are but little more than
arrow-slits ; on that within, facing the town, are well-
proportioned mullioned and transomed windows. The
great ribbed archway is grooved for a portcullis, now removed, and a low doorway on either side gives entrance
to the chambers in the towers. Pottergate was rebuilt in
the eighteenth century and crowns a steep street ; only
four corner-stones marked T indicate the site of Clayport.
No trace of Narrowgate remains." [1]

As the destruction of many of our castles is due to the
action of Cromwell and the Parliament, who caused them
to be "slighted" partly out of revenge upon the loyal
owners who had defended them, so several of our town-
walls were thrown down by order of Charles II at the
Restoration on account of the active assistance which the
townspeople had given to the rebels. The heads of rebels
were often placed on gateways. London Bridge, Lincoln,
Newcastle, York, Berwick, Canterbury, Temple Bar, and
other gates have often been adorned with these gruesome
relics of barbarous punishments.

How were these strong walls ever taken in the days
before gunpowder was extensively used or cannon dis-
charged their devastating shells? Imagine you are present
at a siege. You would see the attacking force advancing
a huge wooden tower, covered with hides and placed on
wheels, towards the walls. Inside this tower were ladders,
and when the "sow" had been pushed towards the wall
the soldiers rushed up these ladders and were able to fight
on a level with the garrison. Perhaps they were repulsed,
and then a shed-like structure would be advanced towards
the wall, so as to enable the men to get close enough to
dig a hole beneath the walls in order to bring them down.
The besieged would not be inactive, but would cast heavy
stones on the roof of the shed. Molten lead and burning
flax were favourite means of defence to alarm and frighten
away the enemy, who retaliated by casting heavy stones
by means of a catapult into the town.

[1] *The Builder*, April 16, 1904.

Fred Roe

Bootham Bar, York

3

Amongst the fragments of walls still standing, those at
Newcastle are very massive, sooty, and impressive. South-
ampton has some grand walls left and a gateway, which
show how strongly the town was fortified. The old
Cinque Port, Sandwich, formerly a great and important
town, lately decayed, but somewhat renovated by golf,
has two gates left, and Rochester and Canterbury have
some fragments of their walls standing. The repair of
the walls of towns was sometimes undertaken by guilds.
Generous benefactors, like Sir Richard Whittington,
frequently contributed to the cost, and sometimes a tax
called murage was levied for the purpose which was
collected by officers named muragers.

The city of York has lost many of its treasures, and the
City Fathers seem to find it difficult to keep their hands
off such relics of antiquity as are left to them. There are
few cities in England more deeply marked with the im-
press of the storied past than York—the long and
moving story of its gates and walls, of the historical
associations of the city through century after century
of English history. About eighty years ago the Corporation destroyed the picturesque old barbicans of the
Bootham, Micklegate, and Monk Bars, and only one,
Walmgate, was suffered to retain this interesting feature.
It is a wonder they spared those curious stone half-length
figures of men, sculptured in a menacing attitude in the
act of hurling large stones downwards, which vaunt
themselves on the summit of Monk Bar—probably intended to deceive invaders—or that interesting stone
platform only twenty-two inches wide, which was the only
foothold available for the martial burghers who guarded
the city wall at Tower Place. A year or two ago the
City Fathers decided, in order to provide work for the
unemployed, to interfere with the city moats by laying
them out as flower-beds and by planting shrubs and
making playgrounds of the banks. The protest of the
Yorks Archæological Society, we believe, stayed their
hands.

The same story can be told of far too many towns and cities. A few years ago several old houses were demolished in the High Street of the city of Rochester to make room for electric tramways. Among these was the old White Hart Inn, built in 1396, the sign being a badge of Richard II, where Samuel Pepys stayed. He found that "the beds were corded, and we had no sheets to our beds, only linen to our mouths" (a narrow strip of linen to prevent the contact of the blanket with the face). With regard to the disappearance of old inns, we must wait until we arrive at another chapter.

We will now visit some old towns where we hope to discover some buildings that are ancient and where all is not distressingly new, hideous, and commonplace. First we will travel to the old-world town of Lynn—"Lynn Regis, vulgarly called King's Lynn," as the royal charter of Henry VIII terms it. On the land side the town was defended by a fosse, and there are still considerable remains of the old wall, including the fine Gothic South Gates. In the days of its ancient glory it was known as Bishop's Lynn, the town being in the hands of the Bishop of Norwich. Bishop Herbert de Losinga built the church of St. Margaret at the beginning of the twelfth century, and gave it with many privileges to the monks of Norwich, who held a priory at Lynn ; and Bishop Turbus did a wonderfully good stroke of business, reclaimed a large tract of land about 1150 A.D., and amassed wealth for his see from his markets, fairs, and mills. Another bishop, Bishop Grey, induced or compelled King John to grant a free charter to the town, but astutely managed to keep all the power in his own hands. Lynn was always a very religious place, and most of the orders—Benedictines, Franciscans, Dominicans, Carmelite and Augustinian Friars, and the Sack Friars—were represented at Lynn, and there were numerous hospitals, a lazar-house, a college of secular canons, and other religious institutions, until they were all swept away by the greed of a rapacious king. There is not much left to-day of all these religious

foundations. The latest authority on the history of Lynn,
Mr. H. J. Hillen, well says : " Time's unpitying plough-
share has spared few vestiges of their achitectural grandeur." A cemetery cross in the museum, the name
" Paradise " that keeps up the remembrance of the cool,
verdant cloister-garth, a brick arch upon the east bank
of the Nar, and a similar gateway in "Austin" Street
are all the relics that remain of the old monastic life,
save the slender hexagonal " Old Tower," the graceful
lantern of the convent of the grey-robed Franciscans.
The above writer also points out the beautifully carved
door in Queen Street, sole relic of the College of Secular
Canons, from which the chisel of the ruthless iconoclast
has chipped off the obnoxious *Orate pro anima.*

The quiet, narrow, almost deserted streets of Lynn, its
port and quays have another story to tell. They proclaim
its former greatness as one of the chief ports in England
and the centre of vast mercantile activity. A thirteenth-
century historian, Friar William Newburg, described
Lynn as "a noble city noted for its trade." It was the
key of Norfolk. Through it flowed all the traffic to and
from northern East Anglia, and from its harbour crowds
of ships carried English produce, mainly wool, to the
Netherlands, Norway, and the Rhine Provinces. Who
would have thought that this decayed harbour ranked
fourth among the ports of the kingdom ? But its glories
have departed. Decay set in. Its prosperity began to
decline.

Railways have been the ruin of King's Lynn. The
merchant princes who once abounded in the town
exist here no longer. The last of the long race died
quite recently. Some ancient ledgers still exist in the
town, which exhibit for one firm alone a turnover of something like a million and a half sterling per annum.
Although possessed of a similarly splendid waterway,
unlike Ipswich, the trade of the town seems to have quite
decayed. Few signs of commerce are visible, except
where the advent of branch stations of enterprising

"Cash" firms has resulted in the squaring up of odd projections and consequent overthrow of certain ancient buildings. There is one act of vandalism which the town has never ceased to regret and which should serve as a warning for the future. This is the demolition of the

Fred Roe Half-timbered House with early Fifteenth-century
Doorway, King's Lynn, Norfolk

house of Walter Coney, merchant, an unequalled speci-men of fifteenth-century domestic architecture, which formerly stood at the corner of the Saturday Market Place and High Street. So strongly was this edifice constructed that it was with the utmost difficulty that it was taken to pieces, in order to make room for the ugly range of white brick buildings which now stands upon its

site.   But Lynn had an era of much prosperity during
the rise of the Townshends, when the agricultural improvements brought about by the second Viscount introduced much wealth to Norfolk.   Such buildings as the
Duke's Head Hotel belong to the second Viscount's
time, and are indicative of the influx of visitors which
the town enjoyed.   In the present day this hotel, though
still a good-sized establishment, occupies only half the
building which it formerly did.   An interesting oak
staircase of fine proportions, though now much warped,
may be seen here.

In olden days the Hanseatic League had an office here.
The Jews were plentiful and supplied capital—you can find
their traces in the name of the " Jews' Lane Ward "—and
then came the industrious Flemings, who brought with
them the art of weaving cloth and peculiar modes of building houses, so that Lynn looks almost like a little Dutch
town.   The old guild life of Lynn was strong and vigorous, from its Merchant Guild to the humbler craft guilds,
of which we are told that there have been no less than
seventy-five.   Part of the old Guildhall, erected in 1421,
with its chequered flint and stone gable still stands facing
the market of St. Margaret with its Renaissance porch,
and a bit of the guild hall of St. George the Martyr remains in King Street.   The custom-house, which was
originally built as an exchange for the Lynn merchants,
is a notable building, and has a statue of Charles II
placed in a niche.

This was the earliest work of a local architect, Henry
Bell, who is almost unknown.   He was mayor of King's
Lynn, and died in 1717, and his memory has been saved
from oblivion by Mr. Beloe of that town, and is enshrined in Mr. Blomfield's *History of Renaissance Architecture* :—

   " This admirable little building originally consisted
of an open loggia about 40 feet by 32 feet outside, with
four columns down the centre, supporting the first floor,
and an attic storey above.   The walls are of Portland

stone, with a Doric order to the ground storey supporting
an Ionic order to the first floor. The cornice is of wood,
and above this is a steep-pitched tile roof with dormers,
surmounted by a balustrade inclosing a flat, from which
rises a most picturesque wooden cupola. The details are
extremely refined, and the technical knowledge and delicate sense of scale and proportion shown in this building
are surprising in a designer who was under thirty, and is
not known to have done any previous work."[1]

A building which the town should make an effort to
preserve is the old "Greenland Fishery House," a tenement dating from the commencement of the seventeenth
century.

The Duke's Head Inn, erected in 1689, now spoilt by its
coating of plaster, a house in Queen's Street, the old
market cross, destroyed in 1831 and sold for old materials,
and the altarpieces of the churches of St. Margaret and
St. Nicholas, destroyed during "restoration," and North
Runcton church, three miles from Lynn, are other works
of this very able artist.

Until the Reformation Lynn was known as Bishop's
Lynn, and galled itself under the yoke of the Bishop of
Norwich; but Henry freed the townsfolk from their bondage and ordered the name to be changed to Lynn Regis.
Whether the good people throve better under the control
of the tyrant who crushed all their guilds and appropriated the spoil than under the episcopal yoke may be
doubtful; but the change pleased them, and with satisfaction they placed the royal arms on their East Gate,
which, after the manner of gates and walls, has been
pulled down. If you doubt the former greatness of this
old seaport you must examine its civic plate. It possesses the oldest and most important and most beautiful
specimen of municipal plate in England, a grand, massive
silver-gilt cup of exquisite workmanship. It is called
"King John's Cup," but it cannot be earlier than the
reign of Edward III. In addition to this there is a superb
sword of state of the time of Henry VIII, another cup,

[1] *History of Renaissance Architecture*, by R. Blomfield.

four silver maces, and other treasures. Moreover, the town
had a famous goldsmiths' company, and several specimens of their handicraft remain. The defences of the
town were sorely tried in the Civil War, when for three
weeks it sustained the attacks of the rebels. The town
was forced to surrender, and the poor folk were obliged
to pay ten shillings a head, besides a month's pay to the
soldiers, in order to save their homes from plunder.
Lynn has many memories. It sheltered King John when
fleeing from the revolting barons, and kept his treasures
until he took them away and left them in a still more
secure place buried in the sands of the Wash. It welcomed Queen Isabella during her retirement at Castle
Rising, entertained Edward IV when he was hotly pursued by the Earl of Warwick, and has been worthy of its
name as a loyal king's town.

Another walled town on the Norfolk coast attracts the
attention of all who love the relics of ancient times, Great
Yarmouth, with its wonderful record of triumphant industry and its associations with many great events in history. Henry III, recognizing the important strategical
position of the town in 1260, granted a charter to the
townsfolk empowering them to fortify the place with a
wall and a moat, but more than a century elapsed before
the fortifications were completed. This was partly owing
to the Black Death, which left few men in Yarmouth to
carry on the work. The walls were built of cut flint and
Caen stone, and extended from the north-east tower in
St. Nicholas Churchyard, called King Henry's Tower, to
Blackfriars Tower at the south end, and from the same
King Henry's Tower to the north-west tower on the bank
of the Bure. Only a few years ago a large portion of this,
north of Ramp Row, now called Rampart Road, was
taken down, much to the regret of many. And here I
may mention a grand movement which might be with
advantage imitated in every historic town. A small
private company has been formed called the "Great
Yarmouth Historical Buildings, Limited." Its object is

Fred Roe
12 Aug 1908

The "Bone Tower"
Town Walls.
Great Yarmouth.

to acquire and preserve the relics of ancient Yarmouth.
The founders deserve the highest praise for their public
spirit and patriotism.   How many cherished objects in
Vanishing England might have been preserved if each
town or county possessed such a valuable association !
This Yarmouth society owns the remains of the cloisters
of Grey Friars and other remains of ancient buildings.
It is only to be regretted that it was not formed earlier.
There were nine gates in the walls of the town, but none
of them are left, and of the sixteen towers which protected the walls only a very few remain.

These walls guard much that is important.   The ecclesiastical buildings are very fine, including the largest
parish church in England, founded by the same Herbert
de Losinga whose good work we saw at King's Lynn.
The church of St. Nicholas has had many vicissitudes,
and is now one of the finest in the country.   It was in
medieval times the church of a Benedictine Priory ; a cell
of the monastery at Norwich and the Priory Hall remains,
and is now restored and used as a school.   Royal guests
have been entertained there, but part of the buildings
were turned into cottages and the great hall into stables.
As we have said, part of the Grey Friars Monastery remains, and also part of the house of the Augustine Friars.
The Yarmouth rows are a great feature of the town.
They are not like the Chester rows, but are long, narrow
streets crossing the town from east to west, only six feet
wide, and one row called Kitty-witches only measures at
one end two feet three inches.   It has been suggested that
this plan of the town arose from the fishermen hanging
out their nets to dry and leaving a narrow passage between each other's nets, and that in course of time these
narrow passages became defined and were permanently
retained.   In former days rich merchants and traders
lived in the houses that line these rows, and had large
gardens behind their dwellings ; and sometimes you can
see relics of former greatness—a panelled room or a
richly decorated ceiling.   But the ancient glory of the

Fred Roe   Row No. 83, Great Yarmouth

rows is past, and the houses are occupied now by fishermen or labourers. These rows are so narrow that no ordinary vehicle could be driven along them. Hence there arose special Yarmouth carts about three and a half feet wide and twelve feet long with wheels underneath the body. Very brave and gallant have always been the fishermen of Yarmouth, not only in fighting the elements, but in defeating the enemies of England. History tells of many a sea-fight in which they did good service to their king and country. They gallantly helped to win the battle of Sluys, and sent forty-three ships and one thousand men to help with the siege of Calais in the time of Edward III. They captured and burned the town and harbour of Cherbourg in the time of Edward I, and performed many other acts of daring.

One of the most interesting houses in the town is the Tolhouse, the centre of the civic life of Yarmouth. It is said to be six hundred years old, having been erected in the time of Henry III, though some of the windows are decorated, but may have been inserted later. Here the customs or tolls were collected, and the Corporation held its meetings. There is a curious open external staircase leading to the first floor, where the great hall is situated. Under the hall is a gaol, a wretched prison wherein the miserable captives were chained to a beam that ran down the centre. Nothing in the town bears stronger witness to the industry and perseverance of the Yarmouth men than the harbour. They have scoured the sea for a thousand years to fill their nets with its spoil, and made their trade of world-wide fame, but their port speaks louder in their praise. Again and again has the fickle sea played havoc with their harbour, silting it up with sand and deserting the town as if in revenge for the harvest they reap from her. They have had to cut out no less than seven harbours in the course of the town's existence, and royally have they triumphed over all difficulties and made Yarmouth a great and prosperous port.

Near Yarmouth is the little port of Gorleston with its old jetty-head, of which we give an illustration. It was once the rival of Yarmouth. The old magnificent church of the Augustine Friars stood in this village and had a lofty, square, embattled tower which was a landmark to sailors. But the church was unroofed and despoiled at the Reformation, and its remains were pulled down in 1760, only a small portion of the tower remaining, and this fell a victim to a violent storm at the beginning of the last century. The grand parish church was much plundered

The Old Jetty, Gorleston

at the Reformation, and left piteously bare by the despoilers.

The town, now incorporated with Yarmouth, has a proud boast :—

> Gorleston was Gorleston ere Yarmouth begun,
> And will be Gorleston when Yarmouth is done.

Another leading East Anglian port in former days was the county town of Suffolk, Ipswich. During the thirteenth and fourteenth centuries ships from most of the countries of Western Europe disembarked their cargoes on its quays—wines from Spain, timber from Norway, cloth from Flanders, salt from France, and "mercerie" from Italy left its crowded wharves to be offered for sale in

the narrow, busy streets of the borough. Stores of fish
from Iceland, bales of wool, loads of untanned hides, as
well as the varied agricultural produce of the district, were
exposed twice in the week on the market stalls.[1]   The
learned editor of the *Memorials of Old Suffolk*, who knows
the old town so well, tells us that the stalls of the
numerous markets lay within a narrow limit of space near
the principal churches of the town—St. Mary-le-Tower,
St. Mildred, and St. Lawrence.   The Tavern Street of
to-day was the site of the flesh market or cowerye.   A

Tudor House, Ipswich, near the Custom House

narrow street leading thence to the Tower Church was the
Poultry, and Cooks' Row, Butter Market, Cheese and
Fish markets were in the vicinity.   The manufacture of
leather was the leading industry of old Ipswich, and there
was a goodly company of skinners, barkers, and tanners
employed in the trade.   Tavern Street had, as its name
implies, many taverns, and was called the Vintry, from the
large number of opulent vintners who carried on their
trade with London and Bordeaux.   Many of these men
were not merely peaceful merchants, but fought with
Edward III in his wars with France and were knighted

[1] Cf. *Memorials of Suffolk*, edited by V. B. Redstone.

for their feats of arms. Ipswich once boasted of a castle
which was destroyed in Stephen's reign. In Saxon times
it was fortified by a ditch and a rampart which were de-

Three-gabled House, Fore Street, Ipswich

stroyed by the Danes, but the fortifications were renewed
in the time of King John, when a wall was built round the
town with four gates which took their names from the
points of the compass. Portions of these remain to bear

witness to the importance of this ancient town.   We give
views of an old building near the custom-house in College
Street and Fore Street, examples of the narrow, tortuous
thoroughfares which modern improvements have not swept
away.

We cannot give accounts of all the old fortified towns
in England and can only make selections.   We have
alluded to the ancient walls of York.   Few cities can rival
it in interest and architectural beauty, its relics of Roman
times, its stately and magnificent cathedral, the beautiful
ruins of St. Mary's Abbey, the numerous churches exhibiting all the grandeur of the various styles of Gothic architecture, the old merchants' hall, and the quaint old narrow
streets with gabled houses and widely projecting storeys.
And then there is the varied history of the place dating from
far-off Roman times.   Not the least interesting feature of
York are its gates and walls.   Some parts of the walls are
Roman, that curious thirteen-sided building called the
multangular tower forming part of it, and also the lower
part of the wall leading from this tower to Bootham Bar,
the upper part being of later origin.   These walls have
witnessed much fighting, and the cannons in the Civil
War during the siege in 1644 battered down some portions of them and sorely tried their hearts.   But they
have been kept in good preservation and repaired at
times, and the part on the west of the Ouse is especially
well preserved.   You can see some Norman and Early
English work, but the bulk of it belongs to Edwardian
times, when York played a great part in the history of
England, and King Edward I made it his capital during
the war with Scotland, and all the great nobles of England sojourned there.   Edward II spent much time there,
and the minster saw the marriage of his son.   These
walls were often sorely needed to check the inroads of
the Scots.   After Bannockburn fifteen thousand of these
northern warriors advanced to the gates of York.   The
four gates of the city are very remarkable.   Micklegate
Bar consists of a square tower built over a circular arch of

Norman date with embattled turrets at the angles. On it
the heads of traitors were formerly exposed. It bears on
its front the arms of France as well as those of England.

"Melia's Passage," York   Fred Roe

Bootham Bar is the main entrance from the north, and
has a Norman arch with later additions and turrets with
narrow slits for the discharge of arrows. It saw the burning of the suburb of Bootham in 1265 and much bloodshed, when a mighty quarrel raged between the citizens

4

and the monks of the Abbey of St. Mary owing to the
abuse of the privilege of sanctuary possessed by the
monastery.   Monk Bar has nothing to do with monks.
Its former name was Goodramgate, and after the Restoration it was changed to Monk Bar in honour of General
Monk.   The present structure was probably built in the
fourteenth century.   Walmgate Bar, a strong, formidable
structure, was built in the reign of Edward I, and as we
have said, it is the only gate that retains its curious barbican, originally built in the time of Edward III and rebuilt
in 1648.   The inner front of the gate has been altered
from its original form in order to secure more accommodation within.   The remains of the Clifford's Tower,
which played an important part in the siege, tell of the
destruction caused by the blowing up of the magazine in
1683, an event which had more the appearance of design
than accident.   York abounds with quaint houses and
narrow streets.   We give an illustration of the curious
Melia's Passage ; the origin of the name I am at a loss to
conjecture.

Chester is, we believe, the only city in England which
has retained the entire circuit of its walls complete.   According to old unreliable legends, Marius, or Marcius,
King of the British, grandson of Cymbeline, who began
his reign A.D. 73, first surrounded Chester with a wall, a
mysterious person who must be classed with Leon Gawr, or
Vawr, a mighty strong giant who founded Chester, digging caverns in the rocks for habitations, and with the
story of King Leir, who first made human habitations in
the future city.   Possibly there was here a British camp.
It was certainly a Roman city, and has preserved the form
and plan which the Romans were accustomed to affect ; its
four principal streets diverging at right angles from a
common centre, and extending north, east, south, and
west, and terminating in a gate, the other streets forming
insulæ as at Silchester.   There is every reason to believe
that the Romans surrounded the city with a wall.   Its
strength was often tried.   Hither the Saxons came under

Ethelfrith and pillaged the city, but left it to the Britons, who were not again dislodged until Egbert came in 828 and recovered it. The Danish pirates came here and were besieged by Alfred, who slew all within its walls. These walls were standing but ruinous when the noble daughter of Alfred, Ethelfleda, restored them in 907. A volume would be needed to give a full account of Chester's varied history, and our main concern is with the treasures that remain. The circumference of the walls is nearly two miles, and there are four principal gates besides posterns —the North, East, Bridge-gate, and Water-gate. The North Gate was in the charge of the citizens; the others were held by persons who had that office by serjeanty under the Earls of Chester, and were entitled to certain tolls, which, with the custody of the gates, were frequently purchased by the Corporation. The custody of the Bridge-gate belonged to the Raby family in the reign of Edward III. It had two round towers, on the westernmost of which was an octagonal water-tower. These were all taken down in 1710–81 and the gate rebuilt. The East Gate was given by Edward I to Henry Bradford, who was bound to find a crannoc and a bushel for measuring the salt that might be brought in. Needless to say, the old gate has vanished. It was of Roman architecture, and consisted of two arches formed by large stones. Between the tops of the arches, which were cased with Norman masonry, was the whole-length figure of a Roman soldier. This gate was a *porta principalis,* the termination of the great Watling Street that led from Dover through London to Chester. It was destroyed in 1768, and the present gate erected by Earl Grosvenor. The custody of the Water-gate belonged to the Earls of Derby. It also was destroyed, and the present arch erected in 1788. A new North Gate was built in 1809 by Robert, Earl Grosvenor. The principal postern-gates were Cale Yard Gate, made by the abbot and convent in the reign of Edward I as a passage to their kitchen garden; Newgate, formerly Woolfield or Wolf-gate, repaired in 1608, also called Pepper-gate ;[1] and Ship-gate, or Hole-in-the-wall, which alone retains its Roman arch, and leads to a ferry across the Dee.

The walls are strengthened by round towers so placed as not to be beyond bowshot of each other, in order that their arrows might reach the enemy who should attempt to scale the walls in the intervals. At the north-east corner is Newton's Tower, better known as the Phœnix from a sculptured figure, the ensign of one of the city guilds, appearing over its door. From this tower Charles I saw the battle of Rowton Heath and the defeat of his troops during the famous siege of Chester. This was one of the most prolonged and deadly in the whole history of the Civil War. It would take many pages to describe the varied fortunes of the gallant Chester men, who were at length constrained to feed on horses, dogs, and cats. There is much in the city to delight the antiquary and the artist—the famous rows, the three-gabled old timber mansion of the Stanleys with its massive staircase, oaken floors, and panelled walls, built in 1591, Bishop Lloyd's house in Water-gate with its timber front sculptured with Scripture subjects, and God's Providence House with its motto "God's Provi-dence is mine inheritance," the inhabitants of which are said to have escaped one of the terrible plagues that used to rage frequently in old Chester.

Journeying southwards we come to Shrewsbury, another walled town, abounding with delightful half-timbered houses, less spoiled than any town we know. It was never a Roman town, though six miles away, at Urico-nium, the Romans had a flourishing city with a great basilica, baths, shops, and villas, and the usual acces-sories of luxury. Tradition says that its earliest Celtic name was Pengwern, where a British prince had his

---

[1] The Chester folk have a proverb, "When the daughter is stolen, shut Pepper-gate"—referring to the well-known story of a daughter of a Mayor of Chester having made her escape with her lover through this gate, which he ordered to be closed, but too late to prevent the fugitives.

NEWMA

Detail of Half-timbered House in
High Street, Shrewsbury

palace ; but the town Scrobbesbyrig came into existence
under Offa's rule in Mercia, and with the Normans came
Roger de Montgomery, Shrewsbury's first Earl, and a
castle and the stately abbey of SS. Peter and Paul.   A
little later the town took to itself walls, which were abundantly necessary on account of the constant inroads of
the wild Welsh.

> For the barbican's massy and high,
>   Bloudie Jacke !
> And the oak-door is heavy and brown ;
> And with iron it's plated and machicolated,
> To pour boiling oil and lead down ;
>   How you'd frown
> Should a ladle-full fall on your crown !
>
> The rock that it stands on is steep,
>   Bloudie Jacke !
> To gain it one's forced for to creep ;
> The Portcullis is strong, and the Drawbridge is long,
> And the water runs all round the Keep ;
>   At a peep
> You can see that the moat's very deep !

So rhymed the author of the *Ingoldsby Legends*, when in
his "Legend of Shropshire" he described the red stone
fortress that towers over the loop of the Severn enclosing
the picturesque old town of Shrewsbury.   The castle, or
rather its keep, for the outworks have disappeared, has
been modernized past antiquarian value now.   Memories
of its importance as the key of the Northern Marches,
and of the ancient custom of girding the knights of the
shire with their swords by the sheriffs on the grass plot
of its inner court, still remain.   The town now stands on
a peninsula girt by the Severn.   On the high ground
between the narrow neck stood the castle, and under its
shelter most of the houses of the inhabitants.   Around
this was erected the first wall.   The latest historian of
Shrewsbury [1] tells us that it started from the gate of the
castle, passed along the ridge at the back of Pride Hill,
at the bottom of which it turned along the line of High

[1] The Rev. T. Auden, *Shrewsbury* (Methuen and Co.).

Street, past St. Julian's Church which overhung it, to the
top of Wyle Cop, when it followed the ridge back to the
castle. Of the part extending from Pride Hill to Wyle
Cop only scant traces exist at the back of more modern
buildings.

The town continued to grow and more extensive
defences were needed, and in the time of Henry III, Mr.
Auden states that this followed the old line at the back of
Pride Hill, but as the ground began to slope downwards,
another wall branched from it in the direction of Rous-
hill and extended to the Welsh Bridge. This became
the main defence, leaving the old wall as an inner rampart. From the Welsh Bridge the new wall turned up
Claremont Bank to where St. Chad's Church now stands,
and where one of the original towers stood. Then it
passed along Murivance, where the only existing tower
is to be seen, and so along the still remaining portion of
the wall to English Bridge, where it turned up the hill at
the back of what is now Dogpole, and passing the Water-
gate, again joined the fortifications of the castle.[1] The
castle itself was reconstructed by Prince Edward, the son
of Henry III, at the end of the thirteenth century, and is
of the Edwardian type of concentric castle. The Norman
keep was incorporated within a larger circle of tower and
wall, forming an inner bailey ; besides this there was
formerly an outer bailey, in which were various buildings,
including the chapel of St. Nicholas. Only part of
the buildings on one side of the inner bailey remains
in its original form, but the massive character of
the whole may be judged from the fragments now
visible.

These walls guarded a noble town full of churches and
monasteries, merchants' houses, guild halls, and much
else. We will glance at the beauties that remain : St.
Mary's, containing specimens of every style of architecture from Norman downward, with its curious foreign
glass ; St. Julian's, mainly rebuilt in 1748, though the

[1] *Ibid.*, p. 48.

Tower on the Town Wall, Shrewsbury

old tower remains; St. Alkmund's; the Church of St. Chad; St. Giles's Church; and the nave and refectory pulpit of the monastery of SS. Peter and Paul. It is distressing to see this interesting gem of fourteenth-century architecture amid the incongruous surroundings of a coalyard. You can find considerable remains of the domestic buildings of the Grey Friars' Monastery near the footbridge across the Severn, and also of the home of the Austin Friars in a builder's yard at the end of Baker Street.

In many towns we find here and there an old half-timbered dwelling, but in Shrewsbury there is a surprising wealth of them—streets full of them, bearing such strange medieval names as "Mardel" or "Wyle Cop." Shrewsbury is second to no other town in England in the interest of its ancient domestic buildings. There is the gatehouse of the old Council House, bearing the date 1620, with its high gable and carved barge-boards, its panelled front, the square spaces between the upright and horizontal timbers being ornamented with cut timber. The old buildings of the famous Shrewsbury School are now used as a Free Library and Museum and abound in interest. The house remains in which Prince Rupert stayed during his sojourn in 1644, then owned by "Master Jones the lawyer," at the west end of St. Mary's Church, with its fine old staircase. Whitehall, a fine mansion of red sandstone, was built by Richard Prince, a lawyer, in 1578–82, "to his great chardge with fame to hym and hys posterite for ever." The Old Market Hall in the Renaissance style, with its mixture of debased Gothic and classic details, is worthy of study. Even in Shrewsbury we have to record the work of the demon of destruction. The erection of the New Market Hall entailed the disappearance of several old picturesque houses. Bellstone House, erected in 1582, is incorporated in the National Provincial Bank. The old mansion known as Vaughan's Place is swallowed up by the music-hall, though part of the ancient dwelling-

place remains. St. Peter's Abbey Church in the commencement of the nineteenth century had an extraordinary
annexe of timber and plaster, probably used at one time
as parsonage house, which, with several buttressed remains of the adjacent conventual buildings, have long
ago been squared up and "improved" out of existence.
Rowley's mansion, in Hill's Lane, built of brick in 1618
by William Rowley, is now a warehouse.   Butcher Row
has some old houses with projecting storeys, including a
fine specimen of a medieval shop.   Some of the houses
in Grope Lane lean together from opposite sides of the
road, so that people in the highest storey can almost
shake hands with their neighbours across the way.   You
can see the " Olde House " in which Mary Tudor is said
to have stayed, and the mansion of the Owens, built in
1592 as an inscription tells us, and that of the Irelands,
with its range of bow-windows, four storeys high, and
terminating in gables, erected about 1579.   The half-
timbered hall of the Drapers' Guild, some old houses in
Frankwell, including the inn with the quaint sign—the
String of Horses, the ancient hostels—the Lion, famous
in the coaching age, the Ship, and the Raven—Bennett's
Hall, which was the mint when Shrewsbury played its
part in the Civil War, and last, but not least, the house
in Wyle Cop, one of the finest in the town, where
Henry Earl of Richmond stayed on his way to Bosworth
field to win the English Crown.   Such are some of the
beauties of old Shrewsbury which happily have not yet
vanished.

Not far removed from Shrewsbury is Coventry, which
at one time could boast of a city wall and a castle.   In
the reign of Richard II this wall was built, strengthened
by towers.   Leland, writing in the time of Henry VIII,
states that the city was begun to be walled in when
Edward II reigned, and that it had six gates, many fair
towers, and streets well built with timber.   Other writers
speak of thirty-two towers and twelve gates.   But few
traces of these remain.   The citizens of Coventry took an

House that the Earl of Richmond stayed in before the Battle of Bosworth, Shrewsbury

active part in the Civil War in favour of the Parliamentary army, and when Charles II came to the throne he ordered these defences to be demolished. The gates were left, but most of them have since been destroyed. Coventry is a city of fine old timber-framed fifteenth-century houses with gables and carved barge-boards and projecting storeys, though many of them are decayed and may not last many years. The city has had a fortunate immunity from serious fires. We give an illustration of one of the old Coventry streets called Spon Street, with its picturesque houses. These old streets are numerous, tortuous and irregular. One of the richest and most interesting examples of domestic architecture in England is St. Mary's Hall, erected in the time of Henry VI. Its origin is connected with ancient guilds of the city, and in it were stored their books and archives. The grotesquely carved roof, minstrels' gallery, armoury, state-chair, great painted window, and a fine specimen of fifteenth-century tapestry are interesting features of this famous hall, which furnishes a vivid idea of the manners and civic customs of the age when Coventry was the favourite resort of kings and princes. It has several fine churches, though the cathedral was levelled with the ground by that arch-destroyer Henry VIII. Coventry remains one of the most interesting towns in England.

One other walled town we will single out for especial notice in this chapter—the quaint, picturesque, peaceful, placid town of Rye on the Sussex coast. It was once wooed by the sea, which surrounded the rocky island on which it stands, but the fickle sea has retired and left it lonely on its hill with a long stretch of marshland between it and the waves. This must have taken place about the fifteenth century. Our illustration of a disused mooring-post (p. 24) is a symbol of the departed greatness of the town as a naval station. The River Rother connects it with the sea, and the few barges and humble craft and a few small shipbuilding yards remind it of its palmy

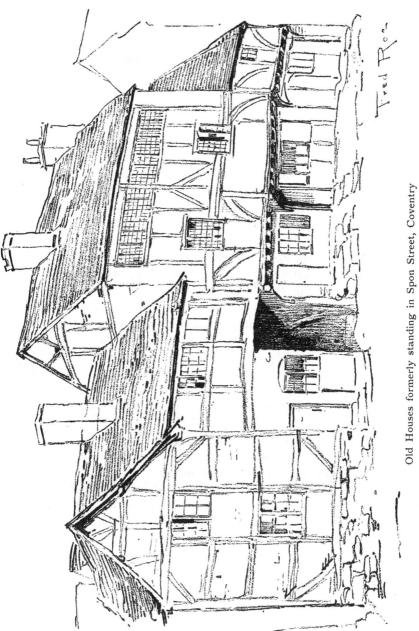

Old Houses formerly standing in Spon Street, Coventry

days when it was a member of the Cinque Ports, a rich
and prosperous town that sent forth its ships to fight the
naval battles of England and win honour for Rye and
St. George. During the French wars English vessels
often visited French ports and towns along the coast and
burned and pillaged them. The French sailors retaliated
with equal zest, and many of our southern towns have
suffered from fire and sword during those adventurous
days.

Rye was strongly fortified by a wall with gates and
towers and a fosse, but the defences suffered grievously
from the attacks of the French, and the folk of Rye
were obliged to send a moving petition to King Richard II,
praying him "to have consideration of the poor town
of Rye, inasmuch as it had been several times taken, and
is unable further to repair the walls, wherefore the
town is, on the sea-side, open to enemies." I am afraid
that the King did not at once grant their petition, as two
years later, in 1380, the French came again and set fire to
the town. With the departure of the sea and the diminishing of the harbour, the population decreased and the
prosperity of Rye declined. Refugees from France have
on two notable occasions added to the number of its
inhabitants. After the Massacre of St. Bartholomew
seven hundred scared and frightened Protestants arrived
at Rye and brought with them their industry, and later
on, after the Revocation of the Edict of Nantes, many
Huguenots settled here and made it almost a French
town. We need not record all the royal visits, the
alarms of attack, the plagues, and other incidents that
have diversified the life of Rye. We will glance at the
relics that remain. The walls seem never to have recovered from the attack of the French, but one gate
is standing—the Landgate on the north-east of the town,
built in 1360, and consisting of a broad arch flanked by
two massive towers with chambers above for archers and
defenders. Formerly there were two other gates, but
these have vanished save only the sculptured arms of the

West Street, Rye

Cinque Ports that once adorned the Strand Gate. The Ypres tower is a memorial of the ancient strength of the town, and was originally built by William de Ypres, Earl of Kent, in the twelfth century, but has received later additions. It has a stern, gaunt appearance, and until recent times was used as a jail. The church possesses many points of unique interest. The builders began in the twelfth century to build the tower and transepts, which are Norman; then they proceeded with the nave, which is Transitional; and when they reached the choir, which is very large and fine, the style had merged into the Early English. Later windows were inserted in the fourteenth and fifteenth centuries. The church has suffered with the town at the hands of the French invaders, who did much damage. The old clock, with its huge swinging pendulum, is curious. The church has a collection of old books, including some old Bibles, including a Vinegar and a Breeches Bible, and some stone cannon-balls, mementoes of the French invasion of 1448.

Near the church is the Town Hall, which contains several relics of olden days. The list of mayors extends from the time of Edward I, and we notice the long continuance of the office in families. Thus the Lambs held office from 1723 to 1832, and the Grebells from 1631 to 1741. A great tragedy happened in the churchyard. A man named Breedes had a grudge against one of the Lambs, and intended to kill him. He saw, as he thought, his victim walking along the dark path through the shrubs in the churchyard, attacked and murdered him. But he had made a mistake; his victim was Mr. Grebell. The murderer was hanged and quartered. The Town Hall contains the ancient pillory, which was described as a very handy affair, handcuffs, leg-irons, special constables' staves, which were always much needed for the usual riots on Gunpowder Plot Day, and the old primitive fire-engine dated 1745. The town has some remarkable plate. There is the mayor's handbell with the inscription :—

O MATER DEI
MEMENTO MEI.
1566.
PETRUS GHEINEUS
ME FECIT.

The maces of Queen Elizabeth with the date 1570 and bearing the fleur-de-lis and the Tudor rose are interesting, and the two silver maces presented by George III,

Monogram and Inscription in the Mermaid Inn, Rye

bearing the arms of Rye and weighing 962 oz., are said to be the finest in Europe.

The chief charm of Rye is to walk along the narrow streets and lanes, and see the picturesque rows and groups of old fifteenth- and sixteenth-century houses with their tiled roofs and gables, weather-boarded or tile-hung after the manner of Sussex cottages, graceful bay-windows—altogether pleasing. Wherever one wanders one meets with these charming dwellings, especially in West Street and Pump Street ; the oldest house in Rye being at the corner of the churchyard. The Mermaid Inn is delightful both outside and inside, with its low panelled rooms, immense fire-places and dog-

5

grates.   We see the monogram and names and dates
carved on the stone fire-places, 1643, 1646, the name
Loffelholtz seeming to indicate some foreign refugee or
settler.   It is pleasant to find at least in one town in
England so much that has been left unaltered and so
little spoilt.

LOEFELHOLTZ I I
1643

Inscription in the Mermaid Inn, Rye

CHAPTER IV

IN STREETS AND LANES

I HAVE said in another place that no country in the
world can boast of possessing rural homes and
villages which have half the charm and picturesqueness of our English cottages and hamlets.[1] They have to
be known in order that they may be loved. The hasty
visitor may pass them by and miss half their attractiveness. They have to be wooed in varying moods in order
that they may display their charms—when the blossoms
are bright in the village orchards, when the sun shines on
the streams and pools and gleams on the glories of old
thatch, when autumn has tinged the trees with golden
tints, or when the hoar frost makes their bare branches
beautiful again with new and glistening foliage. Not even
in their summer garb do they look more beautiful. There
is a sense of stability and a wondrous variety caused by
the different nature of the materials used, the peculiar
stone indigenous in various districts and the individuality
stamped upon them by traditional modes of building.

We have still a large number of examples of the humbler
kind of ancient domestic architecture, but every year sees
the destruction of several of these old buildings, which a
little care and judicious restoration might have saved.
Ruskin's words should be writ in bold, big letters at the
head of the by-laws of every district council.

"Watch an old building with anxious care; guard it as
best you may, and at any cost, from any influence of
dilapidation. Count its stones as you would the jewels of
a crown. Set watchers about it, as if at the gate of a

[1] *The Charm of the English Village* (Batsford).

67

besieged city ; bind it together with iron when it loosens ; stay it with timber when it declines. Do not care about the unsightliness of the aid—better a crutch than a lost limb ; and do this tenderly and reverently and continually, and many a generation will still be born and pass away beneath its shadow."

If this sound advice had been universally taken many a beautiful old cottage would have been spared to us, and our eyes would not be offended by the wondrous creations of the estate agents and local builders, who have no other

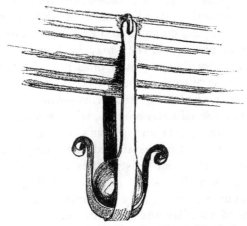

Relic of Lynn Siege in Hampton Court, King's Lynn

ambition but to build cheaply. The contrast between the new and the old is indeed deplorable. The old cottage is a thing of beauty. Its odd, irregular form and various harmonious colouring, the effects of weather, time, and accident, environed with smiling verdure and sweet old-fashioned garden flowers, its thatched roof, high gabled front, inviting porch overgrown with creepers, and case-ment windows, all combine to form a fair and beautiful home. And then look at the modern cottage with its glaring brick walls, slate roof, ungainly stunted chimney, and note the difference. Usually these modern cottages are built in a row, each one exactly like its fellow, with

Fred Roe

Hampton Court, King's Lynn, Norfolk

door and window frames exactly alike, brought over ready-
made from Norway or Sweden.   The walls are thin, and
the winds of winter blow through them piteously, and if
a man and his wife should unfortunately "have words"
(the pleasing country euphemism for a violent quarrel) all
their neighbours can hear them.   The scenery is utterly
spoilt by these ugly eyesores.   Villas at Hindhead seem
to have broken out upon the once majestic hill like a red
skin eruption.   The jerry-built villa is invading our heaths
and pine-woods ; every street in our towns is undergoing
improvement; we are covering whole counties with houses.
In Lancashire no sooner does one village end its mean
streets than another begins.   London is ever enlarging
itself, extending its great maw over all the country round.
The Rev. Canon Erskine Clarke, Vicar of Battersea,
when he first came to reside near Clapham Junction,
remembers the green fields and quiet lanes with trees on
each side that are now built over.   The street leading
from the station lined with shops forty years ago had
hedges and trees on each side.   There were great houses
situated in beautiful gardens and parks wherein resided
some of the great City merchants, county families, the
leaders in old days of the influential "Clapham sect."
These gardens and parks have been covered with streets
and rows of cottages and villas ; some of the great houses
have been pulled down and others turned into schools or
hospitals, valued only at the rent of the land on which
they stand.   All this is inevitable.   You cannot stop all
this any more than Mrs. Partington could stem the
Atlantic tide with a housemaid's mop.   But ere the flood
has quite swallowed up all that remains of England's
natural and architectural beauties, it may be useful to
glance at some of the buildings that remain in town and
country ere they have quite vanished.

Beneath the shade of the lordly castle of Warwick,
which has played such an important part in the history
of England, the town of Warwick sprang into existence,
seeking protection in lawless times from its strong walls

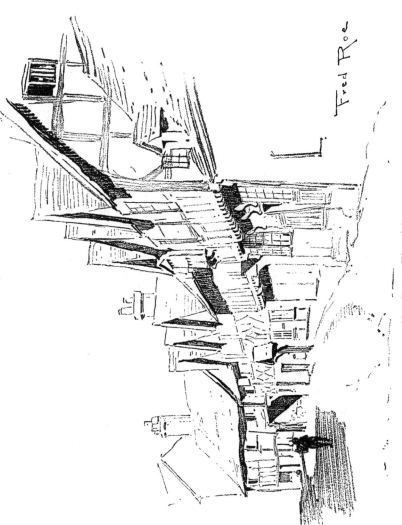

Fred Roe

Mill Street, Warwick

and powerful garrison. Through its streets often rode
in state the proud rulers of the castle with their men-at-
arms—the Beauchamps, the Nevilles, including the great
"King-maker," Richard Neville, the Dudleys, and the
Grevilles. They contributed to the building of their
noble castle, protected the town, and were borne to
their last resting-place in the fine church, where their
tombs remain. The town has many relics of its lords,
and possesses many half-timbered graceful houses. Mill
Street is one of the most picturesque groups of old-time
dwellings, a picture that lingers in our minds long after
we have left the town and fortress of the grim old Earls of
Warwick.

Oxford is a unique city. There is no place like it in
the world. Scholars of Cambridge, of course, will tell
me that I am wrong, and that the town on the Cam is a
far superior place, and then point triumphantly to "the
backs." Yes, they are very beautiful, but as a loyal son
of Oxford I may be allowed to prefer that stately city
with its towers and spires, its wealth of college buildings,
its exquisite architecture unrivalled in the world. Nor is
the new unworthy of the old. The buildings at Magdalen, at Brazenose, and even the New Schools harmo-
nize not unseemly with the ancient structures. Happily
Keble is far removed from the heart of the city, so that
that somewhat unsatisfactory, unsuccessful pile of brickwork interferes not with its joy. In the streets and lanes
of modern Oxford we can search for and discover many
types of old-fashioned, humble specimens of domestic art,
and we give as an illustration some houses which date
back to Tudor times, but have, alas! been recently demolished.

Many conjectures have been made as to the reason why
our forefathers preferred to rear their houses with the
upper storeys projecting out into the streets. We can
understand that in towns where space was limited it
would be an advantage to increase the size of the upper
rooms, if one did not object to the lack of air in the

narrow street and the absence of sunlight. But we find
these same projecting storeys in the depth of the country,
where there could have been no restriction as to the
ground to be occupied by the house. Possibly the

Fred Roe

Tudor Tenements
New Inn Hall St
Oxford
Now demolished

fashion was first established of necessity in towns, and
the traditional mode of building was continued in the
country. Some say that by this means our ancestors
tried to protect the lower part of the house, the foundations, from the influence of the weather; others with

some ingenuity suggest that these projecting storeys were intended to form a covered walk for passengers in the streets, and to protect them from the showers of slops which the careless housewife of Elizabethan times cast recklessly from the upstairs windows. Architects tell us that it was purely a matter of construction. Our fore-fathers used to place four strong corner-posts, framed from the trunks of oak trees, firmly sunk into the ground with their roots left on and placed upward, the roots curving outwards so as to form supports for the upper storeys. These curved parts, and often the posts also, were often elaborately carved and ornamented, as in the example which our artist gives us of a corner-post of a house in Ipswich.

In *The Charm of the English Village* I have tried to describe the methods of the construction of these timber-framed houses,[1] and it is perhaps unnecessary for me to repeat what is there recorded. In fact, there were three types of these dwelling-places, to which have been given the names Post and Pan, Transom Framed, and Intertie Work. In judging of the age of a house it will be remembered that the nearer together the upright posts are placed the older the house is. The builders as time went on obtained greater confidence, set their posts wider apart, and held them together by transoms.

Surrey is a county of good cottages and farm-houses, and these have had their chroniclers in Miss Gertrude Jekyll's delightful *Old West Surrey* and in the more technical work of Mr. Ralph Nevill, F.S.A. The numer-ous works on cottage and farm-house building published by Mr. Batsford illustrate the variety of styles that pre-vailed in different counties, and which are mainly attributable to the variety in the local materials in the counties. Thus in the Cotswolds, Northamptonshire, Derbyshire, Yorkshire, Westmorland, Somersetshire, and elsewhere there is good building-stone ; and there we find charming examples of stone-built cottages and farm-

[1] *The Charm of the English Village*, pp. 50-7.

Gothic Corner-post. The Half Moon Inn, Ipswich

houses, altogether satisfying. In several counties where there is little stone and large forests of timber we find the timber-framed dwelling flourishing in all its native beauty. In Surrey there are several materials for build-

Fred Roe

Timber-built House, Shrewsbury

ing, hence there is a charming diversity of domiciles. Even the same building sometimes shows walls of stone and brick, half-timber and plaster, half-timber and tile-hanging, half-timber with panels filled with red brick, and roofs of thatch or tiles, or stone slates which the Horsham quarries supplied.

These Surrey cottages have changed with age. Originally they were built with timber frames, the panels being filled in with wattle and daub, but the storms of many winters have had their effect upon the structure. Rain drove through the walls, especially when the ends of the wattle rotted a little, and draughts were strong enough to blow out the rushlights and to make the house very uncomfortable. Oak timbers often shrink. Hence the joints came apart, and being exposed to the weather became decayed. In consequence of this the buildings settled,

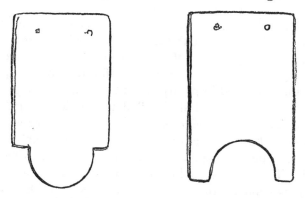

and new methods had to be devised to make them weather-proof. The villages therefore adopted two or three means in order to attain this end. They plastered the whole surface of the walls on the outside, or they hung them with deal boarding or covered them with tiles. In Surrey tile-hung houses are more common than in any other part of the country. This use of weather-tiles is not very ancient, probably not earlier than 1750, and much of this work was done in that century or early in the nineteenth. Many of these tile-hung houses are the old sixteenth-century timber-framed structures in a new shell. Weather-tiles are generally flatter and thinner than those used for roofing, and when bedded in mortar make a thoroughly weather-proof wall. Sometimes they are nailed to boarding, but the former plan makes the work more durable, though the courses are not so regular.

These tiles have various shapes, of which the commonest
is semicircular, resembling a fish-scale. The same form
with a small square shoulder is very generally used, but
there is a great variety, and sometimes those with ornamental ends are blended with plain ones. Age imparts a
very beautiful colour to old tiles, and when covered with
lichen they assume a charming appearance which artists
love to depict.

The mortar used in these old buildings is very strong
and good. In order to strengthen the mortar used in
Sussex and Surrey houses and elsewhere, the process of
"galleting" or "garreting" was adopted. The brick-
layers used to decorate the rather wide and uneven mortar
joint with small pieces of black ironstone stuck into the
mortar. Sussex was once famous for its ironwork, and
ironstone is found in plenty near the surface of the ground
in this district. "Galleting" dates back to Jacobean
times, and is not to be found in sixteenth-century work.

Sussex houses are usually whitewashed and have
thatched roofs, except when Horsham slates or tiles are
used. Thatch as a roofing material will soon have altogether vanished with other features of vanishing England.
District councils in their by-laws usually insert regulations prohibiting thatch to be used for roofing. This is
one of the mysteries of the legislation of district councils.
Rules, suitable enough for towns, are applied to the country
villages, where they are altogether unsuitable or unnecessary. The danger of fire makes it inadvisable to have
thatched roofs in towns, or even in some villages where
the houses are close together, but that does not apply to
isolated cottages in the country. The district councils
do not compel the removal of thatch, but prohibit new
cottages from being roofed with that material. There is,
however, another cause for the disappearance of thatched
roofs, which form such a beautiful feature in the English
landscape. Since mowing-machines came into general
use in the harvest fields the straw is so bruised that it is
not fit for thatching, at least it is not so suitable as the

Missbrook Farm.
Capel.
Surrey

Fred Roe

straw which was cut by the hand. Thatching, too, is
almost a lost art in the country. Indeed ricks have to be
covered with thatch, but "the work for this temporary
purpose cannot compare with that of the old roof-thatcher,
with his 'strood' or 'frail' to hold the loose straw, and
his spars—split hazel rods pointed at each end—that with
a dexterous twist in the middle make neat pegs for the
fastening of the straw rope that he cleverly twists with a
simple implement called a 'wimble.' The lowest course
was finished with an ornamental bordering of rods with a
diagonal criss-cross pattern between, all neatly pegged
and held down by the spars."[1]

Horsham stone makes splendid roofing material. This
stone easily flakes into plates like thick slates, and forms
large grey flat slabs on which "the weather works like a
great artist in harmonies of moss lichen and stain. No
roofing so combines dignity and homeliness, and no
roofing, except possibly thatch (which, however, is short-
lived), so surely passes into the landscape."[2] It is to be
regretted that this stone is no longer used for roofing—
another feature of vanishing England. The stone is
somewhat thick and heavy, and modern rafters are not
adapted to bear their weight. If you want to have a roof
of Horsham stone, you can only accomplish your purpose
by pulling down an old cottage and carrying off the slabs.
Perhaps the small Cotswold stone slabs are even more
beautiful. Old Lancashire and Yorkshire cottages have
heavy stone roofs which somewhat resemble those fashioned
with Horsham slabs.

The builders and masons of our country cottages were
cunning men, and adapted their designs to their materials.
You will have noticed that the pitch of the Horsham-slated
roof is unusually flat. They observed that when the sides
of the roof were deeply sloping, as in the case of thatched
roofs, the heavy stone slates strained and dragged at
the pegs and laths and fell and injured the roof.   Hence

[1] *Old West Surrey*, by Gertrude Jekyll, p. 206.
[2] *Highways and Byways in Sussex*, by E. V. Lucas.

they determined to make the slope less steep. Unfortunately the rain did not then easily run off, and in order to prevent the water penetrating into the house they were obliged to adopt additional precautions. Therefore they cemented their roofs and stopped them with mortar.

Very lovely are these South Country cottages, peaceful,

Cottage at Capel, Surrey

picturesque, pleasant, with their graceful gables and jutting eaves, altogether delightful. Well sang a loyal Sussex poet :—

> If I ever become a rich man,
>   Or if ever I grow to be old,
> I will build a house with deep thatch [1]
>   To shelter me from the cold ;
> And there shall the Sussex songs be sung
>   And the story of Sussex told.

[1] I fear the poet's plans will never be passed by the rural district council.

6

We give some good examples of Surrey cottages at the village of Capel in the neighbourhood of Dorking, a charming region for the study of cottage-building. There you can see some charming ingle-nooks in the interior of the dwellings, and some grand farm-houses. Attached to the ingle-nook is the oven, wherein bread is baked in the

Farm-house, Horsmonden, Kent

old-fashioned way, and the chimneys are large and carried up above the floor of the first storey, so as to form space for curing bacon.

Horsmonden, Kent, near Lamberhurst, is beautifully situated among well-wooded scenery, and the farm-house shown in the illustration is a good example of the pleasant dwellings to be found therein.

East Anglia has no good building-stone, and brick and flint are the principal materials used in that region. The

houses built of the dark, dull, thin old bricks, not of the
great staring modern varieties, are very charming, especially when they are seen against a background of
wooded hills.   We give an illustration of some cottages
at Stow Langtoft, Suffolk.

Seventeenth-century Cottages, Stow Langtoft, Suffolk

The old town of Banbury, celebrated for its cakes, its
Cross, and its fine lady who rode on a white horse accompanied by the sound of bells, has some excellent "black and
white" houses with pointed gables and enriched barge-
boards pierced in every variety of patterns, their finials
and pendants, and pargeted fronts, which give an air of
picturesqueness contrasting strangely with the stiffness of

the modern brick buildings. In one of these is established the old Banbury Cake Shop. In the High Street there is a very perfect example of these Elizabethan houses, erected about the year 1600. It has a fine oak staircase, the newels beautifully carved and enriched with pierced finials and pendants. The market-place has two good specimens of the same date, one of which is probably the front of the Unicorn Inn, and had a fine pair of wooden gates bearing the date 1684, but I am not sure whether they are still there. The Reindeer Inn is one of the chief architectural attractions of the town. We see the dates 1624 and 1637 inscribed on different parts of the building, but its chief glory is the Globe Room, with a large window, rich plaster ceiling, good panelling, elaborately decorated doorways and chimney-piece. The courtyard is a fine specimen of sixteenth-century architecture. A curious feature is the mounting-block near the large oriel window. It must have been designed not for mounting horses, unless these were of giant size, but for climbing to the top of coaches. The Globe Room is a typical example of Vanishing England, as it is reported that the whole building has been sold for transportation to America. We give an illustration of some old houses in Paradise Square, that does not belie its name. The houses all round the square are thatched, and the gardens in the centre are a blaze of colour, full of old-fashioned flowers. The King's Head Inn has a good courtyard. Banbury suffered from a disastrous fire in 1628 which destroyed a great part of the town, and called forth a vehement sermon from the Rev. William Whateley, of two hours' duration, on the depravity of the town, which merited such a severe judgment. In spite of the fire much old work survived, and we give an illustration of a Tudor fire-place which you cannot now discover, as it is walled up into the passage of an ironmonger's shop.

The old ports and harbours are always attractive. The old fishermen mending their nets delight to tell their stories of their adventures, and retain their old customs

The "Fish House," Littleport, Cambs

and usages, which are profoundly interesting to the lovers
of folk-lore.   Their houses are often primitive and quaint.
There is the curious Fish House at Littleport, Cambridgeshire, with part of it built of stone, having a gable and
Tudor weather-moulding over the windows.   The rest of
the building was added at a later date.

In Upper Deal there is an interesting house which

Sixteenth-century Cottage, formerly standing in Upper Deal, Kent

shows Flemish influence in the construction of its picturesque gable and octagonal chimney, and contrasted with it
an early sixteenth-century cottage much the worse for wear.

We give a sketch of a Portsmouth row which resembles
in narrowness those at Yarmouth, and in Crown Street
there is a battered, three-gabled, weather-boarded house
which has evidently seen better days.   There is a fine
canopy over the front door of Buckingham House, wherein
George Villiers, Duke of Buckingham, was assassinated
by John Felton on August 23rd, 1628.

The Vale of Aylesbury is one of the sweetest and most
charmingly characteristic tracts of land in the whole of

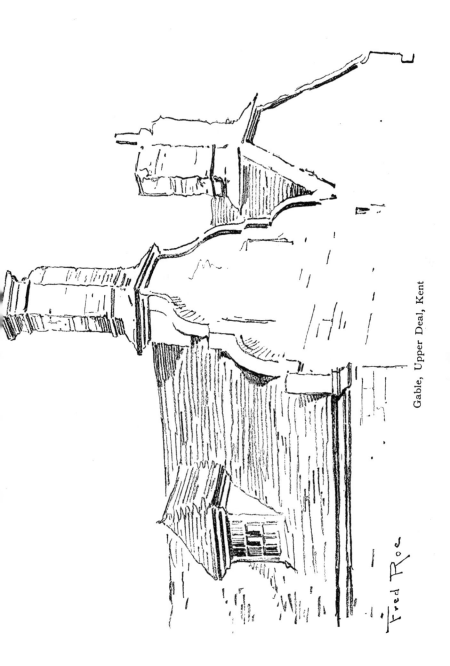

Gable, Upper Deal, Kent

Fred Roe

rural England, abounding with old houses. The whole
countryside literally teems with picturesque evidences of
the past life and history of England. Ancient landmarks
and associations are so numerous that it is difficult to
mention a few without seeming to ignore unfairly their
equally interesting neighbours. Let us take the London
road, which enters the shire from Middlesex and makes
for Aylesbury, a meandering road with patches of scenery
strongly suggestive of Birket Foster's landscapes. Down
a turning at the foot of the lovely Chiltern Hills lies the
secluded village of Chalfont St. Giles. Here Milton, the
poet, sought refuge from plague-stricken London among
a colony of fellow Quakers, and here remains, in a very
perfect state, the cottage in which he lived and was visited
by Andrew Marvel. It is said that his neighbour Elwood,
one of the Quaker fraternity, suggested the idea of " Paradise Regained," and that the draft of the latter poem
was written upon a great oak table which may be seen in
one of the low-pitched rooms on the ground floor. I
fancy that Milton must have beautified and repaired the
cottage at the period of his tenancy. The mantelpiece
with its classic ogee moulding belongs certainly to his
day, and some other minor details may also be noticed
which support this inference. It is not difficult to imagine
that one who was accustomed to metropolitan comforts
would be dissatisfied with the open hearth common to
country cottages of that poet's time, and have it enclosed
in the manner in which we now see it. Outside the
garden is brilliant with old-fashioned flowers, such as the
poet loved. A stone scutcheon may be seen peeping
through the shrubbery which covers the front of the
cottage, but the arms which it displays are those of the
Fleetwoods, one time owners of these tenements. Between
the years 1709 and 1807 the house was used as an inn.
Milton's cottage is one of our national treasures, which
(though not actually belonging to the nation) has successfully resisted purchase by our American cousins and
transportation across the Atlantic.

A Portsmouth "Row"

The entrance to the churchyard in Chalfont St. Giles is through a wonderfully picturesque turnstile or lich-gate under an ancient house in the High Street.   The gate formerly closed itself mechanically by means of a pulley to which was attached a heavy weight.   Unfortunately

Lich-gate, Chalfont St. Giles, Bucks

this weight was not boxed in—as in the somewhat similar example at Hayes, in Middlesex—and an accident which happened to some children resulted in its removal.

A good many picturesque old houses remain in the village, among them being one called Stonewall Farm, a structure of the fifteenth century with an original billet-moulded porch and Gothic barge-boards.

There is a certain similarity about the villages that dot

the Vale of Aylesbury. The old Market House is usually a feature of the High Street—where it has not been spoilt as at Wendover. Groups of picturesque timber cottages, thickest round the church, and shouldered here and there by their more respectable and severe Georgian brethren, are common to all, and vary but little in their general aspect and colouring. Memories and legends haunt every hamlet, the very names of which have an ancient sound carrying us vaguely back to former days. Prince's Risborough, once a manor of the Black Prince; Wendover, the birthplace of Roger of Wendover, the medieval historian, and author of the Chronicle *Flores Historiarum, or History of the World from the Creation to the year 1235,* in modern language a somewhat "large order"; Hampden, identified to all time with the patriot of that name; and so on indefinitely. At Monk's Risborough, another hamlet with an ancient-sounding name, but possessing no special history, is a church

Fifteenth-century Handle on
Church Door, Monk's
Risborough, Bucks

of the Perpendicular period containing some features of exceptional interest, and internally one of the most charmingly picturesque of its kind. The carved tie-beams of the porch with their masks and tracery and the great stone stoup which appears in one corner have an *unrestored* appearance which is quite delightful in these days of over-restoration. The massive oak door has some curious iron fittings, and the interior of the church itself displays such treasures as a magnificent early Tudor roof and an elegant fifteenth-century chancel-screen, on the latter of which some remains of ancient painting exist.[1]

Thame, just across the Oxfordshire border, is another

---

[1] The rood-loft has unfortunately disappeared.

town of the greatest interest.   The noble parish church
here contains a number of fine brasses and tombs, including the recumbent effigies of Lord John Williams of
Thame and his wife, who flourished in the reign of Queen
Mary.   The chancel-screen is of uncommon character, the
base being richly decorated with linen panelling, while
above rises an arcade in which Gothic form mingles freely
with the grotesqueness of the Renaissance.   The choir-
stalls are also lavishly ornamented with the linen-fold
decoration.

The centre of Thame's broad High Street is narrowed
by an island of houses, once termed Middle Row, and
above the jumble of tiled roofs here rises like a watch-
tower a most curious and interesting medieval house
known as the "Bird Cage Inn."   About this structure
little is known ; it is, however, referred to in an old document as the "tenement called the Cage, demised to James
Rosse by indenture for the term of 100 years, yielding
therefor by the year 8s.," and appears to have been
a farm-house.   The document in question is a grant
of Edward IV to Sir John William of the Charity or
Guild of St. Christopher in Thame, founded by Richard
Quartemayne, *Squier*, who died in the year 1460.   This
house, though in some respects adapted during later
years from its original plan, is structurally but little
altered, and should be taken in hand and *intelligently*
restored as an object of local attraction and interest.   The
choicest oaks of a small forest must have supplied its
framework, which stands firm as the day when it was
built.   The fine corner-posts (now enclosed) should be
exposed to view, and the mullioned windows which jut
out over a narrow passage should be opened up.   If this
could be done—and not overdone—the "Bird Cage"
would hardly be surpassed as a miniature specimen of
medieval timber architecture in the county.   A stone
doorway of Gothic form and a kind of almery or safe
exist in its cellars.

A school was founded at Thame by Lord John

Williams, whose recumbent effigy exists in the church, and amongst the students there during the second quarter of the seventeenth century was Anthony Wood, the Oxford antiquary. Thame about this time was the centre of military operations between the King's forces and the rebels, and was continually being beaten up by one side or the other. Wood, though but a boy at the time, has left on record in his narrative some vivid impressions of the conflicts which he personally witnessed, and which bring the disjointed times before us in a vision of strange and absolute reality.

He tells of Colonel Blagge, the Governor of Wallingford Castle, who was on a marauding expedition, being chased through the streets of Thame by Colonel Crafford, who commanded the Parliamentary garrison at Aylesbury, and how one man fell from his horse, and the Colonel "held a pistol to him, but the trooper cried 'Quarter!' and the rebels came up and rifled him and took him and his horse away with them." On another occasion, just as a company of Roundhead soldiers were sitting down to dinner, a Cavalier force appeared "to beat up their quarters," and the Roundheads retired in a hurry, leaving "A. W. and the schoolboys, sojourners in the house," to enjoy their venison pasties.

He tells also of certain doings at the Nag's Head, a house that still exists—a very ancient hostelry, though not nearly so old a building as the Bird Cage Inn. The sign is no longer there, but some interesting features remain, among them the huge strap hinges on the outer door, fashioned at their extremities in the form of fleurs-de-lis. We should like to linger long at Thame and describe the wonders at Thame Park, with its remains of a Cistercian abbey and the fine Tudor buildings of Robert King, last abbot and afterward the first Bishop of Oxford. The three fine oriel windows and stair-turret, the noble Gothic dining-hall and abbot's parlour panelled with oak in the style of the linen pattern, are some of the finest Tudor work in the country. The Prebendal house and chapel built by Grossetête are also worthy of the closest attention.   The chapel is an architectural gem of Early English design, and the rest of the house with its later Perpendicular windows is admirable.   Not far away is the interesting village of Long Crendon, once a market-town, with its fine church and its many picturesque houses, including Staple Hall, near the church, with its noble hall, used for more than five centuries as a manorial court-house on behalf of various lords of the manor, including Queen Katherine, widow of Henry V.   It has now fortunately passed into the care of the National Trust, and its future is secured for the benefit of the nation.   The house is a beautiful half-timbered structure, and was in a terribly dilapidated condition.   It is interesting both historically and architecturally, and is note-worthy as illustrating the continuity of English life, that the three owners from whom the Trust received the build-ing, Lady Kinloss, All Souls' College, and the Eccle-siastical Commissioners, are the successors in title of three daughters of an Earl of Pembroke in the thirteenth century.   It is fortunate that the old house has fallen into such good hands.   The village has a Tudor manor-house which has been restored.

Another court-house, that at Udimore, in Sussex, near Rye, has, we believe, been saved by the Trust, though the owner has retained possession.   It is a picturesque half-timbered building of two storeys with modern wings projecting at right angles at each end.   The older por-tion is all that remains of a larger house which appears to have been built in the fifteenth century.   The manor be-longed to the Crown, and it is said that both Edward I and Edward III visited it.   The building was in a very dilapidated condition, and the owner intended to destroy it and replace it with modern cottages.   We hope that this scheme has now been abandoned, and that the old house is safe for many years to come.

At the other end of the county of Oxfordshire remote from Thame is the beautiful little town of Burford, the

Weather-boarded Houses, Crown Street,
Portsmouth

gem of the Cotswolds. No wonder that my friend
"Sylvanus Urban," otherwise Canon Beeching, sings of
its charm:—

> Oh fair is Moreton in the marsh
>   And Stow on the wide wold,
> Yet fairer far is Burford town
>   With its stone roofs grey and old ;
> And whether the sky be hot and high,
>   Or rain fall thin and chill,
> The grey old town on the lonely down
>   Is where I would be still.
>
> O broad and smooth the Avon flows
>   By Stratford's many piers ;
> And Shakespeare lies by Avon's side
>   These thrice a hundred years ;
> But I would be where Windrush sweet
>   Laves Burford's lovely hill—
> The grey old town on the lonely down
>   Is where I would be still.

It is unlike any other place, this quaint old Burford, a
right pleasing place when the sun is pouring its beams
upon the fantastic creations of the builders of long ago,
and when the moon is full there is no place in England
which surpasses it in picturesqueness. It is very quiet
and still now, but there was a time when Burford cloth,
Burford wool, Burford stone, Burford malt, and Burford
saddles were renowned throughout the land. Did not the
townsfolk present two of its famous saddles to "Dutch
William" when he came to Burford with the view of
ingratiating himself into the affections of his subjects
before an important general election? It has been the
scene of battles. Not far off is Battle Edge, where the
fierce kings of Wessex and Mercia fought in 720 A.D. on
Midsummer Eve, in commemoration of which the good
folks of Burford used to carry a dragon up and down the
streets, the great dragon of Wessex. Perhaps the origin
of this procession dates back to early pagan days before
the battle was fought, but tradition connects it with the
fight. Memories cluster thickly around one as you walk
up the old street. It was the first place in England to
receive the privilege of a Merchant Guild. The gaunt
Earl of Warwick, the King-maker, owned the place, and

appropriated to himself the credit of erecting the alms-houses, though Henry Bird gave the money. You can still see the Earl's signature at the foot of the document relating to this foundation—R. Warrewych—the only signature known save one at Belvoir. You can see the ruined Burford Priory. It is not the conventual build-ing wherein the monks lived in pre-Reformation days and served God in the grand old church that is Burford's chief glory. Edmund Harman, the royal barber-surgeon, re-ceived a grant of the Priory from Henry VIII for curing him from a severe illness. Then Sir Laurence Tanfield, Chief Baron of the Exchequer, owned it, who married a Burford lady, Elizabeth Cobbe. An aged correspondent

Fred Roe.

Inscription on Font, Parish Church, Burford, Oxon

tells me that in the days of her youth there was standing a house called Cobb Hall, evidently the former residence of Lady Tanfield's family. He built a grand Elizabethan mansion on the site of the old Priory, and here was born Lucius Cary, Lord Falkland, who was slain in Newbury fight. That Civil War brought stirring times to Burford. You have heard of the fame of the Levellers, the dis-contented mutineers in Cromwell's army, the followers of John Lilburne, who for a brief space threatened the exist-ence of the Parliamentary regime. Cromwell dealt with them with an iron hand. He caught and surprised them at Burford and imprisoned them in the church, wherein carved roughly on the font with a dagger you can see this touching memorial of one of these poor men :—

ANTHONY SEDLEY PRISNER 1649.

Three of the leaders were shot in the churchyard on the

7

following morning in view of the other prisoners, who were placed on the leaden roof of the church, and you can still see the bullet-holes in the old wall against which the unhappy men were placed. The following

Detail of Fifteenth-century Barge-board, Burford, Oxon.

entries in the books of the church tell the sad story tersely :—

Burials.—" 1649 Three soldiers shot to death in Burford Churchyard May 17th."

" Pd. to Daniel Muncke for cleansinge the Church when the Levellers were taken 3s. 4d."

A walk through the streets of the old town is refreshing to an antiquary's eyes. The old stone buildings grey with age with tile roofs, the old Tolsey much restored, the merchants' guild mark over many of the ancient door-

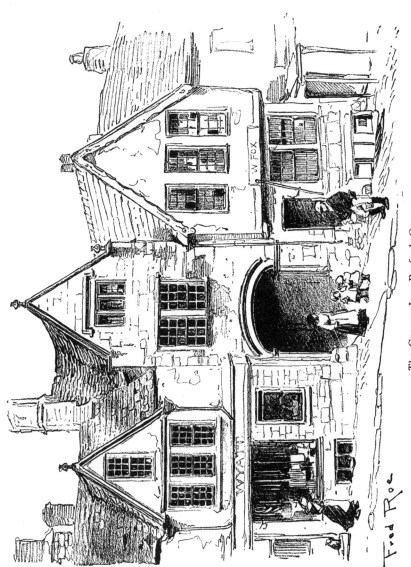

The George Inn, Burford, Oxon

ways, the noble church with its eight chapels and fine
tombs, the plate of the old corporation, now in the custody
of its oldest surviving member (Burford has ceased to be
an incorporated borough), are all full of interest. Vandalism is not, however, quite lacking, even in Burford.
One of the few Gothic chimneys remaining, a gem with a
crocketed and pinnacled canopy, was taken down some
thirty years ago, while the Priory is said to be in danger
of being pulled down, though a later report speaks only
of its restoration. In the coaching age the town was
alive with traffic, and Burford races, established by the
Merry Monarch, brought it much gaiety. At the George
Inn, now degraded from its old estate and cut up into
tenements, Charles I stayed. It was an inn for more than
a century before his time, and was only converted from
that purpose during the early years of the nineteenth
century, when the proprietor of the Bull Inn bought it up
and closed its doors to the public with a view to improving
the prosperity of his own house. The restoration of the
picturesque almshouses founded by Henry Bird in the time
of the King-maker, a difficult piece of work, was well
carried out in the decadent days of the "twenties," and
happily they do not seem to have suffered much in the
process.

During our wanderings in the streets and lanes of rural
England we must not fail to visit the county of Essex. It
is one of the least picturesque of our counties, but it
possesses much wealth of interesting antiquities in the
timber houses at Colchester, Saffron Walden, the old town
of Maldon, the inns at Chigwell and Brentwood, and the
halls of Layer Marney and Horsham at Thaxted. Saffron
Walden is one of those quaint agricultural towns whose
local trade is a thing of the past. From the records which
are left of it in the shape of prints and drawings, the
town in the early part of the nineteenth century must
have been a medieval wonder. It is useless now to rail
against the crass ignorance and vandalism which has
swept away so many irreplaceable specimens of bygone

architecture only to fill their sites with brick boxes, "likely indeed and all alike."

Itineraries of the Georgian period when mentioning Saffron Walden describe the houses as being of "mean appearance,"[1] which remark, taking into consideration the debased taste of the times, is significant. A perfect holocaust followed, which extending through that shocking time known as the Churchwarden Period has not yet spent itself in the present day. Municipal improvements threaten to go further still, and in these commercial days, when combined capital under such appellations as the "Metropolitan Co-operative" or the "Universal Supply Stores" endeavours to increase its display behind plate-glass windows of immodest size, the life of old buildings seems painfully insecure.

A good number of fine early barge-boards still remain in Saffron Walden, and the timber houses which have been allowed to remain speak only too eloquently of the beauties which have vanished. One of these structures— a large timber building or collection of buildings, for the dates of erection are various—stands in Church Street, and was formerly the Sun Inn, a hostel of much importance in bygone times. This house of entertainment is said to have been in 1645 the quarters of the Parliamentary Generals Cromwell, Ireton, and Skippon. In 1870, during the conversion of the Sun Inn into private residences, some glazed tiles were discovered bricked up in what had once been an open hearth. These tiles were collectively painted with a picture on each side of the hearth, and bore the inscription "W. E. 1730," while on one of them a bust of the Lord Protector was depicted, thus showing the tradition to have been honoured during the second George's time.[2] Saffron Walden was the rendezvous of the Parliamentarian forces after the

---

[1] *Excursions in Essex*, published in 1819, states : "The old market cross and gaol are taking down. The market cross has long been considered a nuisance."

[2] These tiles have now found a place in the excellent local museum.

sacking of Leicester, having their encampment on Trip-
low Heath.   A remarkable incident may be mentioned in
connexion with this fact.   In 1826 a rustic, while ploughing some land to the south of the town, turned up with
his share the brass seal of Leicester Hospital, which seal
had doubtless formed part of the loot acquired by the
rebel army.

The Sun Inn, or "House of the Giants," as it has
sometimes been called, from the colossal figures which
appear in the pargeting over its gateway, is a building
which evidently grew with the needs of the town, and
a study of its architectural features is curiously in-
structive.

The following extract from Pepys's *Diary* is interesting
as referring to Saffron Walden :—

" 1659, Feby. 27th.   Up by four o'clock.   Mr. Blayton
and I took horse and straight to Saffron Walden, where at
the White Hart we set up our horses and took the master
to show us Audley End House, where the housekeeper
showed us all the house, in which the stateliness of the
ceilings, chimney-pieces, and form of the whole was ex-
ceedingly worth seeing.   He took us into the cellar,
where we drank most admirable drink, a health to the
King.   Here I played on my flageolette, there being an
excellent echo.   He showed us excellent pictures ; two
especially, those of the four Evangelists and Henry VIII.
In our going my landlord carried us through a very old
hospital or almshouse, where forty poor people were maintained ; a very old foundation, and over the chimney-piece
was an inscription in brass : 'Orato pro animâ Thomae
Bird,' &c.   They brought me a draft of their drink in a
brown bowl, tipt with silver, which I drank off, and at the
bottom was a picture of the Virgin with the child in her
arms done in silver.   So we took leave. . . ."

The inscription and the "brown bowl" (which is a
mazer cup) still remain, but the picturesque front of the
hospital, built in the reign of Edward VI, disappeared
during the awful "improvements" which took place
during the "fifties."   A drawing of it survives in the
local museum.

Maldon, the capital of the Blackwater district, is to the eye of an artist a town for twilight effects. The picturesque skyline of its long, straggling street is accentuated in the early morning or afterglow, when much undesirable detail of modern times below the tiled roofs is blurred and lost. In broad daylight the quaintness of its suburbs towards the river reeks of the salt flavour

Maldon, Essex. Sky-line of the High Street at twilight

of W. W. Jacobs's stories. Formerly the town was rich with such massive timber buildings as still appear in the yard of the Blue Boar—an ancient hostelry which was evidently modernized externally in Pickwickian times. While exploring in the outhouses of this hostel Mr. Roe lighted on a venerable posting-coach of early nineteenth-century origin among some other decaying vehicles, a curiosity even more rare nowadays than the Gothic king-posts to be seen in the picturesque half-timbered billiard-room.

The country around Maldon is dotted plentifully with

evidences of past ages ; Layer Marney, with its famous towers ; D'Arcy Hall, noted for containing some of the finest linen panelling in England ; Beeleigh Abbey, and other old-world buildings.   The sea-serpent may still be seen at Heybridge, on the Norman church-door, one of

St. Mary's Church, Maldon

the best of its kind, and exhibiting almost all its original ironwork, including the chimerical decorative clamp.

The ancient house exhibited at the Franco-British Exhibition at Shepherd's Bush was a typical example of an Elizabethan dwelling.   It was brought from Ipswich, where it was doomed to make room for the extension of Co-operative Stores, but so firmly was it built that, in spite

of its age of three hundred and fifty years, it defied for
some time the attacks of the house-breakers. It was built
in 1563, as the date carved on the solid lintel shows, but
some parts of the structure may have been earlier. All
the oak joists and rafters had been securely mortised into
each other and fixed with stout wooden pins. So securely
were these pins fixed, that after many vain attempts to
knock them out, they had all to be bored out with augers.
The mortises and tenons were found to be as sound and
clean as on the day when they were fitted by the sixteenth-
century carpenters. The foundations and the chimneys
were built of brick. The house contained a large entrance-
hall, a kitchen, a splendidly carved staircase, a living-

Norman Clamp on door of Heybridge Church, Essex

room, and two good bedrooms, on the upper floor. The
whole house was a fine specimen of East Anglian half-
timber work. The timbers that formed the framework
were all straight, the diamond and curved patterns, familiar
in western counties, signs of later construction, being
altogether absent. One of the striking features of this,
as of many other timber-framed houses, is the carved
corner or angle post. It curves outwards as a support to
the projecting first floor to the extent of nearly two feet,
and the whole piece was hewn out of one massive oak
log, the root, as was usual, having been placed upwards,
and beautifully carved with Gothic floriations. The full
overhang of the gables is four feet six inches. In later
examples this distance between the gables and the wall
was considerably reduced, until at last the barge-boards
were flush with the wall. The joists of the first floor project from under a finely carved string-course, and the end
of each joist has a carved finial. All the inside walls
were panelled with oak, and the fire-place is of the typical

old English character, with seats for half a dozen people in the ingle-nook. The principal room had a fine Tudor door, and the frieze and some of the panels were enriched

Tudor Fire-place. Now walled up in the passage of a shop
in Banbury

with an inlay of holly. When the house was demolished many of the choicest fittings which were missing from their places were found carefully stowed under the floor boards. Possibly a raid or a riot had alarmed the owners in some distant period, and they hid their nicest things and then were slain, and no one knew of the secret hiding-place.

The Rector of Haughton calls attention to a curious old house which certainly ought to be preserved if it has not yet quite vanished.

"It is completely hidden from the public gaze. Right away in the fields, to be reached only by footpath, or by strangely circuitous lane, in the parish of Ranton, there stands a little old half-timbered house, known as the Vicarage Farm. Only a very practised eye would suspect the treasures that it contains. Entering through the original door, with quaint knocker intact, you are in the kitchen with a fine open fire-place, noble beam, and walls panelled with oak. But the principal treasure consists in what I have heard called 'The priest's room.' I should venture to put the date of the house at about 1500—certainly pre-Reformation. How did it come to be there? and what purpose did it serve? I have only been able to find one note which can throw any possible light on the matter. Gough says that a certain Rose (Dunston?) brought land at Ranton to her husband John Doiley; and he goes on: 'This man had the consent of William, the Prior of Ranton, to erect a chapel at Ranton.' The little church at Ranton has stood there from the thirteenth century, as the architecture of the west end and south-west doorway plainly testify. The church and cell (or whatever you may call it) must clearly have been an off-shoot from the Priory. But the room: for this is what is principally worth seeing. The beam is richly moulded, and so is the panelling throughout. It has a very well carved course of panelling all round the top, and this is surmounted by an elaborate cornice. The stone mantel-piece is remarkably fine and of unusual character. But the most striking feature of the room is a square-headed arched recess, or niche, with pierced spandrels. What was its use? It is about the right height for a seat, and what may have been the seat is there unaltered. Or was it a niche containing a Calvary, or some figure? I con-fess I know nothing. Is this a unique example? I cannot remember any other. But possibly there may be others, equally hidden away, comparison with which might un-fold its secret. In this room, and in other parts of the house, much of the old ironwork of hinges and door-fasteners remains, and is simply excellent. The old oak sliding shutters are still there, and two more fine stone mantelpieces; on one hearth the original encaustic tiles with patterns, chiefly a Maltese cross, and the oak cill surrounding them, are *in situ*. I confess I tremble for the safety of this priceless relic. The house is in a somewhat dilapidated condition; and I know that one attempt was made to buy the panelling and take it away. Surely such a monument of the past should be in some way guarded by the nation."

The beauty of English cottage-building, its directness, simplicity, variety, and above all its inevitable quality, the intimate way in which the buildings ally themselves with the soil and blend with the ever-varied and exquisite landscape, the delicate harmonies, almost musical in their nature, that grow from their gentle relationship with their surroundings, the modulation from man's handiwork to God's enveloping world that lies in the quiet gardening that binds one to the other without discord or dissonance —all these things are wonderfully attractive to those who have eyes to see and hearts to understand. The English cottages have an importance in the story of the development of architecture far greater than that which concerns their mere beauty and picturesqueness. As we follow the history of Gothic art we find that for the most part the instinctive art in relation to church architecture came to an end in the first quarter of the sixteenth century, but the right impulse did not cease. House-building went on, though there was no church-building, and we admire greatly some of those grand mansions which were reared in the time of Elizabeth and the early Stuarts; but art was declining, a crumbling taste causing disintegration of the sense of real beauty and refinement of detail. A creeping paralysis set in later, and the end came swiftly when the dark days of the eighteenth century blotted out even the memory of a great past. And yet during all this time the people, the poor and middle classes, the yeomen and farmers, were ever building, building,

Witney
Street
Burford

24 May
1908

Fred Roe

quietly and simply, untroubled by any thoughts of style, of Gothic art or Renaissance; hence the cottages and dwellings of the humblest type maintained in all their integrity the real principles that made medieval architecture great. Frank, simple, and direct, built for use and not for the establishment of architectural theories, they have transmitted their messages to the ages and have preserved their beauties for the admiration of mankind and as models for all time.

CHAPTER V

OLD CASTLES

CASTLES have played a prominent part in the making of England. Many towns owe their existence to the protecting guard of an old fortress. They grew up beneath its sheltering walls like children holding the gown of their good mother, though the castle often proved but a harsh and cruel stepmother, and exacted heavy tribute in return for partial security from pillage and rapine. Thus New-castle-upon-Tyne arose about the early fortress erected in 1080 by Robert Curthose to guard the passage of the river at the Pons Aelii. The poor little Saxon village of Monkchester was then its neighbour. But the castle occupying a fine strategic position soon attracted towns-folk, who built their houses 'neath its shadow. The town of Richmond owes its existence to the lordly castle which Alain Rufus, a cousin of the Duke of Brittany, erected on land granted to him by the Conqueror. An old rhyme tells how he

> Came out of Brittany
> With his wife Tiffany,
> And his maid Manfras,
> And his dog Hardigras.

He built his walls of stone. We must not imagine, how-ever, that an early Norman castle was always a vast keep of stone. That came later. The Normans called their earliest strongholds *mottes*, which consisted of a mound with stockades and a deep ditch and a bailey-court also defended by a ditch and stockades. Instead of the great stone keep of later days, "foursquare to every wind that blew," there was a wooden tower for the shelter of the garrison.   You can see in the Bayeux tapestry the followers of William the Conqueror in the act of erecting some such tower of defence.   Such structures were somewhat easily erected, and did not require a long period for their construction.   Hence they were very useful for the holding of a conquered country.   Sometimes advantage was taken of the works that the Romans had left.   The Normans made use of the old stone walls built by the earliest conquerors of Britain.   Thus we find at Pevensey a Norman fortress born within the ancient fortress reared by the Romans to protect that portion of the southern coast from the attacks of the northern pirates.   Porchester Keep rose in the time of the first Henry at the north-west angle of the Roman fort.   William I erected his castle at Colchester on the site of the Roman *castrum*.   The old Roman wall of London was used by the Conqueror for the eastern defence of his Tower that he erected to keep in awe the citizens of the metropolis, and at Lincoln and Colchester the works of the first conquerors of Britain were eagerly utilized by him.

One of the most important Roman castles in the country is Burgh Castle, in North Suffolk, with its grand and noble walls.   The late Mr. G. E. Fox thus described the ruins :—

" According to the plan on the Ordnance Survey map, the walls enclose a quadrangular area roughly 640 feet long by 413 wide, the walls being 9 feet thick with a foundation 12 feet in width.   The angles of the station are rounded.   The eastern wall is strengthened by four solid bastions, one standing against each of the rounded angles, the other two intermediate, and the north and south sides have one each, neither of them being in the centre of the side, but rather west of it. The quaggy ground between the camp and the stream would be an excellent defence against sudden attack."

Burgh Castle, according to the late Canon Raven, was the Roman station *Gariannonum* of the *Notitia Imperii.* Its walls are built of flint-rubble concrete, and there are

Fred Roe.

Burgh Castle

lacing courses of tiles. There is no wall on the west, and
Canon Raven used to contend that one existed there but
has been destroyed. But this conjecture seems improb-
able. That side was probably defended by the sea,
which has considerably receded. Two gates remain,
the principal one being the east gate, commanded by
towers a hundred feet high; while the north is a postern-
gate about five feet wide. The Romans have not left
many traces behind them. Some coins have been found,
including a silver one of Gratian and some of Constantine. Here St. Furseus, an Irish missionary, is said to
have settled with a colony of monks, having been favourably received by Sigebert, the ruler of the East Angles,
in 633 A.D. Burgh Castle is one of the finest specimens
of a Roman fort which our earliest conquerors have
left us, and ranks with Reculver, Richborough, and
Pevensey, those strong fortresses which were erected
nearly two thousand years ago to guard the coasts
against foreign foes.

In early days, ere Norman and Saxon became a united
people, the castle was the sign of the supremacy of the
conquerors and the subjugation of the English. It kept
watch and ward over tumultuous townsfolk and prevented any acts of rebellion and hostility to their new
masters. Thus London's Tower arose to keep the turbulent citizens in awe as well as to protect them from
foreign foes. Thus at Norwich the castle dominated the
town, and required for its erection the destruction of over
a hundred houses. At Lincoln the Conqueror destroyed
166 houses in order to construct a strong *motte* at the
south-west corner of the old *castrum* in order to over-
awe the city. Sometimes castles were erected to protect
the land from foreign foes. The fort at Colchester was
intended to resist the Danes if ever their threatened
invasion came, and Norwich Castle was erected quite
as much to drive back the Scandinavian hosts as to
keep in order the citizens. Newcastle and Carlisle were
of strategic importance for driving back the Scots, and

Lancaster Keep, traditionally said to have been reared by Roger de Poitou, but probably of later date, bore the brunt of many a marauding invasion. To check the incursions of the Welsh, who made frequent and powerful irruptions into Herefordshire, many castles were erected in Shropshire and Herefordshire, forming a chain of fortresses which are more numerous than in any other part of England. They are of every shape and size, from stately piles like Wigmore and Goodrich, to the smallest fortified farm, like Urishay Castle, a house half mansion, half fortress. Even the church towers of Herefordshire, with their walls seven or eight feet thick, such as that at Ewias Harold, look as if they were designed as strongholds in case of need. On the western and northern borders of England we find the largest number of fortresses, erected to restrain and keep back troublesome neighbours.

The story of the English castles abounds in interest and romance. Most of them are ruins now, but fancy pictures them in the days of their splendour, the abodes of chivalry and knightly deeds, of "fair ladies and brave men," and each one can tell its story of siege and battle-cries, of strenuous attack and gallant defence, of prominent parts played in the drama of English history. To some of these we shall presently refer, but it would need a very large volume to record the whole story of our English fortresses.

We have said that the earliest Norman castle was a *motte* fortified by a stockade, an earthwork protected with timber palings. That is the latest theory amongst antiquaries, but there are not a few who maintain that the Normans, who proved themselves such admirable builders of the stoutest of stone churches, would not long content themselves with such poor fortresses. There were stone castles before the Normans, besides the old Roman walls at Pevensey, Colchester, London, and Lincoln. And there came from Normandy a monk named Gundulf in 1070 who was a mighty builder. He was consecrated Bishop

of Rochester and began to build his cathedral with
wondrous architectural skill.   He is credited with devis-
ing a new style of military architecture, and found much
favour with the Conqueror, who at the time especially
needed strong walls to guard himself and his hungry
followers.   He was ordered by the King to build the first
beginnings of the Tower of London.   He probably designed the keep at Colchester and the castle of his
cathedral town, and set the fashion of building these
great ramparts of stone which were so serviceable in the
subjugation and overawing of the English.   The fashion
grew, much to the displeasure of the conquered, who deemed
them "homes of wrong and badges of bondage," hateful
places filled with devils and evil men who robbed and
spoiled them.   And when they were ordered to set to
work on castle-building their impotent wrath knew no
bounds.   It is difficult to ascertain how many were constructed during the Conqueror's reign.   Domesday tells
of forty-nine.   Another authority, Mr. Pearson, mentions
ninety-nine, and Mrs. Armitage after a careful examination
of documents contends for eighty-six.   But there may
have been many others.   In Stephen's reign castles spread
like an evil sore over the land.   His traitorous subjects
broke their allegiance to their king and preyed upon the
country.   The *Anglo-Saxon Chronicle* records that "every
rich man built his castles and defended them against him,
and they filled the land full of castles.   They greatly
oppressed the wretched people by making them work at
these castles, and when the castles were finished they
filled them with devils and evil men.   Then they took
those whom they suspected to have any goods, by night
and by day, seizing both men and women, and they put
them in prison for their gold and silver, and tortured
them with pains unspeakable, for never were any martyrs
tormented as these were.   They hung some up by their
feet and smoked them with foul smoke ; some by their
thumbs or by the head, and they hung burning things on
their feet.   They put a knotted string about their heads,

and twisted it till it went into the brain. They put them into dungeons wherein were adders and snakes and toads, and thus wore them out. Some they put into a crucet-house, that is, into a chest that was short and narrow and not deep, and they put sharp stones in it, and crushed the man therein so that they broke all his limbs. There were hateful and grim things called Sachenteges in many of the castles, and which two or three men had enough to do to carry. The Sachentege was made thus : it was fastened to a beam, having a sharp iron to go round a man's throat and neck, so that he might noways sit, nor lie, nor sleep, but that he must bear all the iron. Many thousands they exhausted with hunger. I cannot, and I may not, tell of all the wounds and all the tortures that they inflicted upon the wretched men of this land ; and this state of things lasted the nineteen years that Stephen was king, and ever grew worse and worse. They were continually levying an exaction from the towns, which they called Tenserie,[1] and when the miserable inhabitants had no more to give, then plundered they and burnt all the towns, so that well mightest thou walk a whole day's journey nor ever shouldest thou find a man seated in a town or its lands tilled."

More than a thousand of these abodes of infamy are said to have been built. Possibly many of them were timber structures only. Countless small towns and villages boast of once possessing a fortress. The name Castle Street remains, though the actual site of the stronghold has long vanished. Sometimes we find a mound which seems to proclaim its position, but memory is silent, and the people of England, if the story of the chronicler be true, have to be grateful to Henry II, who set himself to work to root up and destroy very many of these adulterine castles which were the abodes of tyranny and oppression. However, for the protection of his kingdom, he raised other strongholds, in the south the grand fortress of Dover, which still guards the straits ; in the

---

[1] A payment to the superior lord for protection.

west, Berkeley Castle, for his friend Robert FitzHarding,
ancestor of Lord Berkeley, which has remained in the
same family until the present day ; in the north, Richmond, Scarborough, and Newcastle-upon-Tyne ; and in
the east, Orford Keep.   The same stern Norman keep
remains, but you can see some changes in the architecture.
The projection of the buttresses is increased, and there is
some attempt at ornamentation.   Orford Castle, which
some guide-books and directories will insist on confusing
with Oxford Castle and stating that it was built by
Robert D'Oiley in 1072, was erected by Henry II to
defend the country against the incursions of the Flemings
and to safeguard Orford Haven.   Caen stone was brought
for the stone dressings to windows and doors, parapets
and groins, but masses of septaria found on the shore
and in the neighbouring marshes were utilized with such
good effect that the walls have stood the attacks of besiegers and weathered the storms of the east coast for
more than seven centuries.   It was built in a new fashion
that was made in France, and to which our English eyes
were unaccustomed, and is somewhat similar in plan to
Conisborough Castle, in the valley of the Don.   The plan
is circular with three projecting towers, and the keep was
protected by two circular ditches, one fifteen feet and the
other thirty feet distant from its walls.   Between the two
ditches was a circular wall with parapet and battlements.
The interior of the castle was divided into three floors ;
the towers, exclusive of the turrets, had five, two of which
were entresols, and were ninety-six feet high, the central keep being seventy feet.[1]   The oven was at the top
of the keep.   The chapel is one of the most interesting
chambers, with its original altar still in position, though
much damaged, and also piscina, aumbrey, and ciborium.
This castle nearly vanished with other features of vanishing England in the middle of the eighteenth century,
Lord Hereford proposing to pull it down for the sake of
the material; but "it being a necessary sea-mark, especially

[1] Cf. *Memorials of Old Suffolk*, p. 65.

for ships coming from Holland, who by steering so as to make the castle cover or hide the church thereby avoid a dangerous sandbank called the Whiting, Government interfered and prevented the destruction of the building."[1]

In these keeps the thickness of the walls enabled them to contain chambers, stairs, and passages. At Guildford there is an oratory with rude carvings of sacred subjects, including a crucifixion. The first and second floors were usually vaulted, and the upper ones were of timber. Fireplaces were built in most of the rooms, and some sort of domestic comfort was not altogether forgotten. In the earlier fortresses the walls of the keep enclosed an inner court, which had rooms built up to the great stone walls, the court afterwards being vaulted and floors erected. In order to protect the entrance there were heavy doors with a portcullis, and by degrees the outward defences were strengthened. There was an outer bailey or court surrounded by a strong wall, with a barbican guarding the entrance, consisting of a strong gate protected by two towers. In this lower or outer court are the stables, and the mound where the lord of the castle dispenses justice, and where criminals and traitors are executed. Another strong gateway flanked by towers protects the inner bailey, on the edge of which stands the keep, which frowns down upon us as we enter. An immense household was supported in these castles. Not only were there men-at-arms, but also cooks, bakers, brewers, tailors, carpenters, smiths, masons, and all kinds of craftsmen; and all this crowd of workers had to be provided with accommodation by the lord of the castle. Hence a building in the form of a large hall was erected, sometimes of stone, usually of wood, in the lower or upper bailey, for these soldiers and artisans, where they slept and had their meals.

Amongst other castles which arose during this late Norman and early English period of architecture we may mention Barnard Castle, a mighty stronghold, held

[1] Grose's *Antiquities.*

by the royal house of Balliol, the Prince Bishops of Durham, the Earls of Warwick, the Nevilles, and other powerful families. Sir Walter Scott immortalized the castle in *Rokeby*. Here is his description of the fortress :—

> High crowned he sits, in dawning pale,
> The sovereign of the lovely vale.
> What prospects from the watch-tower high
> Gleam gradual on the warder's eye?
> Far sweeping to the east he sees
> Down his deep woods the course of Tees,
> And tracks his wanderings by the steam
> Of summer vapours from the stream ;
> And ere he pace his destined hour
> By Brackenbury's dungeon tower,
> These silver mists shall melt away
> And dew the woods with glittering spray.
> Then in broad lustre shall be shown
> That mighty trench of living stone.
> And each huge trunk that from the side,
> Reclines him o'er the darksome tide,
> Where Tees, full many a fathom low,
> Wears with his rage no common foe ;
> Nor pebbly bank, nor sand-bed here,
> Nor clay-mound checks his fierce career,
> Condemned to mine a channelled way
> O'er solid sheets of marble grey.

This lordly pile has seen the Balliols fighting with the Scots, of whom John Balliol became king, the fierce contests between the warlike prelates of Durham and Barnard's lord, the triumph of the former, who were deprived of their conquest by Edward I, and then its surrender in later times to the rebels of Queen Elizabeth.

Another northern border castle is Norham, the possession of the Bishop of Durham, built during this period. It was a mighty fortress, and witnessed the gorgeous scene of the arbitration between the rival claimants to the Scottish throne, the arbiter being King Edward I of England, who forgot not to assert his own fancied rights to the overlordship of the northern kingdom. It was, however, besieged by the Scots, and valiant deeds were wrought before its walls by Sir William Marmion and Sir Thomas Grey, but the Scots captured it in 1327 and again in 1513. It is now but a battered ruin. Prudhoe, with its memories of border wars, and Castle Rising, redolent with the memories of the last years of the wicked widow of Edward II, belong to this age of castle-architecture, and also the older portions of Kenilworth.

Pontefract Castle, the last fortress that held out for King Charles in the Civil War, and in consequence slighted and ruined, can tell of many dark deeds and strange events in English history. The De Lacys built it in the early part of the thirteenth century. Its area was seven acres. The wall of the castle court was high and flanked by seven towers; a deep moat was cut on the western side, where was the barbican and drawbridge. It had terrible dungeons, one a room twenty-five feet square, without any entrance save a trap-door in the floor of a turret. The castle passed, in 1310, by marriage to Thomas Earl of Lancaster, who took part in the strife between Edward II and his nobles, was captured, and in his own hall condemned to death. The castle is always associated with the murder of Richard II, but contemporary historians, Thomas of Walsingham and Gower the poet, assert that he starved himself to death; others contend that his starvation was not voluntary; while there are not wanting those who say that he escaped to Scotland, lived there many years, and died in peace in the castle of Stirling, an honoured guest of Robert III of Scotland, in 1419. I have not seen the entries, but I am told in the accounts of the Chamberlain of Scotland there are items for the maintenance of the King for eleven years. But popular tales die hard, and doubtless you will hear the groans and see the ghost of the wronged Richard some moonlight night in the ruined keep of Pontefract. He has many companion ghosts—the Earl of Salisbury, Richard Duke of York, Anthony Wydeville, Earl Rivers and Grey his brother, and Sir Thomas Vaughan, whose feet trod the way to the block, that was worn hard by many victims. The dying days of the old castle made it illustrious. It was besieged three times,

taken and retaken, and saw amazing scenes of gallantry
and bravery. It held out until after the death of the
martyr king ; it heard the proclamation of Charles II,
but at length was compelled to surrender, and "the
strongest inland garrison in the kingdom," as Oliver
Cromwell termed it, was slighted and made a ruin. Its
sister fortress Knaresborough shared its fate. Lord
Lytton, in *Eugene Aram*, wrote of it :—

"You will be at a loss to recognise now the truth of
old Leland's description of that once stout and gallant
bulwark of the north, when 'he numbrid 11 or 12 Toures
in the walles of the Castel, and one very fayre beside
in the second area.' In that castle the four knightly
murderers of the haughty Becket (the Wolsey of his age)
remained for a whole year, defying the weak justice of
the times. There, too, the unfortunate Richard II passed
some portion of his bitter imprisonment. And there, after
the battle of Marston Moor, waved the banner of the
loyalists against the soldiers of Lilburn."

An interesting story is told of the siege. A youth,
whose father was in the garrison, each night went into
the deep, dry moat, climbed up the glacis, and put pro-
visions through a hole where his father stood ready to
receive them. He was seen at length, fired on by the
Parliamentary soldiers, and sentenced to be hanged in
sight of the besieged as a warning to others. But a good
lady obtained his respite, and after the conquest of the
place was released. The castle then, once the residence
of Piers Gaveston, of Henry III, and of John of Gaunt,
was dismantled and destroyed.

During the reign of Henry III great progress was
made in the improvement and development of castle-
building. The comfort and convenience of the dwellers
in these fortresses were considered, and if not very
luxurious places they were made more beautiful by art
and more desirable as residences. During the reigns of
the Edwards this progress continued, and a new type of
castle was introduced. The stern, massive, and high-
towering keep was abandoned, and the fortifications

arranged in a concentric fashion. A fine hall with kitchens occupied the centre of the fortress; a large number of chambers were added. The stronghold itself consisted of a large square or oblong like that at Donnington, Berkshire, and the approach was carefully guarded by strong gateways, advanced works, walled galleries, and barbicans. Deep moats filled with water increased their strength and improved their beauty.

We will give some examples of these Edwardian castles, of which Leeds Castle, Kent, is a fine specimen. It stands on three islands in a sheet of water about fifteen acres in extent, these islands being connected in former times by double drawbridges. It consists of two huge piles of buildings which with a strong gate-house and barbican form four distinct forts, capable of separate defence should any one or other fall into the hands of an enemy. Three causeways, each with its drawbridge, gate, and portcullis, lead to the smallest island or inner barbican, a fortified mill contributing to the defences. A stone bridge connects this island with the main island. There stands the Constable's Tower, and a stone wall surrounds the island and within is the modern mansion. The Maiden's Tower and the Water Tower defend the island on the south. A two-storeyed building on arches now connects the main island with the Tower of the Gloriette, which has a curious old bell with the Virgin and Child, St. George and the Dragon, and the Crucifixion depicted on it, and an ancient clock. The castle withstood a siege in the time of Edward II because Queen Isabella was refused admission. The King hung the Governor, Thomas de Colepepper, by the chain of the drawbridge. Henry IV retired here on account of the Plague in London, and his second wife, Joan of Navarre, was imprisoned here. It was a favourite residence of the Court in the fourteenth and fifteenth centuries. Here the wife of Humphrey, Duke of Gloucester, was tried for witchcraft. Dutch prisoners were confined here in 1666 and contrived to set fire to some of the buildings. It is the

home of the Wykeham Martin family, and is one of the
most picturesque castles in the country.

In the same neighbourhood is Allington Castle, an ivy-
mantled ruin, another example of vanished glory, only
two tenements occupying the princely residence of the
Wyatts, famous in the history of State and Letters. Sir
Henry, the father of the poet, felt the power of the Hunch-
back Richard, and was racked and imprisoned in Scotland, and would have died in the Tower of London but
for a cat. He rose to great honour under Henry VII,
and here entertained the King in great style. At Allington the poet Sir Thomas Wyatt was born, and spent his
days in writing prose and verse, hunting and hawking,
and occasionally dallying after Mistress Anne Boleyn at
the neighbouring castle of Hever. He died here in 1542,
and his son Sir Thomas led the insurrection against
Queen Mary and sealed the fate of himself and his race.

Hever Castle, to which allusion has been made, is an
example of the transition between the old fortress and the
more comfortable mansion of a country squire or mag-
nate. Times were less dangerous, the country more peaceful when Sir Geoffrey Boleyn transformed and rebuilt
the castle built in the reign of Edward III by William de
Hever, but the strong entrance-gate flanked by towers,
embattled and machicolated, and defended by stout doors
and three portcullises and the surrounding moat, shows
that the need of defence had not quite passed away. The
gates lead into a courtyard around which the hall, chapel,
and domestic chambers are grouped. The long gallery
Anne Boleyn so often traversed with impatience still
seems to re-echo her steps, and her bedchamber, which
used to contain some of the original furniture, has
always a pathetic interest. The story of the courtship of
Henry VIII with "the brown girl with a perthroat and
an extra finger," as Margaret More described her, is well
known. Her old home, which was much in decay, has passed
into the possession of a wealthy American gentleman, and
has been recently greatly restored and transformed.

Sussex can boast of many a lordly castle, and in its day Bodiam must have been very magnificent. Even in its decay and ruin it is one of the most beautiful in England. It combined the palace of the feudal lord and the fortress of a knight. The founder, Sir John Dalyngrudge, was a gallant soldier in the wars of Edward III, and spent most of his best years in France, where he had doubtless learned the art of making his house comfortable as well as secure. He acquired licence to fortify his castle in 1385 "for resistance against our enemies." There was need of strong walls, as the French often at that period ravaged the coast of Sussex, burning towns and manor-houses. Clark, the great authority on castles, says that " Bodiam is a complete and typical castle of the end of the fourteenth century, laid out entirely on a new site, and constructed after one design and at one period. It but seldom happens that a great fortress is wholly original, of one, and that a known, date, and so completely free from alterations or additions." It is nearly square, with circular tower sixty-five feet high at the four corners, connected by embattled curtain-walls, in the centre of each of which square towers rise to an equal height with the circular. The gateway is a large structure composed of two flanking towers defended by numerous oiletts for arrows, embattled parapets, and deep machicolations. Over the gateway are three shields bearing the arms of Bodiam, Dalyngrudge, and Wardieu. A huge portcullis still frowns down upon us, and two others opposed the way, while above are openings in the vault through which melted lead, heated sand, pitch, and other disagreeable things could be poured on the heads of the foe. In the courtyard on the south stands the great hall with its oriel, buttery, and kitchen, and amidst the ruins you can discern the chapel, sacristy, ladies' bower, presence chamber. The castle stayed not long in the family of the builder, his son John probably perishing in the wars, and passed to Sir Thomas Lewknor, who opposed Richard III, and was therefore attainted of high treason

and his castle besieged and taken. It was restored to
him again by Henry VII, but the Lewknors never resided
there again. Waller destroyed it after the capture of
Arundel, and since that time it has been left a prey to the
rains and frosts and storms, but manages to preserve much
of its beauty, and to tell how noble knights lived in the
days of chivalry.

Caister Castle is one of the four principal castles in
Norfolk. It is built of brick, and is one of the earliest
edifices in England constructed of that material after its
rediscovery as suitable for building purposes. It stands
with its strong defences not far from the sea on the
barren coast. It was built by Sir John Fastolfe, who
fought with great distinction in the French wars of
Henry V and Henry VI, and was the hero of the Battle
of the Herrings in 1428, when he defeated the French and
succeeded in convoying a load of herrings in triumph to
the English camp before Orleans. It is supposed that he
was the prototype of Shakespeare's Falstaff, but beyond
the resemblance in the names there is little similarity in
the exploits of the two "heroes." Sir John Fastolfe,
much to the chagrin of other friends and relatives, made
John Paston his heir, who became a great and prosperous
man, represented his county in Parliament, and was a
favourite of Edward IV. Paston loved Caister, his "fair
jewell"; but misfortunes befell him. He had great
losses, and was thrice confined in the Fleet Prison and
then outlawed. Those were dangerous days, and friends
often quarrelled. Hence during his troubles the Duke
of Norfolk and Lord Scales tried to get possession of
Caister, and after his death laid siege to it. The Pastons
lacked not courage and determination, and defended it for
a year, but were then forced to surrender. However, it
was restored to them, but again forcibly taken from them.
However, not by the sword but by negotiations and legal
efforts, Sir John again gained his own, and an embattled tower at the north-west corner, one hundred feet
high, and the north and west walls remain to tell the

Caister Castle

Fred Roe
7 Aug 1902

story of this brave old Norfolk family, who by their *Letters* have done so much to guide us through the dark period to which they relate.

We will journey to the West Country, a region of

Defaced Arms, Taunton Castle

castles. The Saxons were obliged to erect their rude earthen strongholds to keep back the turbulent Welsh, and these were succeeded by Norman keeps. Monmouth-shire is famous for its castles. Out of the thousand erected in Norman times twenty-five were built in that county. There is Chepstow Castle with its Early Norman gateway spanned by a circular arch flanked by round towers. In the inner court there are gardens and ruins of a grand hall, and in the outer the remains of a chapel with evidences of beautifully groined vaulting, and also a winding staircase leading to the battlements. In the dungeon of the old keep at the south-east corner of the inner court Roger de Britolio, Earl of Hereford, was imprisoned for rebellion against the Conqueror, and in later times Henry Martin, the regicide, lingered as a prisoner for thirty years, employing his enforced leisure in writing a book in order to prove that it is not right for a man to be governed by one wife. Then there is Glosmont Castle, the fortified residence of the Earl of Lancaster; Skenfrith Castle, White Castle, the *Album Castrum* of the Latin records, the Landreilo of the Welsh, with its six towers, portcullis and drawbridge flanked by massive towers, barbican, and other outworks; and Raglan Castle with its splendid gateway, its Elizabethan banqueting-hall ornamented with rich stone tracery, its bowling-green, garden terraces, and spacious courts—an ideal place for knightly tournaments. Raglan is associated with the gallant defence of the castle by the Marquis of Worcester in the Civil War.

Another famous siege is connected with the old castle of Taunton. Taunton was a noted place in Saxon days, and the castle is the earliest English fortress by some two hundred years of which we have any written historical record.[1] The Anglo-Saxon chronicler states, under the date 722 A.D.: "This year Queen Ethelburge overthrew Taunton, which Ina had before built." The buildings tell their story. We see a Norman keep built to the westward of Ina's earthwork, probably by Henry de Blois, Bishop of Winchester, the warlike brother of King Stephen. The gatehouse with the curtain ending in drum towers, of which one only remains, was first built at the close of the thirteenth century under Edward I; but it was restored with Perpendicular additions by

---

[1] *Taunton and its Castle*, by D. P. Alford (Memorials of Old Somerset), p. 149.

9

Bishop Thomas Langton, whose arms with the date 1495 may be seen on the escutcheon above the arch. Probably Bishop Langton also built the great hall ; whilst Bishop Horne, who is sometimes credited with this work, most likely only repaired the hall, but tacked on to it the southward structure on pilasters, which shows his arms with the date 1577. The hall of the castle was for a long period used as Assize Courts. The castle was purchased by the Taunton and Somerset Archæological Society, and is now most appropriately a museum. Taunton has seen many strange sights. The town was owned by the Bishop of Winchester, and the castle had its constable, an office held by many great men. When Lord Daubeney of Barrington Court was constable in 1497 Taunton saw thousands of gaunt Cornishmen marching on to London to protest against the king's subsidy, and they aroused the sympathy of the kind-hearted Somerset folk, who fed them, and were afterwards fined for " aiding and comforting " them. Again, crowds of Cornishmen here flocked to the standard of Perkin Warbeck. The gallant defence of Taunton by Robert Blake, aided by the townsfolk, against the whole force of the Royalists, is a matter of history, and also the rebellion of Monmouth, who made Taunton his head-quarters. This castle, like every other one in England, has much to tell us of the chief events in our national annals.

In the principality of Wales we find many noted strongholds—Conway, Harlech, and many others. Carnarvon Castle, the repair of which is being undertaken by Sir John Puleston, has no rival among our medieval fortresses for the grandeur and extent of the ruins. It was commenced about 1283 by Edward I, but took forty years to complete. In 1295 a playful North Walian, named Madoc, who was an illegitimate son of Prince David, took the rising stronghold by surprise upon a fair day, massacred the entire garrison, and hanged the constable from his own half-finished walls. Sir John Puleston, the present constable, though he derives his patronymic

from the " base, bloody, and brutal Saxon," is really a
warmly patriotic Welshman, and is doing a good work
in preserving the ruins of the fortress of which he is the
titular governor.

We should like to record the romantic stories that have
woven themselves around each crumbling keep and bailey-
court, to see them in the days of their glory when warders
kept the gate and watching archers guarded the wall, and
the lord and lady and their knights and esquires dined in
the great hall, and knights practised feats of arms in the
tilting-ground, and the banner of the lord waved over the
battlements, and everything was ready for war or sport,
hunting or hawking.   But all the glories of most of the
castles of England have vanished, and naught is to be
seen but ruined walls and deserted halls.   Some few have
survived and become royal palaces or noblemen's mansions.   Such are Windsor, Warwick, Raby, Alnwick,
and Arundel, but the fate of most of them is very similar.
The old fortress aimed at being impregnable in the days
of bows and arrows ; but the progress of guns and artillery
somewhat changed the ideas with regard to their security.
In the struggle between Yorkists and Lancastrians many
a noble owner lost his castle and his head.   Edward IV
thinned down castle-ownership, and many a fine fortress
was left to die.   When the Spaniards threatened our
shores those who possessed castles tried to adapt them for
the use of artillery, and when the Civil War began many
of them were strengthened and fortified and often made
gallant defences against their enemies, such as Donnington, Colchester, Scarborough, and Pontefract.   When the
Civil War ended the last bugle sounded the signal for
their destruction.   Orders were issued for their destruction, lest they should ever again be thorns in the sides of
the Parliamentary army.   Sometimes they were destroyed
for revenge, or because of their materials, which were sold
for the benefit of the Government or for the satisfaction of
private greed.   Lead was torn from the roofs of chapels
and banqueting-halls.   The massive walls were so strong

that they resisted to the last and had to be demolished
with the aid of gunpowder. They became convenient
quarries for stone and furnished many a farm, cottage and
manor-house with materials for their construction. Hence-
forth the old castle became a ruin. In its silent marshy
moat reeds and rushes grow, and ivy covers its walls, and
trees have sprung up in the quiet and deserted courts.
Picnic parties encamp on the green sward, and excursion-
ists amuse themselves in strolling along the walls and
wonder why they were built so thick, and imagine that the
castle was always a ruin erected for the amusement of the
cheap-tripper for jest and playground. Happily care is
usually bestowed upon the relics that remain, and diligent
antiquaries excavate and try to rear in imagination the
stately buildings. Some have been fortunate enough to
become museums, and some modernized and restored are
private residences. The English castle recalls some of
the most eventful scenes in English history, and its bones
and skeleton should be treated with respect and veneration as an important feature of vanishing England.

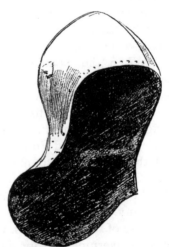

Knightly Bascinet (*temp.* Henry V) in Norwich Castle

CHAPTER VI

VANISHING OR VANISHED CHURCHES

NO buildings have suffered more than our parish churches in the course of ages. Many have vanished entirely. A few stones or ruins mark the site of others, and iconoclasm has left such enduring marks on the fabric of many that remain that it is difficult to read their story and history. A volume, several volumes, would be needed to record all the vandalism that has been done to our ecclesiastical structures in the ages that have passed. We can only be thankful that some churches have survived to proclaim the glories of English architecture and the skill of our masons and artificers who wrought so well and worthily in olden days.

In the chapter that relates to the erosion of our coasts we have mentioned many of the towns and villages which have been devoured by the sea with their churches. These now lie beneath the waves, and the bells in their towers are still said to ring when storms rage. We need not record again the submerged Ravenspur, Dunwich, Kilnsea, and other unfortunate towns with their churches where now only mermaids can form the congregation.

> And as the fisherman strays
> When the clear cold eve's declining,
> He sees the round tower of other days
> In the wave beneath him shining.

In the depths of the country, far from the sea, we can find many deserted shrines, many churches that once echoed with the songs of praise of faithful worshippers, wherein were celebrated the divine mysteries, and organs

pealed forth celestial music, but now forsaken, desecrated,
ruined, forgotten.

> The altar has vanished, the rood screen flown,
> Foundation and buttress are ivy-grown ;
> The arches are shattered, the roof has gone,
> The mullions are mouldering one by one ;
> Foxglove and cow-grass and waving weed
> Grow over the scrolls where you once could read
> Benedicite.

Many of them have been used as quarries, and only a
few stones remain to mark the spot where once stood
a holy house of God.   Before the Reformation the land
must have teemed with churches.   I know not the exact
number of monastic houses once existing in England.
There must have been at least a thousand, and each had
its church.   Each parish had a church.   Besides these
were the cathedrals, chantry chapels, chapels attached to
the mansions, castles, and manor-houses of the lords and
squires, to almshouses and hospitals, pilgrim churches by
the roadside, where bands of pilgrims would halt and pay
their devotions ere they passed along to the shrine of
St. Thomas at Canterbury or to Our Lady at Walsingham.
When chantries and guilds as well as monasteries were
suppressed, their chapels were no longer used for divine
service ; some of the monastic churches became cathedrals or parish churches, but most of them were pillaged,
desecrated, and destroyed.   When pilgrimages were
declared to be "fond things vainly invented," and the
pilgrim bands ceased to travel along the pilgrim way, the
wayside chapel fell into decay, or was turned into a barn
or stable.

It is all very sad and deplorable.   But the roll of
abandoned shrines is not complete.   At the present day
many old churches are vanishing.   Some have been
abandoned or pulled down because they were deemed too
near to the squire's house, and a new church erected at
a more respectful distance.   " Restoration " has doomed
many to destruction.   Not long ago the new scheme for
supplying Liverpool with water necessitated the converting

of a Welsh valley into a huge reservoir and the consequent destruction of churches and villages. A new scheme for supplying London with water has been mooted, and would entail the damming up of a river at the end of a valley and the overwhelming of several prosperous old villages and churches which have stood there for centuries. The destruction of churches in London on account of the value of their site and the migration of the population, westward and eastward, has been frequently deplored. With the exception of All Hallows, Barking; St. Andrew's Undershaft; St. Catherine Cree; St. Dunstan's, Stepney; St. Giles', Cripplegate; All Hallows, Staining; St. James's, Aldgate; St. Sepulchre's; St. Mary Woolnoth; all the old City churches were destroyed by the Great Fire, and some of the above were damaged and repaired. "Destroyed by the Great Fire, rebuilt by Wren," is the story of most of the City churches of London. To him fell the task of rebuilding the fallen edifices. Well did he accomplish his task. He had no one to guide him ; no school of artists or craftsmen to help him in the detail of his buildings; no great principles of architecture to direct him. But he triumphed over all obstacles and devised a style of his own that was well suitable for the requirements of the time and climate and for the form of worship of the English National Church. And how have we treated the buildings which his genius devised for us? Eighteen of his beautiful buildings have already been destroyed, and fourteen of these since the passing of the Union of City Benefices Act in 1860 have succumbed. With the utmost difficulty vehement attacks on others have been warded off, and no one can tell how long they will remain. Here is a very sad and deplorable instance of the vanishing of English architectural treasures. While we deplore the destructive tendencies of our ancestors we have need to be ashamed of our own.

We will glance at some of these deserted shrines on the sites where formerly they stood. The Rev. Gilbert Twenlow Royds, Rector of Haughton and Rural Dean

of Stafford, records three of these in his neighbourhood,
and shall describe them in his own words :—

"On the main road to Stafford, in a field at the top of
Billington Hill, a little to the left of the road, there once
stood a chapel.   The field is still known as Chapel Hill ;
but not a vestige of the building survives ; no doubt the
foundations were grubbed up for ploughing purposes.
In a State paper, describing 'The State of the Church
in Staffs. in 1586,' we find the following entry : 'Billington Chappell ; reader, a husbandman ; pension 16
groats ; no preacher.'   This is under the heading of
Bradeley, in which parish it stood.   I have made a wide
search for information as to the dates of the building and
destruction of this chapel.   Only one solitary note has
come to my knowledge.   In Mazzinghi's *History of Castle
Church* he writes : 'Mention is made of Thomas Salt
the son of Richard Salt and C(lem)ance his wife as
Christened at Billington Chapel in 1600.'   Local tradition says that within the memory of the last generation
stones were carted from this site to build the churchyard
wall of Bradley Church.   I have noticed several re-used
stones ; but perhaps if that wall were to be more closely
examined or pulled down, some further history might
disclose itself.   Knowing that some of the stones were
said to be in a garden on the opposite side of the road,
I asked permission to investigate.   This was most kindly
granted, and I was told that there was a stone 'with
some writing on it' in a wall.   No doubt we had the
fragment of a gravestone ! and such it proved to be.
With some difficulty we got the stone out of the wall ;
and, being an expert in palæography, I was able to
decipher the inscription.   It ran as follows : 'FURy.
Died Feb. 28, 1864.'   A skilled antiquary would probably pronounce it to be the headstone of a favourite dog's
grave ; and I am inclined to think that we have here
a not unformidable rival of the celebrated

✠

BIL ST
U M
PS HI
S.M.
A R K

of the *Pickwick Papers*.

"Yet another vanished chapel, of which I have even less
to tell you.   On the right-hand side of the railway line

running towards Stafford, a little beyond Stallbrook Crossing, there is a field known as Chapel Field. But there is nothing but the name left. From ancient documents I have learnt that a chapel once stood there, known as Derrington Chapel (I think in the thirteenth century), in Seighford parish, but served from Ranton Priory. In 1847 my father built a beautiful little church at Derrington, in the Geometrical Decorated style, but not on the Chapel Field. I cannot tell you what an immense source of satisfaction it would be to me if I could gather some further reliable information as to the history, style, and annihilation of these two vanished chapels. It is unspeakably sad to be forced to realize that in so many of our country parishes no records exist of things and events of surpassing interest in their histories.

"I take you now to where there is something a little more tangible. There stand in the park of Creswell Hall, near Stafford, the ruins of a little thirteenth-century chapel. I will describe what is left. I may say that some twenty years ago I made certain excavations, which showed the ground plan to be still complete. So far as I remember, we found a chamfered plinth all round the nave, with a west doorway. The chancel and nave are of the same width, the chancel measuring about 21 ft. long and the nave c. 33 ft. The ground now again covers much of what we found. The remains above ground are those of the chancel only. Large portions of the east and north walls remain, and a small part of the south wall. The north wall is still c. 12 ft. high, and contains two narrow lancets, quite perfect. The east wall reaches c. 15 ft., and has a good base-mould. It contains the opening, without the head, of a three-light window, with simply moulded jambs, and the glass-line remaining. A string-course under the window runs round the angle buttresses, or rather did so run, for I think the north buttress has been rebuilt, and without the string. The south buttress is complete up to two weatherings, and has two strings round it. It is a picturesque and valuable ruin, and well worth a visit. It is amusing to notice that Creswell now calls itself a rectory, and an open-air service is held annually within its walls. It was a prebend of S. Mary's, Stafford, and previously a Free Chapel, the advowson belonging to the Lord of the Manor; and it was sometimes supplied with preachers from Ranton Priory. Of the story of its destruction I

can discover nothing. It is now carefully preserved and,
I have heard it suggested that it might some day be
rebuilt to meet the spiritual needs of its neighbourhood.

"We pass now to the most stately and beautiful object
in this neighbourhood. I mean the tower of Ranton
Priory Church. It is always known here as Ranton
Abbey. But it has no right to the title. It was an off-
shoot of Haughmond Abbey, near Shrewsbury, and
was a Priory of Black Canons, founded *temp*. Henry II.
The church has disappeared entirely, with the exception
of a bit of the south-west walling of the nave and a
Norman doorway in it. This may have connected the
church with the domestic build ngs. In Gough's Collection in the Bodleian, dated 1731, there is a sketch of
the church. What is shown there is a simple parallelo-
gram, with the usual high walls, in Transition-Norman
style, with flat pilaster buttresses, two strings running
round the walls, the upper one forming the dripstones
of lancet windows, a corbel-table supporting the eaves-
course, and a north-east priest's door. But whatever the
church may have been (and the sketch represents it as
being of severe simplicity), some one built on to it a
west tower of great magnificence. It is of early Perpendicular date, practically uninjured, the pinnacles only
being absent, though, happily, the stumps of these remain. Its proportion appears to me to be absolutely
perfect, and its detail so good that I think you would
have to travel far to find its rival. There is a very
interesting point to notice in the beautiful west doorway.
It will be seen that the masonry of the lower parts of its
jambs is quite different from that of the upper parts, and
there can, I think, be no doubt that these lower stones
have been re-used from a thirteenth-century doorway of
some other part of the buildings. There is a tradition
that the bells of Gnosall Church were taken from this
tower. I can find no confirmation of this, and I cannot
believe it. For the church at Gnosall is of earlier date
and greater magnificence than that of Ranton Priory,
and was, I imagine, quite capable of having bells of its
own."

It would be an advantage to archæology if every one
were such a careful and accurate observer of local antiquarian remains as the Rural Dean of Stafford. Wherever

we go we find similar deserted and abandoned shrines. In Derbyshire alone there are over a hundred destroyed or disused churches, of which Dr. Cox, the leading authority on the subject, has published a list. Nottinghamshire abounds in instances of the same kind. As late as 1892 the church at Colston Bassett was deliberately turned into a ruin. There are only mounds and a few stones to show the site of the parish church of Thorpe-in-the-fields, which in the seventeenth century was actually used as a beer-shop. In the fields between Elston and East Stoke is a disused church with a south Norman doorway. The old parochial chapel of Aslacton was long desecrated, and used in comparatively recent days as a beer-shop. The remains of it have, happily, been reclaimed, and now serve as a mission-room. East Anglia, famous for its grand churches, has to mourn over many which have been lost, many that are left roofless and ivy-clad, and some ruined indeed, though some fragment has been made secure enough for the holding of divine service. Whitling has a roofless church with a round Norman tower. The early Norman church of St. Mary at Kirby Bedon has been allowed to fall into decay, and for nearly two hundred years has been ruinous. St. Saviour's Church, Surlingham, was pulled down at the beginning of the eighteenth century on the ground that one church in the village was sufficient for its spiritual wants, and its materials served to mend roads.

A strange reason has been given for the destruction of several of these East Anglian churches. In Norfolk there were many recusants, members of old Roman Catholic families, who refused in the sixteenth and seventeenth centuries to obey the law requiring them to attend their parish church. But if their church were in ruins no service could be held, and therefore they could not be compelled to attend. Hence in many cases the churches were deliberately reduced to a ruinous state. Bowthorpe was one of these unfortunate churches which met its fate in the days of Queen Elizabeth. It stands in a farm-yard, and the nave made an excellent barn and the steeple a dovecote. The lord of the manor was ordered to restore it at the beginning of the seventeenth century. This he did, and for a time it was used for divine service. Now it is deserted and roofless, and sleeps placidly girt by a surrounding wall, a lonely shrine. The church of St. Peter, Hungate, at Norwich, is of great historical interest and contains good architectural features, including a very fine roof. It was rebuilt in the fifteenth century by John Paston and Margaret, his wife, whose letters form part of that extraordinary series of medieval correspondence which throws so much light upon the social life of the period. The church has a rudely carved record of their work outside the north door. This unhappy church has fallen into disuse, and it has been proposed to follow the example of the London citizens to unite the benefice with another and to destroy the building. Thanks to the energy and zeal of His Highness Prince Frederick Duleep Singh, delay in carrying out the work of destruction has been secured, and we trust that his efforts to save the building will be crowned with the success they deserve.

Not far from Norwich are the churches of Keswick and Intwood. Before 1600 A.D. the latter was deserted and desecrated, being used for a sheep-fold, and the people attended service at Keswick. Then Intwood was restored to its sacred uses, and poor Keswick church was compelled to furnish materials for its repair. Keswick remained ruinous until a few years ago, when part of it was restored and used as a cemetery chapel. Ringstead has two ruined churches, St. Andrew's and St. Peter's. Only the tower of the latter remains. Roudham church two hundred years ago was a grand building, as its remains plainly testify. It had a thatched roof, which was fired by a careless thatcher, and has remained roofless to this day. Few are acquainted with the ancient hamlet of Liscombe, situated in a beautiful

Dorset valley. It now consists of only one or two
houses, a little Norman church, and an old monastic
barn. The little church is built of flint, stone, and large
blocks of hard chalk, and consists of a chancel and nave
divided by a Transition-Norman arch with massive
rounded columns. There are Norman windows in the
chancel, with some later work inserted. A fine niche,
eight feet high, with a crocketed canopy, stood at the
north-east corner of the chancel, but has disappeared.
The windows of the nave and the west doorway have
perished. It has been for a long time desecrated. The
nave is used as a bakehouse. There is a large open
grate, oven, and chimney in the centre, and the chancel
is a storehouse for logs. The upper part of the building
has been converted into an upper storey and divided into
bedrooms, which have broken-down ceilings. The roof
is of thatch. Modern windows and a door have been
inserted. It is a deplorable instance of terrible desecration.

The growth of ivy unchecked has caused many a ruin.
The roof of the nave and south aisle of the venerable
church of Chingford, Essex, fell a few years ago entirely
owing to the destructive ivy which was allowed to work
its relentless will on the beams, tiles, and rafters of this
ancient structure.

Besides those we have mentioned there are about sixty
other ruined churches in Norfolk, and in Suffolk many
others, including the magnificent ruins of Covehithe,
Flixton, Hopton, which was destroyed only forty-four
years ago through the burning of its thatched roof, and
the Old Minster, South Elmham.

Attempts have been made by the National Trust and
the Society for the Protection of Ancient Buildings to
save Kirkstead Chapel, near Woodhall Spa, Lincolnshire.
It is one of the very few surviving examples of the
capella extra portas, which was a feature of every Cistercian abbey, where women and other persons who were
not allowed within the gates could hear Mass. The

abbey was founded in 1139, and the chapel, which is
private property, is one of the finest examples of Early
English architecture remaining in the country. It is in
a very decaying condition. The owner has been ap-
proached, and the officials of the above societies have
tried to persuade him to repair it himself or to allow them
to do so. But these negotiations have hitherto failed. It
is very deplorable when the owners of historic buildings
should act in this "dog-in-the-manger" fashion, and
surely the time has come when the Government should
have power to compulsorily acquire such historic monuments when their natural protectors prove themselves to
be incapable or unwilling to preserve and save them from
destruction.

We turn from this sorry page of wilful neglect to one
that records the grand achievement of modern antiquaries,
the rescue and restoration of the beautiful specimen of
Saxon architecture, the little chapel of St. Lawrence at
Bradford-on-Avon.   Until 1856 its existence was entirely
unknown, and the credit of its discovery was due to the
Rev. Canon Jones, Vicar of Bradford.   At the Reformation with the dissolution of the abbey at Shaftesbury it
had passed into lay hands.   The chancel was used as a
cottage.   Round its walls other cottages arose.   Perhaps
part of the building was at one time used as a charnel-
house, as in an old deed it is called the Skull House.   In
1715 the nave and porch were given to the vicar to be
used as a school.   But no one suspected the presence of
this exquisite gem of Anglo-Saxon architecture, until
Canon Jones when surveying the town from the height of
a neighbouring hill recognized the peculiarity of the roof
and thought that it might indicate the existence of a
church.   Thirty-seven years ago the Wiltshire antiquaries
succeeded in purchasing the building.   They cleared away
the buildings, chimney-stacks, and outhouses that had
grown up around it, and revealed the whole beauties of
this lovely shrine.   Archæologists have fought many battles
over it as to its date.   Some contend that it is the identical

Saxon Doorway in St. Lawrence's Church, Bradford-on-Avon, Wilts

church which William of Malmesbury tells us St. Aldhelm built at Bradford-on-Avon about 700 A.D., others assert that it cannot be earlier than the tenth century. It was a monastic cell attached to the Abbey of Malmesbury, but Ethelred II gave it to the Abbess of Shaftesbury in 1001 as a secure retreat for her nuns if Shaftesbury should be threatened by the ravaging Danes. We need not describe the building, as it is well known. Our artist has furnished us with an admirable illustration of it. Its great height, its characteristic narrow Saxon doorways, heavy plain imposts, the string-courses surrounding the building, the arcades of pilasters, the carved figures of angels are some of its most important features. It is cheering to find that amid so much that has vanished we have here at Bradford a complete Saxon church that differs very little from what it was when it was first erected.

Other Saxon remains are not wanting. Wilfrid's Crypt at Hexham, that at Ripon, Brixworth Church, the church within the precincts of Dover Castle, the towers of Barnack, Barton-upon-Humber, Stow, Earl's Barton, Sompting, Stanton Lacy show considerable evidences of Saxon work. Saxon windows with their peculiar baluster shafts can be seen at Bolam and Billingham, Durham; St. Andrew's, Bywell, Monkwearmouth, Ovington, Sompting, St. Mary Junior, York, Hornby, Wickham (Berks), Waithe, Holton-le-Clay, Glentworth and Clee (Lincoln), Northleigh, Oxon, and St. Alban's Abbey. Saxon arches exist at Worth, Corhampton, Escomb, Deerhurst, St. Benet's, Cambridge, Brigstock, and Barnack. Triangular arches remain at Brigstock, Barnack, Deerhurst, Aston Tirrold, Berks. We have still some Saxon fonts at Potterne, Wilts; Little Billing, Northants; Edgmond and Bucknell, Shropshire; Penmon, Anglesey; and South Hayling, Hants. Even Saxon sundials exist at Winchester, Corhampton, Bishopstone, Escomb, Aldborough, Edston, and Kirkdale. There is also one at Daglingworth, Gloucestershire. Some hours of the

Saxon's day in that village must have fled more swiftly than others, as all the radii are placed at the same angle. Even some mural paintings by Saxon artists exist at St. Mary's, Guildford ; St. Martin's, Canterbury; and faint traces at Britford, Headbourne, Worthing, and St. Nicholas, Ipswich, and some painted consecration crosses are believed to belong to this period.

Recent investigations have revealed much Saxon work in our churches, the existence of which had before been unsuspected. Many circumstances have combined to obliterate it. The Danish wars had a disastrous effect on many churches reared in Saxon times. The Norman Conquest caused many of them to be replaced by more highly finished structures. But frequently, as we study the history written in the stonework of our churches, we find beneath coatings of stucco the actual walls built by Saxon builders, and an arch here, a column there, which link our own times with the distant past, when England was divided into eight kingdoms and when Danegelt was levied to buy off the marauding strangers.

It is refreshing to find these specimens of early work in our churches. Since then what destruction has been wrought, what havoc done upon their fabric and furniture ! At the Reformation iconoclasm raged with unpitying ferocity. Everybody from the King to the churchwardens, who sold church plate lest it should fall into the hands of the royal commissioners, seems to have been engaged in pillaging churches and monasteries. The plunder of chantries and guilds followed. Fuller quaintly describes this as "the last dish of the course, and after cheese nothing is to be expected." But the coping-stone was placed on the vast fabric of spoliation by sending commissioners to visit all the cathedrals and parish churches, and seize the superfluous plate and ornaments for the King's use. Even quite small churches possessed many treasures which the piety of many generations had bestowed upon them.

There is a little village in Berkshire called Boxford,

10

quite a small place. Here is the list of church goods
which the commissioners found there, and which had
escaped previous ravages :—

"One challice, a cross of copper & gilt, another cross
of timber covered with brass, one cope of blue velvet
embroidered with images of angles, one vestment of the
same suit with an albe of Lockeram,[1] two vestments of
Dornexe,[2] and three other very old, two old & coarse
albes of Lockeram, two old copes of Dornexe, iiij altar
cloths of linen cloth, two corporals with two cases whereof one is embroidered, two surplices, & one rochet, one
bible & the paraphrases of Erasmus in English, seven
banners of lockeram & one streamer all painted, three
front cloths for altars whereof one of them is with panes
of white damask & black satin, & the other two of old
vestments, two towels of linen, iiij candlesticks of latten[3]
& two standertes[4] before the high altar of latten, a lent
vail[5] before the high altar with panes blue and white, two
candlesticks of latten and five branches, a peace,[6] three
great bells with one saunce bell xx, one canopy of cloth,
a covering of Dornixe for the Sepulchre, two cruets of
pewter, a holy-water pot of latten, a linen cloth to draw
before the rood. And all the said parcels safely to be
kept & preserved, & all the same & every parcel thereof
to be forthcoming at all times when it shall be of them
[the churchwardens] required."

This inventory of the goods of one small church enables
us to judge of the wealth of our country churches before
they were despoiled. Of private spoliators their name
was legion. The arch-spoliator was Protector Somerset,
the King's uncle, Edward Seymour, formerly Earl of
Hertford and then created Duke of Somerset. He ruled
England for three years after King Henry's death. He
was a glaring and unblushing church-robber, setting an
example which others were only too ready to follow.
Canon Overton[7] tells how Somerset House remains as a

---

[1] A fine linen cloth made in Brittany (cf. *Coriolanus*, Act ii. sc. 1).

[2] A rich sort of stuff interwoven with gold and silver, made at Tournay,
which was formerly called Dorneck, in Flanders.

[3] An alloy of copper and zinc.   [4] Large standard candlesticks.

[5] The Lent cloth, hung before the altar during Lent.   [6] A Pax

[7] *History of the Church in England*, p. 401.

standing memorial of his rapacity. In order to provide materials for building it he pulled down the church of St. Mary-le-Strand and three bishops' houses, and was proceeding also to pull down the historical church of St. Margaret, Westminster; but public opinion was too strong against him, the parishioners rose and beat off his workmen, and he was forced to desist, and content himself with violating and plundering the precincts of St. Paul's. Moreover, the steeple and most of the church of St. John of Jerusalem, Smithfield, were mined and blown up with gunpowder that the materials might be utilized for the ducal mansion in the Strand. He turned Glastonbury, with all its associations dating from the earliest introduction of Christianity into our island, into a worsted manufactory, managed by French Protestants. Under his auspices the splendid college of St. Martin-le-Grand in London was converted into a tavern, and St. Stephen's Chapel, Westminster, served the scarcely less incongruous purpose of a Parliament House. All this he did, and when his well-earned fall came the Church fared no better under his successor, John Dudley, Earl of Warwick, and afterwards Duke of Northumberland.

Another wretch was Robert, Earl of Sussex, to whom the King gave the choir of Atleburgh, in Norfolk, because it belonged to a college. "Being of a covetous disposition, he not only pulled down and spoiled the chancel, but also pulled up many fair marble gravestones of his ancestors with monuments of brass upon them, and other fair good pavements, and carried them and laid them for his hall, kitchen, and larder-house." The church of St. Nicholas, Yarmouth, has many monumental stones, the brasses of which were in 1551 sent to London to be cast into weights and measures for the use of the town. The shops of the artists in brass in London were full of broken brass memorials torn from tombs. Hence arose the making of palimpsest brasses, the carvers using an old brass and on the reverse side cutting a memorial of a more recently deceased person.

After all this iconoclasm, spoliation, and robbery it is surprising that anything of value should have been left in our churches. But happily some treasures escaped, and the gifts of two or three generations added others. Thus I find from the will of a good gentleman, Mr. Edward Ball, that after the spoliation of Barkham Church he left the sum of five shillings for the providing of a processional cross to be borne before the choir in that church, and I expect that he gave us our beautiful Elizabethan chalice of the date 1561. The Church had scarcely recovered from its spoliation before another era of devastation and robbery ensued. During the Cromwellian period much destruction was wrought by mad zealots of the Puritan faction. One of these men and his doings are mentioned by Dr. Berwick in his *Querela Cantabrigiensis :*—

"One who calls himself John [it should be William] Dowsing and by Virtue of a pretended Commission, goes about yᵉ country like a Bedlam, breaking glasse windows, having battered and beaten downe all our painted glasses, not only in our Chappels, but (contrary to order) in our Publique Schools, Colledge Halls, Libraries, and Chambers, mistaking, perhaps, yᵉ liberall Artes for Saints (which they intend in time to pull down too) and having (against an order) defaced and digged up yᵉ floors of our Chappels, many of which had lien so for two or three hundred years together, not regarding yᵉ dust of our founders and predecessors who likely were buried there; compelled us by armed Souldiers to pay forty shillings a Colledge for not mending what he had spoyled and defaced, or forth with to goe to prison."

We meet with the sad doings of this wretch Dowsing in various places in East Anglia. He left his hideous mark on many a fair church. Thus the churchwardens of Walberswick, in Suffolk, record in their accounts :—

"1644, April 8th, paid to Martin Dowson, that came with the troopers to our church, about the taking down of Images and Brasses off Stones 0 6 0."
"1644 paid that day to others for taking up the brasses of grave stones before the officer Dowson came 0 1 0."

St. George's Church, Great Yarmouth

The record of the ecclesiastical exploits of William
Dowsing has been preserved by the wretch himself in a
diary which he kept. It was published in 1786, and the
volume provides much curious reading. With reference
to the church of Toffe he says :—

"Will : Disborough Church Warden Richard Basly
and John Newman Cunstable, 27 Superstitious pictures
in glass and ten other in stone, three brass inscriptions,
Pray for yᵉ Soules, and a Cross to be taken of the Steeple
(6s. 8d.) and there was divers Orate pro Animabus in
ye windows, and on a Bell, Ora pro Anima Sanctæ
Catharinæ."

"*Trinity Parish, Cambridge*, M. Frog, Churchwarden,
December 25, we brake down 80 Popish pictures, and
one of Christ and God yᵉ Father above."

"At *Clare* we brake down 1000 pictures superstitious."

"*Cochie*, there were divers pictures in the Windows
which we could not reach, neither would they help us to
raise the ladders."

"1643, Janʸ 1, Edwards parish, we digged up the steps,
and brake down 40 pictures, and took off ten superstitious inscriptions."

It is terrible to read these records, and to imagine all the
beautiful works of art that this ignorant wretch ruthlessly
destroyed. To all the inscriptions on tombs containing
the pious petition *Orate pro anima*—his ignorance is
palpably displayed by his *Orate pro animabus*—he paid
special attention. Well did Mr. Cole observe concerning
the last entry in Dowsing's diary :—

"From this last Entry we may clearly see to whom we
are obliged for the dismantling of almost all the gravestones that had brasses on them, both in town and
country : a sacrilegious sanctified rascal that was afraid,
or too proud, to call it St. Edward's Church, but not
ashamed to rob the dead of their honours and the Church
of its ornaments.—W. C."

He tells also of the dreadful deeds that were being
done at Lowestoft in 1644 :—

"In the same year, also, on the 12th of June, there
came one Jessop, with a commission from the Earl of

Manchester, to take away from gravestones all inscriptions on which he found *Orate pro anima*—a wretched
Commissioner not able to read or find out that which his
commission enjoyned him to remove—he took up in our
Church so much brasse, as he sold to Mr. Josiah Wild
for five shillings, which was afterwards (contrary to my
knowledge) runn into the little bell that hangs in the
Town-house. There were taken up in the Middle Ayl
twelve pieces belonging to twelve generations of the
Jettours."

The same scenes were being enacted in many parts of
England. Everywhere ignorant commissioners were ram-
paging about the country imitating the ignorant ferocity
of this Dowsing and Jessop. No wonder our churches
were bare, pillaged, and ruinated. Moreover, the conception of art and the taste for architecture were dead or
dying, and there was no one who could replace the
beautiful objects which these wretches destroyed or
repair the desolation they had caused.

Another era of spoliation set in in more recent times,
when the restorers came with vitiated taste and the worst
ideals to reconstruct and renovate our churches which
time, spoliation, and carelessness had left somewhat
the worse for wear. The Oxford Movement taught men
to bestow more care upon the houses of God in the
land, to promote His honour by more reverent worship,
and to restore the beauty of His sanctuary. A rector
found his church in a dilapidated state and talked over
the matter with the squire. Although the building was
in a sorry condition, with a cracked ceiling, hideous
galleries, and high pews like cattle-pens, it had a Norman
doorway, some Early English carved work in the chancel,
a good Perpendicular tower, and fine Decorated windows.
These two well-meaning but ignorant men decided that a
brand-new church would be a great improvement on this
old tumble-down building. An architect was called in,
or a local builder ; the plan of a new church was speedily
drawn, and ere long the hammers and axes were let loose
on the old church and every vestige of antiquity

destroyed. The old Norman font was turned out of the church, and either used as a cattle-trough or to hold a flower-pot in the rectory garden. Some of the beautifully carved stones made an excellent rockery in the squire's garden, and old woodwork, perchance a fourteenth-century rood-screen, encaustic tiles bearing the arms of the abbey with which in former days the church was connected, monuments and stained glass, are all carted away and destroyed, and the triumph of vandalism is complete.

That is an oft-told tale which finds its counterpart in many towns and villages, the entire and absolute destruction of the old church by ignorant vandals who work endless mischief and know not what they do. There is the village of Little Wittenham, in our county of Berks, not far from Sinodun Hill, an ancient earthwork covered with trees, that forms so conspicuous an object to the travellers by the Great Western Railway from Didcot to Oxford. About forty years ago terrible things were done in the church of that village. The vicar was a Goth. There was a very beautiful chantry chapel on the south side of the choir, full of magnificent marble monuments to the memory of various members of the Dunce family. This family, once great and powerful, whose great house stood hard by on the north of the church—only the terraces of which remain—is now, it is believed, extinct. The vicar thought that he might be held responsible for the dilapidations of this old chantry; so he pulled it down, and broke all the marble tombs with axes and hammers. You can see the shattered remains that still show signs of beauty in one of the adjoining barns. Some few were set up in the tower, the old font became a pig-trough, the body of the church was entirely renewed, and vandalism reigned supreme. In our county of Berks there were at the beginning of the last century 170 ancient parish churches. Of these, thirty have been pulled down and entirely rebuilt, six of them on entirely new sites; one has been burnt down, one disused; before 1890 one hundred were restored, some of them most drastically, and several others have been restored since, but with greater respect to old work.

A favourite method of "restoration" was adopted in many instances. A church had a Norman doorway and pillars in the nave ; sundry additions and alterations had been made in subsequent periods, and examples of Early English, Decorated, and Perpendicular styles of architecture were observable, with, perhaps, a Renaissance porch or other later feature. What did the early restorers do ? They said, "This is a Norman church ; all its details should be Norman too." So they proceeded to take away these later additions and imitate Norman work as much as they could by breaking down the Perpendicular or Decorated tracery in the windows and putting in large round-headed windows—their conception of Norman work, but far different from what any Norman builder would have contrived. Thus these good people entirely destroyed the history of the building, and caused to vanish much that was interesting and important. Such is the deplorable story of the "restoration" of many a parish church.

An amusing book, entitled *Hints to Some Church-wardens, with a few Illustrations Relative to the Repair and Improvement of Parish Churches*, was published in 1825. The author, with much satire, depicts the "very many splendid, curious, and convenient ideas which have emanated from those churchwardens who have attained perfection as planners and architects." He apologises for not giving the names of these superior men and the dates of the improvements they have achieved, but is sure that such works as theirs must immortalize them, not only in their parishes, but in their counties, and, he trusts, in the kingdom at large. The following are some of the "hints" :—

"*How to affix a porch to an old church.*

"If the church is of stone, let the porch be of brick, the roof slated, and the entrance to it of the improved

Gothic called modern, being an arch formed by an acute angle. The porch should be placed so as to stop up what might be called a useless window ; and as it sometimes happens that there is an ancient Saxon [1] entrance, let it be carefully bricked up, and perhaps plastered, so as to conceal as much as possible of the zigzag ornament used in buildings of this kind. Such improvements cannot fail to ensure celebrity to churchwardens of future ages.

" How to add a vestry to an old church.

" The building here proposed is to be of bright brick, with a slated roof and sash windows, with a small door on one side ; and it is, moreover, to be adorned with a most tasty and ornamental brick chimney, which terminates at the chancel end. The position of the building should be against two old Gothic windows ; which, having the advantage of hiding them nearly altogether, when contrasted with the dull and uniform surface of an old stone church, has a lively and most imposing effect.

" How to ornament the top or battlements of a tower belonging to an ancient church.

"Place on each battlement, vases, candlesticks, and pineapples alternately, and the effect will be striking. Vases have many votaries amongst those worthy members of society, the churchwardens. Candlesticks are of ancient origin, and represent, from the highest authority, the light of the churches : but as in most churches weathercocks are used, I would here recommend the admirers of novelty and improvement to adopt a pair of snuffers, which might also be considered as a useful emblem for reinvigorating the lights from the candlesticks. The pineapple ornament having in so many churches been judiciously substituted for Gothic, cannot fail to please. Some such ornament should also be placed at the top of the church, and at the chancel end. But as this publication does not restrict any churchwarden of real taste, and as the ornaments here recommended are in a common way made of stone, if any would wish to distinguish his year of office, perhaps he would do it brilliantly by painting them all bright red. . . ."

Other valuable suggestions are made in this curious and amusing work, such as " how to repair Quartre-feuille

[1] Doubtless our author means Norman.

windows" by cutting out all the partitions and making them quite round ; "how to adapt a new church to an old tower with most taste and effect," the most attractive features being light iron partitions instead of stone mullions for the windows, with shutters painted yellow, bright brick walls and slate roof, and a door painted sky-blue. You can best ornament a chancel by placing colossal figures of Moses and Aaron supporting the altar, huge tables of the commandments, and clusters of grapes and pomegranates in festoons and clusters of monuments. Vases upon pillars, the commandments in sky-blue, clouds carved out of wood supporting angels, are some of the ideas recommended. Instead of a Norman font you can substitute one resembling a punch-bowl,[1] with the pedestal and legs of a round claw table ; and it would be well to rear a massive pulpit in the centre of the chancel arch, hung with crimson and gold lace, with gilt chandeliers, large sounding-board with a vase at the top. A stove is always necessary. It can be placed in the centre of the chancel, and the stove-pipe can be carried through the upper part of the east window, and then by an elbow conveyed to the crest of the roof over the window, the cross being taken down to make room for the chimney. Such are some of the recommendations of this ingenious writer, which are ably illustrated by effective drawings. They are not all imaginative. Many old churches tell the tragic story of their mutilation at the hands of a rector who has discovered Parker's *Glossary*, knows nothing about art, but " does know what he likes," advised by his wife who has visited some of the cathedrals, and by an architect who has been elaborately educated in the principles of Roman Renaissance, but who knows no more of Lombard, Byzantine, or Gothic art than he does of the dynasties of ancient Egypt. When a church has fallen into the hands of such renovators and been heavily " restored," if the ghost of one of its medieval builders came

---

[1] A china punch-bowl was actually presented by Sir T. Drake to be used as a font at Woodbury, Devon.

to view his work he would scarcely recognize it. Well says Mr. Thomas Hardy : " To restore the great carcases of mediævalism in the remote nooks of western England seems a not less incongruous act than to set about renovating the adjoining crags themselves,"and well might he sigh over the destruction of the grand old tower of Endelstow Church and the erection of what the vicar called "a splendid tower, designed by a first-rate London man—in the newest style of Gothic art and full of Christian feeling."

The novelist's remarks on " restoration " are most valuable :—

" Entire destruction under the saving name has been effected on so gigantic a scale that the protection of structures, their being kept wind and weather-proof, counts as nothing in the balance. Its enormous magnitude is realized by few who have not gone personally from parish to parish through a considerable district, and compared existing churches there with records, traditions, and memories of what they formerly were. The shifting of old windows and other details irregularly spaced, and spacing them at exact distances, has been one process. The deportation of the original chancel arch to an obscure nook and the insertion of a wider new one, to throw open the view of the choir, is a practice by no means extinct. Next in turn to the re-designing of old buildings and parts of them comes the devastation caused by letting restorations by contract, with a clause in the specification requesting the builder to give a price for ' old materials,' such as the lead of the roofs, to be replaced by tiles or slates, and the oak of the pews, pulpit, altar-rails, etc., to be replaced by deal. Apart from these irregularities it has been a principle that anything later than Henry VIII is anathema and to be cast out. At Wimborne Minster fine Jacobean canopies have been removed from Tudor stalls for the offence only of being Jacobean. At a hotel in Cornwall a tea-garden was, and probably is still, ornamented with seats constructed of the carved oak from a neighbouring church—no doubt the restorer's perquisite.

" Poor places which cannot afford to pay a clerk of the works suffer much in these ecclesiastical convulsions. In one case I visited, as a youth, the careful repair of an interesting Early English window had been specified, but it was gone. The contractor, who had met me on the spot,

replied genially to my gaze of concern: 'Well, now, I said
to myself when I looked at the old thing, I won't stand
upon a pound or two. I'll give 'em a new winder now
I am about it, and make a good job of it, howsomever.'
A caricature in new stone of the old window had taken its
place. In the same church was an old oak rood-screen in
the Perpendicular style with some gilding and colouring
still remaining. Some repairs had been specified, but I beheld in its place a new screen of varnished deal. 'Well,'
replied the builder, more genial than ever, 'please God,
now I am about it, I'll do the thing well, cost what it
will.' The old screen had been used up to boil the workmen's kettles, though 'a were not much at that.'"

Such is the terrible report of this amazing iconoclasm.

Some wiseacres, the vicar and churchwardens, once
determined to pull down their old church and build a new
one. So they met in solemn conclave and passed the
following sagacious resolutions :—

1. That a new church should be built.
2. That the materials of the old church should be used
   in the construction of the new.
3. That the old church should not be pulled down until
   the new one be built.

How they contrived to combine the second and third
resolutions history recordeth not.

Even when the church was spared the "restorers"
were guilty of strange enormities in the embellishment
and decoration of the sacred building. Whitewash was
vigorously applied to the walls and pews, carvings,
pulpit, and font. If curious mural paintings adorned
the walls, the hideous whitewash soon obliterated every
trace and produced "those modest hues which the native
appearance of the stone so pleasingly bestows." But
whitewash has one redeeming virtue, it preserves and
saves for future generations treasures which otherwise
might have been destroyed. Happily all decoration of
churches has not been carried out in the reckless fashion
thus described by a friend of the writer. An old Cambridgeshire incumbent, who had done nothing to his

church for many years, was bidden by the archdeacon to
" brighten matters up a little." The whole of the woodwork wanted repainting and varnishing, a serious matter
for a poor man. His wife, a very capable lady, took the
matter in hand. She went to the local carpenter and
wheelwright and bought up the whole of his stock of
that particular paint with which farm carts and wagons
are painted, coarse but serviceable, and of the brightest
possible red, blue, green, and yellow hues. With her
own hands she painted the whole of the interior—pulpit,
pews, doors, etc., and probably the wooden altar, using
the colours as her fancy dictated, or as the various colours
held out. The effect was remarkable. A succeeding

Carving on Rood-screen, Alcester Church, Warwick

rector began at once the work of restoration, scraping off the
paint and substituting oak varnish ; but when my friend
took a morning service for him the work had not been
completed, and he preached from a bright green pulpit.

The contents of our parish churches, furniture and
plate, are rapidly vanishing. England has ever been
remarkable for the number and beauty of its rood-screens.
At the Reformation the roods were destroyed and many
screens with them, but many of the latter were retained,
and although through neglect or wanton destruction they
have ever since been disappearing, yet hundreds still
exist.[1] Their number is, however, sadly decreased. In
Cheshire " restoration " has removed nearly all examples,
except Ashbury, Mobberley, Malpas, and a few others.
The churches of Bunbury and Danbury have lost some
good screen-work since 1860. In Derbyshire screens

[1] *English Church Furniture*, by Dr. Cox and A. Harvey.

suffered severely in the nineteenth century, and the
records of each county show the disappearance of many
notable examples, though happily Devonshire, Somerset,
and several other shires still possess some beautiful
specimens of medieval woodwork. A large number of
Jacobean pulpits with their curious carvings have
vanished. A pious donor wishes to give a new pulpit
to a church in memory of a relative, and the old pulpit
is carted away to make room for its modern and often
inferior substitute. Old stalls and misericordes, seats and
benches with poppy-head terminations have often been
made to vanish, and the pillaging of our churches at the
Reformation and during the Commonwealth period and
at the hands of the "restorers" has done much to deprive our churches of their ancient furniture.

Most churches had two or three chests or coffers for the
storing of valuable ornaments and vestments. Each
chantry had its chest or ark, as it was sometimes called,
e.g. the collegiate church of St. Mary, Warwick, had in
1464, "ij old irebound coofres," "j gret olde arke to put
in vestments," "j olde arke at the autere ende, j old coofre
irebonde having a long lok of the olde facion, and j lasse
new coofre having iij loks called the tresory cofre and
certain almaries." "In the inner house j new hie almarie
with ij dores to kepe in the evidence of the Churche and j
great old arke and certain olde Almaries, and in the house
afore the Chapter house j old irebounde cofre having hie
feet and rings of iron in the endes thereof to heve it bye."

"It is almost exceptional to find any parish of five
hundred inhabitants which does not possess a parish
chest. The parish chest of the parish in which I am
writing is now in the vestry of the church here. It has
been used for generations as a coal box. It is exceptional
to find anything so useful as wholesome fuel inside these
parish chests; their contents have in the great majority
of instances utterly perished, and the miserable destruction
of those interesting parish records testifies to the almost
universal neglect which they have suffered at the hands,
not of the parsons, who as a rule have kept with remark-

able care the register books for which they have always been responsible, but of the churchwardens and overseers, who have let them perish without a thought of their value.

"As a rule the old parish chests have fallen to pieces, or worse, and their contents have been used to light the church stove, except in those very few cases where the chests were furnished with two or more keys, each key being of different wards from the other, and each being handed over to a different functionary when the time of the parish meeting came round."[1]

When the ornaments and vestments were carted away from the church in the time of Edward VI, many of the church chests lost their use, and were sold or destroyed, the poorest only being kept for registers and documents. Very magnificent were some of these chests which have survived, such as that at Icklington, Suffolk, Church Brampton, Northants, Rugby, Westminster Abbey, and Chichester. The old chest at Heckfield may have been one of those ordered in the reign of King John for the collection of the alms of the faithful for the fifth crusade. The artist, Mr. Fred Roe, has written a valuable work on chests, to which those who desire to know about these interesting objects can refer.

Another much diminishing store of treasure belonging to our churches is the church plate. Many churches possess some old plate — perhaps a pre-Reformation chalice. It is worn by age, and the clergyman, ignorant of its value, takes it to a jeweller to be repaired. He is told that it is old and thin and cannot easily be repaired, and is offered very kindly by the jeweller in return for this old chalice a brand-new one with a paten added. He is delighted, and the old chalice finds its way to Christie's, realizes a large sum, and goes into the collection of some millionaire. Not long ago the Council of the Society of Antiquaries issued a memorandum to the bishops and archdeacons of the Anglican Church calling attention to the increasing frequency of the sale of old or obsolete church plate. This is of two kinds : (1) pieces of plate

[1] *The Parish Councillor*, an article by Dr. Jessop, September 20, 1895.

Fred Roe.

Fourteenth-century Coffer in Faversham Church, Kent

From *Old Oak Furniture*, by Fred Roe

11

or other articles of a domestic character not especially made, nor perhaps well fitted for the service of the Church; (2) chalices, patens, flagons, or plate generally, made especially for ecclesiastical use, but now, for reasons of change of fashion or from the articles themselves being worn out, no longer desired to be used. A church possibly is in need of funds for restoration, and an effort is naturally made to turn such articles into money. The officials decide to sell any objects the church may have of the first kind. Thus the property of the Church of England finds its way abroad, and is thus lost to the nation. With regard to the sacred vessels of the second class, it is undignified, if not a desecration, that vessels of such a sacred character should be subjected to a sale by auction and afterwards used as table ornaments by collectors to whom their religious significance makes no appeal. We are reminded of the profanity of Belshazzar's feast.[1] It would be far better to place such objects for safe custody and preservation in some local museum. Not long ago a church in Knightsbridge was removed and rebuilt on another site. It had a communion cup presented by Archbishop Laud. Some addition was required for the new church, and it was proposed to sell the chalice to help in defraying the cost of this addition. A London dealer offered five hundred guineas for it, and doubtless by this time it has passed into private hands and left the country. This is only one instance out of many of the depletion of the Church of its treasures. It must not be forgotten that although the vicar and churchwardens are for the time being trustees of the church plate and furniture, yet the property really is vested in the parishioners. It ought not to be sold without a faculty, and the chancellors of dioceses ought to be extremely careful ere they allow such sales to take place. The learned Chancellor of Exeter very wisely recently

---

[1] Canon F. E. Warren recently reported to the Suffolk Institute of Archæology that while he was dining at a friend's house he saw two chalices on the table.

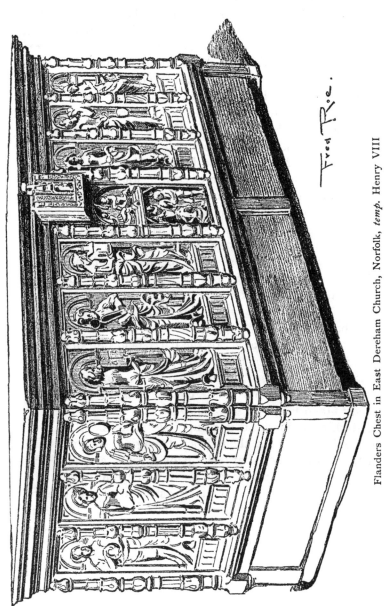

Fred Roe.

Flanders Chest in East Dereham Church, Norfolk, *temp.* Henry VIII

From *Old Oak Furniture*, by Fred Roe

refused to allow the rector of Churchstanton to sell a
chalice of the date 1660 A.D., stating that it was painfully
repugnant to the feelings of many Churchmen that it
should be possible that a vessel dedicated to the most sacred
service of the Church should figure upon the dinner-table
of a collector.   He quoted a case of a chalice which had disappeared from a church and been found afterwards with an
inscription showing that it had been awarded as a prize at
athletic sports. Such desecration is too deplorable for words
suitable to describe it.   If other chancellors took the same
firm stand as Mr. Chadwyck-Healey, of Exeter, we should
hear less of such alienation of ecclesiastical treasure.

Another cause of mutilation and the vanishing of
objects of interest and beauty is the iconoclasm of visitors,
especially of American visitors, who love our English
shrines so much that they like to chip off bits of statuary
or wood-carving to preserve as mementoes of their visit.
The fine monuments in our churches and cathedrals are
especially convenient to them for prey.   Not long ago
the best portions of some fine carving were ruthlessly cut
and hacked away by a party of American visitors.   The
verger explained that six of the party held him in conversation at one end of the building while the rest did their
deadly and nefarious work at the other.   One of the most
beautiful monuments in the country, that of the tomb of
Lady Maud FitzAlan at Chichester, has recently been cut
and chipped by these unscrupulous visitors.   It may be
difficult to prevent them from damaging such works of
art, but it is hoped that feelings of greater reverence may
grow which would render such vandalism impossible.
All civilized persons would be ashamed to mutilate the
statues of Greece and Rome in our museums.   Let them
realize that these monuments in our cathedrals and
churches are just as valuable, as they are the best of
English art, and then no sacrilegious hand would dare to
injure them or deface them by scratching names upon
them or by carrying away broken chips as souvenirs.

Playful boys in churchyards sometimes do much mischief. In Shrivenham churchyard there is an ancient full-sized effigy, and two village urchins were recently seen amusing themselves by sliding the whole length of the figure. This must be a common practice of the boys of the village, as the effigy is worn almost to an inclined plane. A tradition exists that the figure represents a man who was building the tower and fell and was killed. Both tower and effigy are of the same period—Early English—and it is quite possible that the figure may be that of the founder of the tower, but its head-dress seems to show that it represents a lady. Whipping-posts and stocks are too light a punishment for such vandalism.

The story of our vanished and vanishing churches, and of their vanished and vanishing contents, is indeed a sorry one. Many efforts are made in these days to educate the public taste, to instil into the minds of their custodians a due appreciation of their beauties and of the principles of English art and architecture, and to save and protect the treasures that remain. That these may be crowned with success is the earnest hope and endeavour of every right-minded Englishman.

Reversed Rose carved on "Miserere" in
Norwich Cathedral

CHAPTER VII

OLD MANSIONS

ONE of the most deplorable features of vanishing England is the gradual disappearance of its grand old manor-houses and mansions. A vast number still remain, we are thankful to say. We have still left to us Haddon and Wilton, Broughton, Penshurst, Hardwick, Welbeck, Bramshill, Longleat, and a host of others; but every year sees a diminution in their number. The great enemy they have to contend with is fire, and modern conveniences and luxuries, electric lighting and the heating apparatus, have added considerably to their danger. The old floors and beams are unaccustomed to these insidious wires that have a habit of fusing, hence we often read in the newspapers: "DISASTROUS FIRE— HISTORIC MANSION ENTIRELY DESTROYED." Too often not only is the house destroyed, but most of its valuable contents is devoured by the flames. Priceless pictures by Lely and Vandyke, miniatures of Cosway, old furniture of Chippendale and Sheraton, and the countless treasures which generations of cultured folk with ample wealth have accumulated, deeds, documents and old papers that throw valuable light on the manners and customs of our forefathers and on the history of the country, all disappear and can never be replaced. A great writer has likened an old house to a human heart with a life of its own, full of sad and sweet reminiscences. It is deplorably sad when the old mansion disappears in a night, and to find in the morning nothing but blackened walls—a grim ruin.

Our forefathers were a hardy race, and did not require

hot-water pipes and furnaces to keep them warm. Moreover, they built their houses so surely and so well that
they scarcely needed these modern appliances. They
constructed them with a great square courtyard, so that
the rooms on the inside of the quadrangle were protected

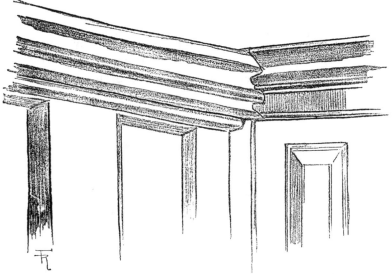

Oak Panelling. Wainscot of Fifteenth Century, with addition
circa late Seventeenth Century, fitted on to it in angle of
room in the Church House, Goudhurst, Kent

from the winds. They sang truly in those days, as in
these :—

> Sing heigh ho for the wind and the rain,
> For the rain it raineth every day.

So they sheltered themselves from the wind and rain by
having a courtyard or by making an E or H shaped
plan for their dwelling-place. Moreover, they made their
walls very thick in order that the winds should not blow
or the rain beat through them. Their rooms, too, were
panelled or hung with tapestry—famous things for
making a room warm and cosy. We have plaster
walls covered with an elegant wall-paper which has

always a cold surface, hence the air in the room, heated by the fire, is chilled when it comes into contact with the cold wall and creates draughts. But oak panelling or woollen tapestry soon becomes warm, and gives back its heat to the room, making it delightfully comfortable and cosy.

One foolish thing our forefathers did, and that was to allow the great beams that help to support the upper floor to go through the chimney. How many houses have been burnt down owing to that fatal beam! But our ancestors were content with a dog-grate and wood

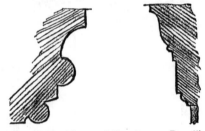

Section of Mouldings of Cornice on Panelling,
the Church House, Goudhurst

fires; they could not foresee the advent of the modern range and the great coal fires, or perhaps they would have been more careful about that beam.

Fire is, perhaps, the chief cause of the vanishing of old houses, but it is not the only cause. The craze for new fashions at the beginning of the last century doomed to death many a noble mansion. There seems to have been a positive mania for pulling down houses at that period. As I go over in my mind the existing great houses in this country, I find that by far the greater number of the old houses were wantonly destroyed about the years 1800–20, and new ones in the Italian or some other incongruous style erected in their place. Sometimes, as at Little Wittenham, you find the lone lorn terraces of the gardens of the house, but all else has disappeared. As Mr. Allan Fea says : " When an old landmark disappears,

The Wardrobe
House.
The Close.
Salisbury
Evening

Fred Roe   6 Oct: 1900

who does not feel a pang of regret at parting with something which linked us with the past? Seldom an old house is threatened with demolition but there is some protest, more perhaps from the old associations than from any particular architectural merit the building may have." We have many pangs of regret when we see such wanton destruction. The old house at Weston, where the Throckmortons resided when the poet Cowper lived at the lodge, and when leaving wrote on a window-shutter—

> Farewell, dear scenes, for ever closed to me ;
> Oh ! for what sorrows must I now exchange ye !

may be instanced as an example of a demolished mansion. Nothing is now left of it but the entrance-gates and a part of the stables. It was pulled down in 1827. It is described as a fine mansion, possessing secret chambers which were occupied by Roman Catholic priests when it was penal to say Mass. One of these chambers was found to contain, when the house was pulled down, a rough bed, candlestick, remains of food, and a breviary. A Roman Catholic school and presbytery now occupy its site. It is a melancholy sight to see the " Wilderness" behind the house, still adorned with busts and urns, and the graves of favourite dogs, which still bear the epitaphs written by Cowper on Sir John Throckmorton's pointer and Lady Throckmorton's pet spaniel. " Capability Brown " laid his rude, rough hand upon the grounds, but you can still see the " prosed alcove " mentioned by Cowper, a wooden summer-house, much injured

> By rural carvers, who with knives deface
> The panels, leaving an obscure rude name.

Sometimes, alas ! the old house has to vanish entirely through old age. It cannot maintain its struggle any longer. The rain pours through the roof and down the insides of the walls. And the family is as decayed as their mansion, and has no money wherewith to defray the cost of reparation.

Our artist, Mr. Fred Roe, in his search for the picturesque, had one sad and deplorable experience, which he
shall describe in his own words:—

"One of the most weird and, I may add, chilling ex-
periences in connection with the decline of county families
which it was my lot to experience, occurred a year or two
ago in a remote corner of the eastern counties. I had
received, through a friend, an invitation to visit an old
mansion before the inmates (descendants of the owners in
Elizabethan times) left and the contents were dispersed.
On a comfortless January morning, while rain and sleet
descended in torrents to the accompaniment of a biting
wind, I detrained at a small out-of-the-way station in
——folk. A weather-beaten old man in a patched great-
coat, with the oldest and shaggiest of ponies and the
smallest of governess-traps, awaited my arrival. I, having
wedged myself with the Jehu into this miniature vehicle,
was driven through some miles of muddy ruts, until turning through a belt of wooded land the broken outlines of
an extensive dilapidated building broke into view. This
was —— Hall.

"I never in my life saw anything so weirdly picturesque
and suggestive of the phrase 'In Chancery' as this semi-
ruinous mansion. Of many dates and styles of architecture, from Henry VIII to George III, the whole seemed
to breathe an atmosphere of neglect and decay. The
waves of affluence and successive rise of various members
of the family could be distinctly traced in the enlarge-
ments and excrescences which contributed to the casual
plan and irregular contour of the building. At one part
an addition seemed to denote that the owner had acquired
wealth about the time of the first James, and promptly
directed it to the enlargement of his residence. In another
a huge hall with classic brick frontage, dating from the
commencement of the eighteenth century, spoke of an
increase of affluence—probably due to agricultural prosperity—followed by the dignity of a peerage. The latest
alterations appear to have been made during the
Strawberry Hill epoch, when most of the mullioned
windows had been transformed to suit the prevailing
taste. Some of the building—a little of it—seemed
habitable, but in the greater part the gables were
tottering, the stucco frontage peeling and falling, and
the windows broken and shuttered. In front of this

wreck of a building stretched the overgrown remains
of what once had been a terrace, bounded by large
stone globes, now moss-grown and half hidden under
long grass. It was the very picture of desolation and
proud poverty.

"We drove up to what had once been the entrance to
the servants' hall, for the principal doorway had long
been disused, and descending from the trap I was con-
ducted to a small panelled apartment, where some freshly
cut logs did their best to give out a certain amount of
heat. Of the hospitality meted out to me that day I can
only hint with mournful appreciation. I was made
welcome with all the resources which the family had
available. But the place was a veritable vault, and cold
and damp as such. I think that this state of things had
been endured so long and with such haughty silence by
the inmates that it had passed into a sort of normal condition with them, and remained unnoticed except by new-
comers. A few old domestics stuck by the family in its
fallen fortunes, and of these one who had entered into
their service some quarter of a century previous waited
upon us at lunch with dignified ceremony. After lunch
a tour of the house commenced. Into this I shall not
enter into in detail; many of the rooms were so bare that
little could be said of them, but the Great Hall, an apartment modelled somewhat on the lines of the more palatial
Rainham, needs the pen of the author of *Lammermoor*
to describe. It was a very large and lofty room in the
pseudo-classic style, with a fine cornice, and hung round
with family portraits so bleached with damp and neglect
that they presented but dim and ghostly presentments of
their originals. I do not think a fire could have been lit
in this ghostly gallery for many years, and some of the
portraits literally sagged in their frames with accumula-
tions of rubbish which had dropped behind the canvases.
Many of the pictures were of no value except for their
associations, but I saw at least one Lely, a family group,
the principal figure in which was a young lady displaying too little modesty and too much bosom. Another
may have been a Vandyk, while one or two were early
works representing gallants of Elizabeth's time in ruffs
and feathered caps. The rest were for the most part but
wooden ancestors displaying curled wigs, legs which
lacked drawing, and high-heeled shoes. A few old
cabinets remained, and a glorious suite of chairs of

Queen Anne's time—these, however, were perishing, like the rest—from want of proper care and firing.

"The kitchens, a vast range of stone-flagged apartments, spoke of mighty hospitality in bygone times, containing fire-places fit to roast oxen at whole, huge spits and countless hooks, the last exhibiting but one dependent—the skin of the rabbit shot for lunch. The atmosphere was, if possible, a trifle more penetrating than that of the Great Hall, and the walls were discoloured with damp.

"Upstairs, besides the bedrooms, was a little chapel with some remains of Gothic carving, and a few interesting pictures of the fifteenth century; a cunningly contrived priest-hole, and a long gallery lined with dusty books, whither my lord used to repair on rainy days. Many of the windows were darkened by creepers, and over one was a flap of half-detached plaster work which hung like a shroud. But, oh, the stained glass! The eighteenth-century renovators had at least respected these, and quarterings and coats of arms from the fifteenth century downwards were to be seen by scores. What an opportunity for the genealogist with a history in view, but that opportunity I fear has passed for ever. The —— Hall estate was evidently mortgaged up to the hilt, and nothing intervened to prevent the dispersal of these treasures, which occurred some few months after my visit. Large though the building was, I learned that its size was once far greater, some two-thirds of the old building having been pulled down when the hall was constituted in its present form. Hard by on an adjoining estate a millionaire manufacturer (who owned several motor-cars) had set up an establishment, but I gathered that his tastes were the reverse of antiquarian, and that no effort would be made to restore the old hall to its former glories and preserve such treasures as yet remained intact—a golden opportunity to many people of taste with leanings towards a country life. But time fled, and the ragged retainer was once more at the door, so I left —— Hall in a blinding storm of rain, and took my last look at its gaunt façade, carrying with me the seeds of a cold which prevented me from visiting the Eastern Counties for some time to come."

Some historic houses of rare beauty have only just escaped destruction. Such an one is the ancestral house

of the Comptons, Compton Wynyates, a vision of colour
and architectural beauty—

> A Tudor-chimneyed bulk
> Of mellow brickwork on an isle of bowers.

Owing to his extravagance and the enormous expenses
of a contested election in 1768, Spencer, the eighth Earl
of Northampton, was reduced to cutting down the timber
on the estate, selling his furniture at Castle Ashby and
Compton, and spending the rest of his life in Switzerland.
He actually ordered Compton Wynyates to be pulled
down, as he could not afford to repair it; happily the
faithful steward of the estate, John Berrill, did not obey
the order.   He did his best to keep out the weather and
to preserve the house, asserting that he was sure the
family would return there some day. Most of the
windows were bricked up in order to save the window-
tax, and the glorious old building within whose walls
kings and queens had been entertained remained bare
and desolate for many years, excepting a small portion
used as a farm-house. All honour to the old man's
memory, the faithful servant, who thus saved his master's
noble house from destruction, the pride of the Midlands.
Its latest historian, Miss Alice Dryden,[1] thus describes
its appearance :—

"On approaching the building by the high road, the
entrance front now bursts into view across a wide stretch
of lawn, where formerly it was shielded by buildings
forming an outer court. It is indeed a most glorious pile
of exquisite colouring, built of small red bricks widely
separated by mortar, with occasional chequers of blue
bricks; the mouldings and facings of yellow local stone,
the woodwork of the two gables carved and black with
age, the stone slates covered with lichens and mellowed
by the hand of time; the whole building has an in-
describable charm. The architecture, too, is all irregular;
towers here and there, gables of different heights, any
straight line embattled, few windows placed exactly over
others, and the whole fitly surmounted by the elaborate

---

[1] *Memorials of Old Warwickshire*, edited by Miss Alice Dryden.

brick chimneys of different designs, some fluted, others zigzagged, others spiral, or combined spiral and fluted."

An illustration is given of one of these chimneys which form such an attractive feature of the house.

It is unnecessary to record the history of Compton Wynyates. The present owner, the Marquis of North-

ampton, has written an admirable mono-
graph on the annals of the house of his
ancestors. Its builder was Sir William
Compton,[1] who by his valour in arms
and his courtly ways gained the favour
of Henry VIII, and was promoted to
high honour at the Court. Dugdale
states that in 1520 he obtained licence
to impark two thousand acres at Over-
compton and Nethercompton, *alias*
Compton Vyneyats, where he built a
"fair mannour house," and where he
was visited by the King, "for over
the gateway are the arms of France and
England, under a crown, supported by
the greyhound and griffin, and sided
by the rose and the crown, probably in
memory of Henry VIII's visit here."[2]
The Comptons ever basked in the smiles
of royalty. Henry Compton, created
baron, was the favourite of Queen
Elizabeth, and his son William succeeded in marrying the daughter of Sir

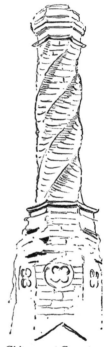

Chimney at Compton Wynyates

John Spencer, richest of City merchants. All the world knows of his ingenious craft in carrying off the lady in a baker's basket, of his wife's disinheritance by the irate father, and of the subsequent reconciliation through the

[1] The present Marquis of Northampton in his book contends that the house was mainly built in the reign of Henry VII by Edmund Compton, Sir William's father, and that Sir William only enlarged and added to the house. We have not space to record the arguments in favour of or against this view.

[2] *The Progresses of James I*, by Nichols.

intervention of Queen Elizabeth at the baptism of the
son of this marriage. The Comptons fought bravely for
the King in the Civil War. Their house was captured by
the enemy, and besieged by James Compton, Earl of
Northampton, and the story of the fighting about the
house abounds in interest, but cannot be related here.
The building was much battered by the siege and by
Cromwell's soldiers, who plundered the house, killed the
deer in the park, defaced the monuments in the church,
and wrought much mischief. Since the eighteenth-
century disaster to the family it has been restored, and

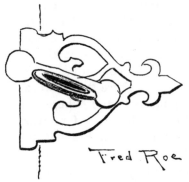

Window-catch, Brockhall, Northants

remains to this day one of the most charming homes in
England.

"The greatest advantages men have by riches are to
give, to build, to plant, and make pleasant scenes." So
wrote Sir William Temple, diplomatist, philosopher, and
true garden-lover. And many of the gentlemen of England seem to have been of the same mind, if we may
judge from the number of delightful old country-houses
set amid pleasant scenes that time and war and fire have
spared to us. Macaulay draws a very unflattering picture
of the old country squire, as of the parson. His untruths
concerning the latter I have endeavoured to expose in
another place.[1] The manor-houses themselves declare

[1] *Old-time Parson*, by P. H. Ditchfield, 1908.

the historian's strictures to be unfounded. Is it possible that men so ignorant and crude could have built for themselves residences bearing evidence of such good taste, so full of grace and charm, and surrounded by such rare blendings of art and nature as are displayed so often in park and garden? And it is not, as a rule, in the greatest mansions, the vast piles erected by the great nobles of the Court, that we find such artistic qualities, but most often in the smaller manor-houses of knights and squires. Certainly many higher-cultured people of Macaulay's time and our own could learn a great deal from them of the art of making beautiful homes.

Holinshed, the Chronicler, writing during the third quarter of the sixteenth century, makes some illuminating observations on the increasing preference shown in his time for stone and brick buildings in place of timber and plaster. He wrote:—

Gothic Chimney, Norton
St. Philip, Somerset

"The ancient maners and houses of our gentlemen are yet for the most part of strong timber. How beit such as be lately buylded are commonly either of bricke or harde stone, their rowmes large and stately, and houses of office farder distant fro their lodgings. Those of the nobilitie are likewise wrought with bricke and harde stone, as provision may best be made; but so magnificent and stately, as the basest house of a barren doth often match with some honours of princes in olde tyme: so that if ever curious buylding did flourishe in Englande it is in these our dayes, wherein our worckemen excel and are in maner comparable in skill with old Vitruvius and Serle."

He also adds the curious information that "there are olde men yet dwelling in the village where I remayn, which have noted three things to be marveylously altered

in Englande within their sound remembrance. One is,
the multitude of chimnies lately erected, whereas, in their
young dayes there were not above two or three, if so
many, in most uplandish townes of the realme (the religious houses and mannour places of their lordes alwayes
excepted, and peradventure some great personages [par-
sonages]), but each one made his fire against a reredosse
in the halle, where he dined and dressed his meate."
This want of chimneys is noticeable in many pictures of,
and previous to, the time of Henry VIII. A timber farm-
house yet remains (or did until recently) near Folkestone,
which shows no vestige of either chimney or hearth.

Most of our great houses and manor-houses sprang up
in the great Elizabethan building epoch, when the untold
wealth of the monasteries which fell into the hands of the
courtiers and favourites of the King, the plunder of gold-
laden Spanish galleons, and the unprecedented prosperity
in trade gave such an impulse to the erection of fine
houses that the England of that period has been described
as "one great stonemason's yard." The great noblemen
and gentlemen of the Court were filled with the desire for
extravagant display, and built such clumsy piles as Wolla-
ton and Burghley House, importing French and German
artisans to load them with bastard Italian Renaissance
detail. Some of these vast structures are not very admirable with their distorted gables, their chaotic proportions,
and their crazy imitations of classic orders. But the typical Elizabethan mansion, whose builder's means or good
taste would not permit of such a profusion of these architectural luxuries, is unequalled in its combination of stateliness with homeliness, in its expression of the manner of
life of the class for which it was built. And in the humbler
manors and farm-houses the latter idea is even more per-
fectly expressed, for houses were affected by the new
fashions in architecture generally in proportion to their
size.

Holinshed tells of the increased use of stone or brick
in his age in the district wherein he lived. In other parts

The Moat, Crowhurst Place, Surrey

of England, where the forests supplied good timber, the builders stuck to their half-timbered houses and brought the "black and white" style to perfection. Plaster was extensively used in this and subsequent ages, and often the whole surface of the house was covered with rough-cast, such as the quaint old house called Broughton Hall, near Market Drayton. Avebury Manor, Wiltshire, is an attractive example of the plastered house. The irregular roof-line, the gables, and the white-barred windows, and the contrast of the white walls with the rich green of the vines and surrounding trees combine to make a picture of rare beauty. Part of the house is built of stone and part half-timber, but a coat of thin plaster covers the stone-work and makes it conform with the rest. To plaster over stone-work is a somewhat daring act, and is not archi-tecturally correct, but the appearance of the house is altogether pleasing.

The Elizabethan and Jacobean builder increased the height of his house, sometimes causing it to have three storeys, besides rooms in attics beneath the gabled roof. He also loved windows. "Light, more light," was his continued cry. Hence there is often an excess of win-dows, and Lord Bacon complained that there was no comfortable place to be found in these houses, "in sum-mer by reason of the heat, or in winter by reason of the cold." It was a sore burden to many a house-owner when Charles II imposed the iniquitous window-tax, and so heavily did this fall upon the owners of some Elizabethan houses that the poorer ones were driven to the necessity of walling up some of the windows which their ancestors had provided with such prodigality. You will often see to this day bricked-up windows in many an old farm-house. Not every one was so cunning as the parish clerk of Bradford-on-Avon, Orpin, who took out the window-frames from his interesting little house near the church and inserted numerous small single-paned win-dows which escaped the tax.

Surrey and Kent afford an unlimited field for the study

of the better sort of houses, mansions, and manor-houses. We have already alluded to Hever Castle and its memories of Anne Boleyn. Then there is the historic Penshurst, the home of the Sidneys, haunted by the shades of Sir Philip, "Sacharissa," the ill-fated Algernon, and his handsome brother. You see their portraits on the walls, the fine gallery, and the hall, which reveals the exact condition of an ancient noble's hall in former days.

Not far away are the manors of Crittenden, Puttenden,

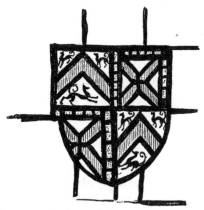

Arms of the Gaynesfords in window, Crowhurst Place, Surrey

and Crowhurst. This last is one of the most picturesque in Surrey, with its moat, across which there is a fine view of the house, its half-timber work, the straight uprights placed close together signifying early work, and the striking character of the interior. The Gaynesford family became lords of the manor of Crowhurst in 1337, and continued to hold it until 1700, a very long record. In 1903 the Place was purchased by the Rev. — Gaynesford, of Hitchin, a descendant of the family of the former owners. This is a [rare instance of the repossession of a medieval residence by an ancient family after the lapse of two hundred years. It was built in the fifteenth century, and is a complete specimen of its age and style, having been unspoilt by later alterations and additions. The part nearer the moat is, however, a little later than the gables further back. The dining-room is the contracted remains of the great hall of Crowhurst Place, the upper part of which was converted into a series of bedrooms in the eighteenth century. We give an illustration of a very fine hinge to a cupboard door in one of the bedrooms, a good example of the blacksmith's skill. It is noticeable that the points of the linen-fold in the panelling of the

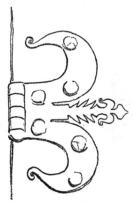

Cupboard Hinge,
Crowhurst Place, Surrey

door are undercut and project sharply. We see the open framed floor with moulded beams. Later on the fashion changed, and the builders preferred to have square-shaped beams. We notice the fine old panelling, the elaborate mouldings, and the fixed bench running along one end of the chamber, of which we give an illustration. The design and workmanship of this fixture show it to belong to the period of Henry VIII. All the work is of stout timber, save the fire-place. The smith's art is shown in the fine candelabrum and in the knocker or ring-plate, perforated with Gothic design, still backed with its original morocco leather. It is worthy of a sanctuary, and doubtless many generations of Crowhurst squires have found a very dear sanctuary in this grand old English home. This ring-plate is in one of the original bedrooms. Immense labour was often bestowed upon the mouldings of beams in these fifteenth-century houses. There was a very fine moulded beam in a farm-house in my own parish, but a recent restoration has, alas! covered it. We give some illustrations of the cornice mouldings of the Church House, Goudhurst, Kent, and of a fine Gothic door-head.

It is impossible for us to traverse many shires in our

search for old houses. But a word must be said for the priceless contents of many of our historic mansions and manors. These often vanish and are lost for ever. I have alluded to the thirst of American millionaires for these valuables, which causes so many of our treasures to cross the Atlantic and find their home in the palaces of Boston and Washington and elsewhere. Perhaps if our valuables must leave their old resting-places and go out

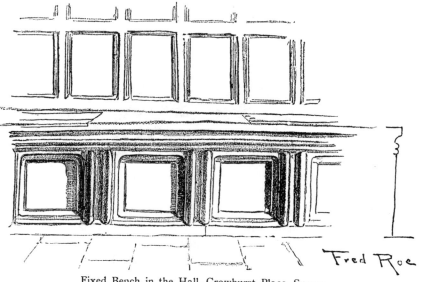

Fixed Bench in the Hall, Crowhurst Place, Surrey

of the country, we should prefer them to go to America than to any other land. Our American cousins are our kindred; they know how to appreciate the treasures of the land that, in spite of many changes, is to them their mother-country. No nation in the world prizes a high lineage and a family tree more than the Americans, and it is my privilege to receive many inquiries from across the Atlantic for missing links in the family pedigree, and the joy that a successful search yields compensates for all one's trouble. So if our treasures must go we should rather send them to America than to Germany.

It is, however, distressing to see pictures taken from the place where they have hung for centuries and sent to Christie's, to see the dispersal of old libraries at Sotherby's, and the contents of a house, amassed by generations of cultured and wealthy folk, scattered to the four winds and bought up by the *nouveaux riches*.

There still remain in many old houses collections of armour that bears the dints of many fights. Swords, helmets, shields, lances, and other weapons of warfare often are seen hanging on the walls of an ancestral hall. The buff coats of Cromwell's soldiers, tilting-helmets, guns and pistols of many periods are all there, together with man-traps—the cruel invention of a barbarous age.

Gothic Door-head, Goudhurst, Kent

The historic hall of Littlecote bears on its walls many suits worn during the Civil War by the Parliamentary troopers, and in countless other halls you can see specimens of armour. In churches also much armour has been stored. It was the custom to suspend over the tomb the principal arms of the departed warrior, which had previously been carried in the funeral procession. Shakespeare alludes to this custom when, in *Hamlet*, he makes Laertes say :—

> His means of death, his obscure burial—
> No trophy, sword, nor hatchment o'er his bones,
> No noble rite, nor formal ostentation.

You can see the armour of the Black Prince over his tomb at Canterbury, and at Westminster the shield of Henry V that probably did its duty at Agincourt. Several of our churches still retain the arms of the heroes who lie buried beneath them, but occasionally it is not the actual

armour but sham, counterfeit helmets and breastplates
made for the funeral procession and hung over the
monument. Much of this armour has been removed from
churches and stored in museums. Norwich Museum has
some good specimens, of which we give some illustrations. There is a knight's basinet which belongs to the
time of Henry V (*circa* 1415). We can compare this with
the salads, which came into use shortly after this period,

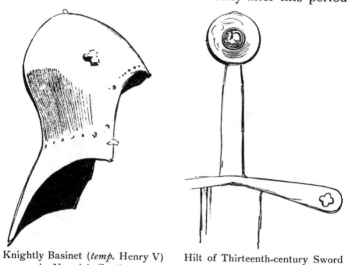

Knightly Basinet (*temp.* Henry V)   Hilt of Thirteenth-century Sword
in Norwich Castle   in Norwich Museum

an example of which may be seen at the Porte d'Hal,
Brussels. We also show a thirteenth-century sword,
which was dredged up at Thorpe, and believed to have
been lost in 1277, when King Edward I made a military
progress through Suffolk and Norfolk, and kept his
Easter at Norwich. The blade is scimitar-shaped, is one-
edged, and has a groove at the back. We may compare
this with the sword of the time of Edward IV now in the
possession of Mr. Seymour Lucas. The development of
riding-boots is an interesting study. We show a drawing
of one in the possession of Mr. Ernest Crofts, R.A.,
which was in use in the time of William III.

An illustration is given of a chapel-de-fer which re-

poses in the noble hall of Ockwells, Berkshire, much
dented by use. It has evidently seen service. In the same
hall is collected by the friends of the author, Sir Edward
and Lady Barry, a vast store of armour and most interesting examples of ancient furniture worthy of the beautiful
building in which they are placed. Ockwells Manor
House is goodly to look upon, a perfect example of
fifteenth-century residence with its noble hall and min-

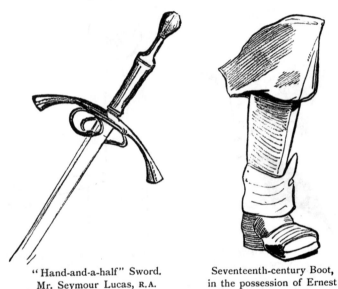

"Hand-and-a-half" Sword.
Mr. Seymour Lucas, R.A.

Seventeenth-century Boot,
in the possession of Ernest
Crofts, Esq., R.A.

strels' gallery, its solar, kitchens, corridors, and gardens.
Moreover, it is now owned by those who love and respect
antiquity and its architectural beauties, and is in every
respect an old English mansion well preserved and
tenderly cared for. Yet at one time it was almost doomed
to destruction. Not many years ago it was the property
of a man who knew nothing of its importance. He
threatened to pull it down or to turn the old house into
a tannery. Our Berks Archæological Society endeavoured to raise money for its purchase in order to preserve it. This action helped the owner to realise that the

house was of some commercial value. Its destruction
was stayed, and then, happily, it was purchased by the
present owners, who have done so much to restore its
original beauties.

Ockwells was built by Sir John Norreys about the year
1466. The chapel was not completed at his death in
1467, and he left money in his will "to the full bilding
and making uppe of the Chapell with the Chambres
ajoyng with'n my manoir of Okholt in the p'rish of Bray
aforsaid not yet finisshed XL li." This chapel was burnt
down in 1778. One of the most important features of the

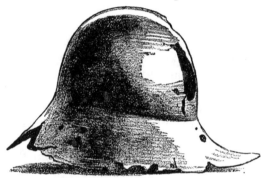

Chapel de Fer at Ockwells, Berks

hall is the heraldic glass, commemorating eighteen
worthies, which is of the same date as the house. The
credit of identifying these worthies is due to Mr. Everard
Green, Rouge Dragon, who in 1899 communicated the
result of his researches to Viscount Dillon, President of
the Society of Antiquaries. There are eighteen shields
of arms. Two are royal and ensigned with royal crowns.
Two are ensigned with mitres and fourteen with mantled
helms, and of these fourteen, thirteen support a crest.
Each achievement is placed in a separate light on an
ornamental background composed of quarries and alter-
nate diagonal stripes of white glass bordered with gold,
on which the motto

ffeyth-fully-serbe

is inscribed in black-letter. This motto is assigned by

some to the family of Norreys and by others as that of the Royal Wardrobe. The quarries in each light have the same badge, namely, three golden distaffs, one in pale and two in saltire, banded with a golden and tasselled ribbon, which badge some again assign to the family of Norreys and others to the Royal Wardrobe. If, however, the Norreys arms are correctly set forth in a compartment of a door-head remaining in the north wall, and also in one of the windows—namely, argent a chevron between three ravens' heads erased sable, with a beaver for a dexter supporter—the second conjecture is doubtless correct.

These shields represent the arms of Sir John Norreys, the builder of Ockwells Manor House, and of his sovereign, patrons, and kinsfolk. It is a *liber amicorum* in glass, a not unpleasant way for light to come to us, as Mr. Everard Green pleasantly remarks. By means of heraldry Sir John Norreys recorded his friendships, thereby adding to the pleasures of memory as well as to the splendour of his great hall. His eye saw the shield, his memory supplied the story, and to him the lines of George Eliot,

O memories,
O Past that is,

were made possible by heraldry.

The names of his friends and patrons so recorded in glass by their arms are : Sir Henry Beauchamp, sixth Earl of Warwick ; Sir Edmund Beaufort, K.G. ; Margaret of Anjou, Queen of Henry VI, "the dauntless queen of tears, who headed councils, led armies, and ruled both king and people" ; Sir John de la Pole, K.G.; Henry VI ; Sir James Butler ; the Abbey of Abingdon ; Richard Beauchamp, Bishop of Salisbury from 1450 to 1481 ; Sir John Norreys himself; Sir John Wenlock, of Wenlock, Shropshire ; Sir William Lacon, of Stow, Kent, buried at Bray ; the arms and crest of a member of the Mortimer family ; Sir Richard Nanfan, of Birtsmorton Court, Worcestershire ; Sir John Norreys with his arms quar-

tered with those of Alice Merbury, of Yattendon, his first
wife ; Sir John Langford, who married Sir John Norreys's
granddaughter ; a member of the De la Beche family (?) ;
John Purye, of Thatcham, Bray, and Cookham ; Richard
Bulstrode, of Upton, Buckinghamshire, Keeper of the
Great Wardrobe to Queen Margaret of Anjou, and afterwards Comptroller of the Household to Edward IV.
These are the worthies whose arms are recorded in the
windows of Ockwells. Nash gave a drawing of the house
in his *Mansions of England in the Olden Time*, showing
the interior of the hall, the porch and corridor, and the
east front ; and from the hospitable door is issuing a
crowd of gaily dressed people in Elizabethan costume,
such as was doubtless often witnessed in days of yore.
It is a happy and fortunate event that this noble house
should in its old age have found such a loving master
and mistress, in whose family we hope it may remain for
many long years.

Another grand old house has just been saved by the
National Trust and the bounty of an anonymous benefac-
tor. This is Barrington Court, and is one of the finest
houses in Somerset. It is situated a few miles east of
Ilminster, in the hundred of South Petherton. Its exact
age is uncertain, but it seems probable that it was built
by Henry, Lord Daubeney, created Earl of Bridgewater
in 1539, whose ancestors had owned the place since early
Plantagenet times. At any rate, it appears to date from
about the middle of the sixteenth century, and it is a very
perfect example of the domestic architecture of that period.
From the Daubeneys it passed successively to the Duke
of Suffolk, the Crown, the Cliftons, the Phelips's, the
Strodes ; and one of this last family entertained the Duke
of Monmouth there during his tour in the west in 1680.
The house, which is E-shaped, with central porch and
wings at each end, is built of the beautiful Ham Hill
stone which abounds in the district ; the colour of this
stone greatly enhances the appearance of the house and
adds to its venerable aspect. It has little ornamental

detail, but what there is is very good, while the loftiness and general proportions of the building—its extent and solidity of masonry, and the taste and care with which every part has been designed and carried out, give it an air of dignity and importance.

"The angle buttresses to the wings and the porch rising to twisted terminals are a feature surviving from mediæval times, which disappeared entirely in the buildings of Stuart times. These twisted terminals with cupola-like tops are also upon the gables, and with the chimneys, also twisted, give a most pleasing and attractive character to the structure. We may go far, indeed, before we find another house of stone so lightly and gracefully adorned, and the detail of the mullioned windows with their arched heads, in every light, and their water-tables above, is admirable. The porch also has a fine Tudor arch, which might form the entrance to some college quadrangle, and there are rooms above and gables on either hand. The whole structure breathes the spirit of the Tudor age, before the classic spirit had exercised any marked influence upon our national architecture, while the details of the carving are almost as rich as is the moulded and sculptured work in the brick houses of East Anglia. The features in other parts of the exterior are all equally good, and we may certainly say of Barrington Court that it occupies a most notable place in the domestic architecture of England. It is also worthy of remark that such houses as this are far rarer than those of Jacobean times."[1]

But Barrington Court has fallen on evil days ; one half of the house only is now habitable, the rest having been completely gutted about eighty years ago. The great hall is used as a cider store, the wainscoting has been ruthlessly removed, and there have even been recent suggestions of moving the whole structure across England and re-erecting it in a strange county. It has several times changed hands in recent years, and under these circumstances it is not surprising that but little has been done to ensure the preservation of what is indeed an architectural gem. But the walls are in excellent condition and the roofs fairly

[1] *Country Life*, September 17th, 1904.

sound. The National Trust, like an angel of mercy, has spread its protecting wings over the building; friends have been found to succour the Court in its old age; and there is every reason to hope that its evil days are past, and that it may remain standing for many generations.

The wealth of treasure to be found in many country houses is indeed enormous. In Holinshed's *Chronicle of Englande, Scotlande and Irelande*, published in 1577,

Tudor Dresser Table, in the possession of Sir Alfred Dryden,
Canon's Ashby, Northants

there is a chapter on the "maner of buylding and furniture of our Houses," wherein is recorded the costliness of the stores of plate and tapestry that were found in the dwellings of nobility and gentry and also in farm-houses, and even in the homes of "inferior artificers." Verily the spoils of the monasteries and churches must have been fairly evenly divided. These are his words:—

"The furniture of our houses also exceedeth, and is growne in maner even to passing delicacie; and herein I do not speake of the nobilitie and gentrie onely, but even of the lowest sorte that have anything to take to. Certes in noble men's houses it is not rare to see abundance of array, riche hangings of tapestry, silver vessell, and so much other plate as may furnish sundrie cupbordes to the summe ofte times of a thousand or two thousand pounde at the leaste ; wherby the value of this and the reast of their stuffe doth grow to be inestimable. Likewise in the houses of knightes, gentlemen, marchauntmen, and other wealthie citizens, it is not geson to beholde generallye their great provision of tapestrie Turkye worke, *pewter*, *brasse*, fine linen, and thereto costly cupbords of plate woorth five or six hundred pounde, to be demed by estimation. But as herein all these sortes doe farre exceede their elders and predecessours, so in tyme past the costly furniture *stayed there*, whereas now it is descended yet lower, even unto the inferior artificiers and most fermers[1] who have learned to garnish also their cupbordes with plate, their beddes with tapestrie and silk hanginges, and their table with fine naperie whereby the wealth of our countrie doth infinitely appeare. . . ."

Much of this wealth has, of course, been scattered. Time, poverty, war, the rise and fall of families, have caused the dispersion of these treasures. Sometimes you find valuable old prints or china in obscure and unlikely places. A friend of the writer, overtaken by a storm, sought shelter in a lone Welsh cottage. She admired and bought a rather curious jug. It turned out to be a somewhat rare and valuable ware, and a sketch of it has since been reproduced in the *Connoisseur*. I have myself discovered three Bartolozzi engravings in cottages in this parish. We give an illustration of a seventeenth-century powder-horn which was found at Glastonbury by Charles Griffin in 1833 in the wall of an old house which formerly stood where the Wilts and Dorset Bank is now erected. Mr. Griffin's account of its discovery is as follows :—

" When I was a boy about fifteen years of age I took a ladder up into the attic to see if there was anything hid in some holes that were just under the roof. . . . Pushing my hand in the wall . . . I pulled out this carved horn,

---

[1] Farmers.

which then had a metal rim and cover—of silver, I think. A man gave me a shilling for it, and he sold it to Mr. Porch."

It is stated that a coronet was engraved or stamped on the silver rim which has now disappeared.

Monmouth's harassed army occupied Glastonbury on

Seventeenth-century Powder-horn, found in the wall of an old house at Glastonbury. Now in Glastonbury Museum

the night of June 22, 1685, and it is extremely probable that the powder-horn was deposited in its hiding-place by some wavering follower who had decided to abandon the Duke's cause. There is another relic of Monmouth's rebellion, now in the Taunton Museum, a spy-glass, with the aid of which Mr. Sparke, from the tower of Chedzoy, discovered the King's troops marching down Sedgemoor

13

on the day previous to the fight, and gave information thereof to the Duke, who was quartered at Bridgwater. It was preserved by the family for more than a century, and given by Miss Mary Sparke, the great-granddaughter of the above William Sparke, in 1822 to a Mr. Stradling, who placed it in the museum. The spy-glass, which is of very primitive construction, is in four sections or tubes of bone covered with parchment. Relics of war and fighting are often stored in country houses. Thus at Swallowfield Park, the residence of Lady Russell, was found, when an old tree was grubbed up, some gold and silver coins of the reign of Charles I.

Seventeenth-century Spy-glass in Taunton Museum

It is probable that a Cavalier, when hard pressed, threw his purse into a hollow tree, intending, if he escaped, to return and rescue it. This, for some reason, he was unable to do, and his money remained in the tree until old age necessitated its removal. The late Sir George Russell, Bart., caused a box to be made of the wood of the tree, and in it he placed the coins, so that they should not be separated after their connexion of two centuries and a half.

We give an illustration of a remarkable flagon of bell-metal for holding spiced wine, found in an old manor-house in Norfolk. It is of English make, and was manufactured about the year 1350. It is embossed with the old Royal Arms of England crowned and repeated several times, and has an inscription in Gothic letters:—

𝔊𝔬𝔡 𝔦𝔰 𝔤𝔯𝔞𝔠𝔢 𝔅𝔢 𝔦𝔫 𝔱𝔥𝔦𝔰 𝔭𝔩𝔞𝔠𝔢.
𝔄𝔪𝔢𝔫.
𝔖𝔱𝔞𝔫𝔡 𝔲𝔱𝔱𝔦𝔯[1] 𝔣𝔯𝔬𝔪 𝔱𝔥𝔢 𝔣𝔦𝔢𝔯
𝔄𝔫𝔡 𝔩𝔢𝔱 𝔬𝔫𝔧𝔲𝔰𝔱[2] 𝔠𝔬𝔪𝔢 𝔫𝔢𝔯𝔢.

[1] Stand away.   [2] One just.

Fourteenth-century Flagon
From an old Manor House in Norfolk

Fred Roe

This interesting flagon was bought from the Robinson Collection in 1879 by the nation, and is now in the Victoria and Albert Museum.

Many old houses, happily, contain their stores of ancient furniture. Elizabethan bedsteads wherein, of course, the Virgin Queen reposed (she made so many royal progresses that it is no wonder she slept in so many places), expanding tables, Jacobean chairs and sideboards, and later on the beautiful productions of Chippendale, Sheraton, and Hipplethwaite. Some of the family chests are elaborate works of art. We give as an illustration a fine example of an Elizabethan chest. It is made of oak, inlaid with holly, dating from the last quarter of the sixteenth century. Its length is 5 ft. 2 in., its height 2 ft. 11 in. It is in the possession of Sir Coleridge Grove, K.C.B., of the manor-house, Warborough, in Oxfordshire. The staircases are often elaborately carved, which form a striking feature of many old houses. The old Aldermaston Court was burnt down, but fortunately the huge figures on the staircase were saved and appear again in the new Court, the residence of a distinguished antiquary, Mr. Charles Keyser, F.S.A. Hartwell House, in Buckinghamshire, once the residence of the exiled French Court of Louis XVIII during the Revolution and the period of the ascendancy of Napoleon I, has some curiously carved oaken figures adorning the staircase, representing Hercules, the Furies, and various knights in armour. We give an illustration of the staircase newel in Cromwell House, Highgate, with its quaint little figure of a man standing on a lofty pedestal.

Sometimes one comes across strange curiosities in old houses, the odds and ends which Time has accumulated. On p. 201 is a representation of a water-clock or clepsydra which was made at Norwich by an ingenious person named Parson in 1610. It is constructed on the same principle as the timepieces used by the Greeks and Romans. The brass tube was filled with water, which

Elizabethan Chest, in the possession of Sir Coleridge Grove, K.C.B.
Height, 2 ft. 11 in.; length, 5 ft. 2 in.

Fred Roe

was allowed to run out slowly at the bottom. A cork floated at the top of the water in the tube, and as it descended the hour was indicated by the pointer on the dial above. This ingenious clock has now found its way into the museum in Norwich Castle. The interesting contents of old houses would require a volume for their complete enumeration.

In looking at these ancient buildings, which time has spared us, we seem to catch a glimpse of the Lamp of Memory which shines forth in the illuminated pages of Ruskin. The men, our forefathers, who built these houses, built them to last, and not for their own generation. It would have grieved them to think that their earthly abode, which had seen and seemed almost to sympathize in all their honour, their gladness or their suffering—that this, with all the record it bare of them, and of all material things that they had loved and ruled over, and set the stamp of themselves upon—was to be swept away as soon as there was room made for them in the grave. They valued and prized the house that they had reared, or added to, or improved. Hence they loved to carve their names or their initials on the lintels of their doors or on the walls of their houses with the date. On the stone houses of the Cotswolds, in Derbyshire, Lancashire, Cumberland, wherever good building stone abounds, you can see these inscriptions, initials usually those of husband and wife, which preserved the memorial of their names as long as the house remained in the family. Alas! too often the memorial conveys no meaning, and no one knows the names they represent. But it was a worthy feeling that prompted this building for futurity. There is a mystery about the inscription recorded in the illustration " T. D. 1678." It was discovered, together with a sword (temp. Charles II), between the ceiling and the floor when an old farm-house called Gundry's, at Stoke-under-Ham, was pulled down. The year was one of great political disturbance, being that in which the so-called " Popish Plot " was exploited by

Staircase Newel
Cromwell House, Highgate

Titus Oates. Possibly "T.D." was fearful of being implicated, concealed this inscription, and effected his escape.

Our forefathers must have been animated by the spirit which caused Mr. Ruskin to write : "When we build, let us think that we build for ever. Let it not be for present delight, nor for present use alone ; let it be such work as our descendants will thank us for, and let us think, as we lay stone on stone, that a time is to come when those stones will be held sacred because our hands have touched them, and that men will say as they look

Piece of Wood Carved with Inscription
Found with a sword (*temp.* Charles II) in an old house at Stoke-
under-Ham, Somerset

upon the labour and wrought substance of them, 'See ! this our fathers did for us.'"

Contrast these old houses with the modern suburban abominations, "those thin tottering foundationless shells of splintered wood and imitated stone," "those gloomy rows of formalised minuteness, alike without difference and without fellowship, as solitary as similar," as Ruskin calls them. These modern erections have no more relation to their surroundings than would a Pullman-car or a newly painted piece of machinery. Age cannot improve the appearance of such things. But age only mellows and improves our ancient houses. Solidly built of good materials, the golden stain of time only adds to their beauties. The vines have clothed their walls and the green lawns about them have grown smoother and thicker, and the passing of the centuries has served but to tone them down and bring them into closer harmony

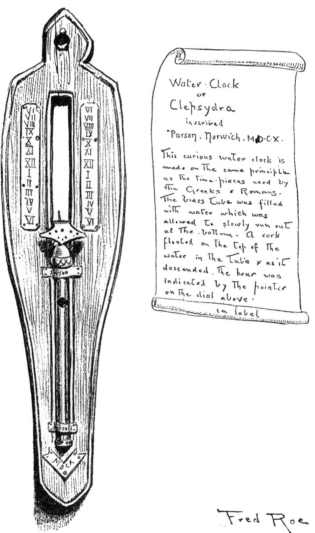

Water·Clock
or
Clepsydra
inscribed
"Parson. Norwich. M·D·C·X.

This curious water clock is
made on The same principle
as The time·pieces used by
The Greeks & Romans.
The brass tube was filled
with water which was
allowed to slowly run out
at The bottom. A cork
floated on The top of The
water in The tube & as it
descended The hour was
indicated by The pointer
on The dial above·
see label

Fred Roe

Seventeenth-century Water-clock, in Norwich Museum

with nature. With their garden walls and hedges they almost seem to have grown in their places as did the great trees that stand near by. They have nothing of the uneasy look of the parvenu about them. They have an air of dignified repose; the spirit of ancient peace seems to rest upon them and their beautiful surroundings.

Sun-dial
The Manor House, Sutton Courtenay

CHAPTER VIII

THE DESTRUCTION OF PREHISTORIC
REMAINS

W E still find in various parts of the country traces
of the prehistoric races who inhabited our
island and left their footprints behind them,
which startle us as much as ever the print of Friday's feet
did the indomitable Robinson Crusoe. During the last
fifty years we have been collecting the weapons and implements of early man, and have learnt that the history of
Britain did not begin with the year B.C. 55, when Julius
Cæsar attempted his first conquest of our island. Our
historical horizon has been pushed back very considerably,
and every year adds new knowledge concerning the
Palæolithic and Neolithic races, and the first users of
bronze and iron tools and weapons. We have learnt to
prize what they have left, to recognize the immense
archæological value of these remains, and of their inestimable prehistoric interest. It is therefore very deplorable
to discover that so much has been destroyed, obliterated,
and forgotten.

We have still some left. Examples are still to be
seen of megalithic structures, barrows, cromlechs, camps,
earthen or walled castles, hut-circles, and other remains
of the prehistoric inhabitants of these islands. We have
many monoliths, called in Wales and Cornwall, as also
in Brittany, menhirs, a name derived from the Celtic word
maen or *men*, signifying a stone, and *hir* meaning tall.
They are also called logan stones and " hoar " stones, *hoar*
meaning a boundary, inasmuch as they were frequently

used in later times to mark the boundary of an estate, parish, or manor. A vast number have been torn down and used as gateposts or for building purposes, and a recent observer in the West Country states that he has looked in vain for several where he knew that not long ago they existed. If in the Land's End district you climb the ascent of Bolleit, the Place of Blood, where Athelstan fought and slew the Britons, you can see "the Pipers," two great menhirs, twelve and sixteen feet high, and the Holed Stone, which is really an ancient cross, but you will be told that the cruel Druids used to tie their human victims for sacrifice to this stone, and you would shudder at the memory if you did not know that the Druids were very philosophical folk, and never did such dreadful deeds.

Another kind of megalithic monument are the stone circles, only they are circles no longer, many stones having been carted away to mend walls. If you look at the ordnance map of Penzance you will find large numbers of these circles, but if you visit the spots where they are supposed to be, you will find that many have vanished. The "Merry Maidens," not far from the "Pipers," still remain—nineteen great stones, which fairy-lore perhaps supposes to have been once fair maidens who danced to the tune the pipers played ere a Celtic Medusa gazed at them and turned them into stone. Every one knows the story of the Rollright stones, a similar stone circle in Oxfordshire, which were once upon a time a king and his army, and were converted into stone by a witch who cast a fatal spell upon them by the words—

> Move no more ; stand fast, stone ;
> King of England thou shalt none.

The solitary stone is the ambitious monarch who was told by an oracle that if he could see Long Compton he would be king of England ; the circle is his army, and the five "Whispering Knights" are five of his chieftains, who were hatching a plot against him when the magic spell was uttered. Local legends have sometimes helped to preserve these stones. The farmers around Rollright say that if these stones are removed from the spot they will never rest, but make mischief till they are restored. There is a well-known cromlech at Stanton Drew, in Somerset, and there are several in Scotland, the Channel Islands, and Brittany. Some sacrilegious persons transported a cromlech from the Channel Islands, and set it up at Park Place, Henley-on-Thames. Such an act of antiquarian barbarism happily has few imitators.

Stonehenge, with its well-wrought stones and gigantic trilitha, is one of the latest of the stone circles, and was doubtless made in the Iron Age, about two hundred years before the Christian era. Antiquarians have been very anxious about its safety. In 1900 one of the great upright stones fell, bringing down the cross-piece with it, and several learned societies have been invited by the owner, Sir Edmund Antrobus, to furnish recommendations as to the best means of preserving this unique memorial of an early race. We are glad to know that all that can be done will be done to keep Stonehenge safe for future generations.

We need not record the existence of dolmens, or table-stones, the remains of burial mounds, which have been washed away by denudation, nor of what the French folk call *alignements*, or lines of stones, which have suffered like other megalithic monuments. Barrows or tumuli are still plentiful, great mounds of earth raised to cover the prehistoric dead. But many have disappeared. Some have been worn down by ploughing, as on the Berkshire Downs. Others have been dug into for gravel. The making of golf-links has disturbed several, as at Sunningdale, where several barrows were destroyed in order to make a good golf-course. Happily their contents were carefully guarded, and are preserved in the British Museum and in that of Reading. Earthworks and camps still guard the British ancient roads and trackways, and you still admire their triple vallum and their cleverly protected entrance. Happily the Earthworks Committee of the Congress of Archæological Societies watches over them, and strives to protect them from injury. Pit-dwellings and the so-called "ancient British villages" are in many instances sorely neglected, and are often buried beneath masses of destructive briers and ferns. We can still trace the course of several of the great tribal boundaries of prehistoric times, the Grim's dykes that are seen in various parts of the country, gigantic earthworks that so surprised the Saxon invaders that they attributed them to the agency of the Devil or Grim. Here and there much has vanished, but stretches remain with a high bank twelve or fourteen feet high and a ditch; the labour of making these earthen ramparts must have been immense in the days when the builders of them had only picks made out of stag's horns and such simple tools to work with.

Along some of our hillsides are curious turf-cut monuments, which always attract our gaze and make us wonder who first cut out these figures on the face of the chalk hill. There is the great White Horse on the Berkshire Downs above Uffington, which we like to think was cut out by Alfred's men after his victory over the Danes on the Ashdown Hills. We are told, however, that that cannot be, and that it must have been made at least a thousand years before King Alfred's glorious reign. Some of these monuments are in danger of disappearing. They need scouring pretty constantly, as the weeds and grass will grow over the face of the bare chalk and tend to obliterate the figures. The Berkshire White Horse wanted grooming badly a short time ago, and the present writer was urged to approach the noble owner, the Earl of Craven, and urge the necessity of a scouring. The Earl, however, needed no reminder, and the White Horse is now thoroughly groomed, and looks as fit and active as ever. Other steeds on our hillsides have in modern times been so cut and altered in shape that their nearest relations would not know them. Thus the White Horse at Westbury, in Wiltshire, is now a sturdy-looking little cob, quite up to date and altogether modern, very different from the old shape of the animal.

The vanishing of prehistoric monuments is due to various causes. Avebury had at one time within a great rampart and a fosse, which is still forty feet deep, a large circle of rough unhewn stones, and within this two circles each containing a smaller concentric circle. Two avenues of stones led to the two entrances to the space surrounded by the fosse. It must have been a vast and imposing edifice, much more important than Stonehenge, and the area within this great circle exceeds twenty-eight acres, with a diameter of twelve hundred feet. But the spoilers have been at work, and "Farmer George" and other depredators have carted away so many of the stones, and done so much damage, that much imagination is needed to construct in the eye of the mind this wonder of the world.

Every one who journeys from London to Oxford by the Great Western Railway knows the appearance of the famous Wittenham Clumps, a few miles from historic Wallingford. If you ascend the hill you will find it a paradise for antiquaries. The camp itself occupies a commanding position overlooking the valley of the Thames, and has doubtless witnessed many tribal fights, and the great contest between the Celts and the Roman invaders. In the plain beneath is another remarkable earthwork. It was defended on three sides by the Thames, and a strong double rampart had been made across the cord of the bow formed by the river. There was also a trench which in case of danger could have been filled with water. But the spoiler has been at work here. In 1870 a farmer employed his men during a hard winter in digging down the west side of the rampart and flinging the earth into the fosse. The farmer intended to perform a charitable act, and charity is said to cover a multitude of sins; but his action was disastrous to antiquaries and has almost destroyed a valuable prehistoric monument. There is a noted camp at Ashbury, erroneously called "Alfred's Castle," on an elevated part of Swinley Down, in Berkshire, not far from Ashdown Park, the seat of the Earl of Craven. Lysons tells us that formerly there were traces of buildings here, and Aubrey says that in his time the earthworks were "almost quite defaced by digging for sarsden stones to build my Lord Craven's house in the park." Borough Hill Camp, in Boxford parish, near Newbury, has little left, so much of the earth having been removed at various times. Rabbits, too, are great destroyers, as they disturb the original surface of the ground and make it difficult for investigators to make out anything with certainty.

Sometimes local tradition, which is wonderfully long-lived, helps the archæologist in his discoveries. An old man told an antiquary that a certain barrow in his parish was haunted by the ghost of a soldier who wore golden armour. The antiquary determined to investigate and dug into the barrow, and there found the body of a man with a gold or bronze breastplate. I am not sure whether the armour was gold or bronze. Now here is an amazing instance of folk-memory. The chieftain was buried probably in Anglo-Saxon times, or possibly earlier. During thirteen hundred years, at least, the memory of that burial has been handed down from father to son until the present day. It almost seems incredible.

It seems something like sacrilege to disturb the resting-places of our prehistoric ancestors, and to dig into barrows and examine their contents. But much knowledge of the history and manners and customs of the early inhabitants of our island has been gained by these investigations. Year by year this knowledge grows owing to the patient labours of industrious antiquaries, and perhaps our predecessors would not mind very much the disturbing of their remains, if they reflected that we are getting to know them better by this means, and are almost on speaking terms with the makers of stone axes, celts and arrow-heads, and are great admirers of their skill and ingenuity. It is important that all these monuments of antiquity should be carefully preserved, that plans should be made of them, and systematic investigations undertaken by competent and skilled antiquaries. The old stone monuments and the later Celtic crosses should be rescued from serving such purposes as brook bridges, stone walls, stepping-stones, and gate-posts and reared again on their original sites. They are of national importance, and the nation should do this.

Half-timber Cottages, Waterside, Evesham

CHAPTER IX

CATHEDRAL CITIES AND ABBEY TOWNS

THERE is always an air of quietude and restfulness about an ordinary cathedral city. Some of our cathedrals are set in busy places, in great centres of population, wherein the high towering minster looks down with a kind of pitying compassion upon the toiling folk and invites them to seek shelter and peace and the consolations of religion in her quiet courts. For ages she has watched over the city and seen generation after generation pass away. Kings and queens have come to lay their offerings on her altars, and have been borne there amid all the pomp of stately mourning to lie in the gorgeous tombs that grace her choir. She has seen it all—times of pillage and alarm, of robbery and spoliation, of change and disturbance, but she lives on, ever calling men with her quiet voice to look up in love and faith and prayer.

But many of our cathedral cities are quite small places which owe their very life and existence to the stately church which pious hands have raised centuries ago. There age after age the prayer of faith, the anthems of praise, and the divine services have been offered.

In the glow of a summer's evening its heavenly architecture stands out, a mass of wondrous beauty, telling of the skill of the masons and craftsmen of olden days who put their hearts into their work and wrought so surely and so well. The greensward of the close, wherein the rooks caw and guard their nests, speaks of peace and joy that is not of earth. We walk through the fretted cloisters

that once echoed with the tread of sandalled monks and
saw them illuminating and copying wonderful missals,
antiphonaries, and other manuscripts which we prize so
highly now.   The deanery is close at hand, a venerable
house of peace and learning ; and the canons' houses tell
of centuries of devoted service to God's Church, wherein
many a distinguished scholar, able preacher, and learned
writer has lived and sent forth his burning message to
the world, and now lies at peace in the quiet minster.

The fabric of the cathedrals is often in danger of becoming part and parcel of vanishing England.   Every
one has watched with anxiety the gallant efforts that have
been made to save Winchester.   The insecure foundations,
based on timbers that had rotted, threatened to bring
down that wondrous pile of masonry.   And now Canterbury is in danger.

The Dean and Chapter of Canterbury having recently
completed the reparation of the central tower of the
cathedral, now find themselves confronted with responsi-
bilities which require still heavier expenditure.   It has
recently been found that the upper parts of the two
western towers are in a dangerous condition.   All the
pinnacles of these towers have had to be partially removed in order to avoid the risk of dangerous injury
from falling stones, and a great part of the external work
of the two towers is in a state of grievous decay.

The Chapter were warned by the architect that they
would incur an anxious responsibility if they did not at
once adopt measures to obviate this danger.

Further, the architect states that there are some fissures
and shakes in the supporting piers of the central tower
within the cathedral, and that some of the stonework
shows signs of crushing.   He further reports that there
is urgent need of repair to the nave windows, the south
transept roof, the Warriors' Chapel, and several other
parts of the building.   The nave pinnacles are reported
by him to be in the last stage of decay, large portions
falling frequently, or having to be removed.

In these modern days we run "tubes" and underground railways in close proximity to the foundations of historic buildings, and thereby endanger their safety. The grand cathedral of St. Paul, London, was threatened by a "tube," and only saved by vigorous protest from having its foundations jarred and shaken by rumbling trains in the bowels of the earth. Moreover, by sewers and drains the earth is made devoid of moisture, and therefore is liable to crack and crumble, and to disturb the foundations of ponderous buildings. St. Paul's still causes anxiety on this account, and requires all the care and vigilance of the skilful architect who guards it.

The old Norman builders loved a central tower, which they built low and squat. Happily they built surely and well, firmly and solidly, as their successors loved to pile course upon course upon their Norman towers, to raise a massive superstructure, and often crown them with a lofty, graceful, but heavy spire. No wonder the early masonry has, at times, protested against this additional weight, and many mighty central towers and spires have fallen and brought ruin on the surrounding stonework. So it happened at Chichester and in several other noble churches. St. Alban's tower very nearly fell. There the ingenuity of destroyers and vandals at the Dissolution had dug a hole and removed the earth from under one of the piers, hoping that it would collapse. The old tower held on for three hundred years, and then the mighty mass began to give way, and Sir Gilbert Scott tells the story of its reparation in 1870, of the triumphs of the skill of modern builders, and their bravery and resolution in saving the fall of that great tower. The greatest credit is due to all concerned in that hazardous and most difficult task. It had very nearly gone. The story of Peterborough, and of several others, shows that many of these vast fanes which have borne the storms and frosts of centuries are by no means too secure, and that the skill of wise architects and the wealth of the Englishmen of to-day are sorely needed to prevent them from vanish-

ing. If they fell, new and modern work would scarcely
compensate us for their loss.

We will take Wells as a model of a cathedral city which
entirely owes its origin to the noble church and palace
built there in early times. The city is one of the most
picturesque in England, situated in the most delightful
country, and possessing the most perfect ecclesiastical
buildings which can be conceived. Jocelyn de Wells,
who lived at the beginning of the thirteenth century
(1206–39), has for many years had the credit of building
the main part of this beautiful house of God. It is hard
to have one's beliefs and early traditions upset, but modern
authorities, with much reason, tell us that we are all
wrong, and that another Jocelyn—one Reginald Fitz-Jocelyn (1171–91)—was the main builder of Wells Cathedral.
Old documents recently discovered decide the question,
and, moreover, the style of architecture is certainly
earlier than the fully developed Early English of Jocelyn
de Wells.   The latter, and also Bishop Savaricus (1192–
1205), carried out the work, but the whole design and
a considerable part of the building are due to Bishop
Reginald Fitz-Jocelyn.   His successors, until the middle
of the fifteenth century, went on perfecting the wondrous
shrine, and in the time of Bishop Beckington Wells was
in its full glory.   The church, the outbuildings, the
episcopal palace, the deanery, all combined to form a
wonderful architectural triumph, a group of buildings
which represented the highest achievement of English
Gothic art.

Since then many things have happened. The cathedral,
like all other ecclesiastical buildings, has passed through
three great periods of iconoclastic violence.   It was shorn
of some of its glory at the Reformation, when it was
plundered of the treasures which the piety of many generations had heaped together.   Then the beautiful Lady
Chapel in the cloisters was pulled down, and the infamous
Duke of Somerset robbed it of its wealth and medi-
tated further sacrilege.   Amongst these desecrators and

despoilers there was a mighty hunger for lead. "I would that they had found it scalding," exclaimed an old chaplain of Wells; and to get hold of the lead that covered the roofs—a valuable commodity—Somerset and his kind did much mischief to many of our cathedrals and churches. An infamous bishop of York, at this period, stripped his fine palace that stood on the north of York Minster, "for the sake of the lead that covered it," and shipped it off to London, where it was sold for £1000; but of this sum he was cheated by a noble duke, and therefore gained nothing by his infamy. During the Civil War it escaped fairly well, but some damage was done, the palace was despoiled; and at the Restoration of the Monarchy much repair was needed. Monmouth's rebels wrought havoc. They came to Wells in no amiable mood, defaced the statues on the west front, did much wanton mischief, and would have caroused about the altar had not Lord Grey stood before it with his sword drawn, and thus preserved it from the insults of the ruffians. Then came the evils of "restoration." A terrible renewing was begun in 1848, when the old stalls were destroyed and much damage done. Twenty years later better things were accomplished, save that the grandeur of the west front was belittled by a pipey restoration, when Irish limestone, with its harsh hue, was used to embellish it.

A curiosity at Wells are the quarter jacks over the clock on the exterior north wall of the cathedral. Local tradition has it that the clock with its accompanying figures was part of the spoil removed from Glastonbury Abbey. The ecclesiastical authorities at Wells assert in contradiction to this that the clock was the work of one Peter Lightfoot, and was placed in the cathedral in the latter part of the fourteenth century. A minute is said to exist in the archives of repairs to the clock and figures in 1418. It is Mr. Roe's opinion that the defensive armour on the quarter jacks dates from the first half of the fifteenth century, the plain oviform breastplates and basinets, as well as the con-

Quarter Jacks over the Clock on exterior of North Wall of Wells Cathedral

tinuation of the tassets round the hips, being very characteristic features of this period. The halberds in the hands
of the figures are evidently restorations of a later time. It
may be mentioned that in 1907, when the quarter jacks were
painted, it was discovered that though the figures themselves were carved out of solid blocks of oak hard as iron,
the arms were of elm bolted and braced thereon. Though
such instances of combined materials are common enough
among antiquities of medieval times, it may yet be sur-
mised that the jar caused by incessant striking may in
time have necessitated repairs to the upper limbs. The
arms are immovable, as the figures turn on pivots to
strike.

An illustration is given of the palace at Wells, which
is one of the finest examples of thirteenth-century houses
existing in England. It was begun by Jocelyn. The
great hall, now in ruins, was built by Bishop Burnell at
the end of the thirteenth century, and was destroyed by
Bishop Barlow in 1552. The chapel is Decorated. The
gatehouse, with its drawbridge, moat, and fortifications,
was constructed by Bishop Ralph, of Shrewsbury, who
ruled from 1329 to 1363. The deanery was built by Dean
Gunthorpe in 1475, who was chaplain to Edward IV.
On the north is the beautiful vicar's close, which has
forty-two houses, constructed mainly by Bishop Beckington (1443-64), with a common hall erected by Bishop
Ralph in 1340 and a chapel by Budwith (1407-64), but
altered a century later. You can see the old fireplace,
the pulpit from which one of the brethren read aloud
during meals, and an ancient painting representing
Bishop Ralph making his grant to the kneeling figures,
and some additional figures painted in the time of Queen
Elizabeth.

When we study the cathedrals of England and try to
trace the causes which led to the destruction of so much
that was beautiful, so much of English art that has
vanished, we find that there were three great eras of
iconoclasm. First there were the changes wrought at

The Gate House, Bishop's Palace, Wells

Fred Roe

the time of the Reformation, when a rapacious king and his greedy ministers set themselves to wring from the treasures of the Church as much gain and spoil as they were able. These men were guilty of the most daring acts of shameless sacrilege, the grossest robbery. With them nothing was sacred. Buildings consecrated to God, holy vessels used in His service, all the works of sacred art, the offerings of countless pious benefactors were deemed as mere profane things to be seized and polluted by their sacrilegious hands. The land was full of the most beautiful gems of architectural art, the monastic churches. We can tell something of their glories from those which were happily spared and converted into cathderals or parish churches. Ely, Peterborough the pride of the Fenlands, Chester, Gloucester, Bristol, Westminster, St. Albans, Beverley, and some others proclaim the grandeur of hundreds of other magnificent structures which have been shorn of their leaden roofs, used as quarries for building-stone, entirely removed and obliterated, or left as pitiable ruins which still look beautiful in their decay. Reading, Tintern, Glastonbury, Fountains, and a host of others all tell the same story of pitiless iconoclasm. And what became of the contents of these churches? The contents usually went with the fabric to the spoliators. The halls of country-houses were hung with altar-cloths; tables and beds were quilted with copes; knights and squires drank their claret out of chalices and watered their horses in marble coffins. From the accounts of the royal jewels it is evident that a great deal of Church plate was delivered to the king for his own use, besides which the sum of £30,360 derived from plate obtained by the spoilers was given to the proper hand of the king.

The iconoclasts vented their rage in the destruction of stained glass and beautiful illuminated manuscripts, priceless tomes and costly treasures of exceeding rarity. Parish churches were plundered everywhere. Robbery was in the air, and clergy and churchwardens sold sacred vessels and appropriated the money for parochial purposes rather than they should be seized by the king. Commissioners were sent to visit all the cathedral and parish

House in which Bishop Hooper was imprisoned,
Westgate Street, Gloucester

churches and seize the superfluous ornaments for the king's use. Tithes, lands, farms, buildings belonging to the church all went the same way, until the hand of the iconoclast was stayed, as there was little left to steal or to be destroyed. The next era of iconoclastic zeal was that of the Civil War and the Cromwellian period. At Rochester the soldiers profaned the cathedral by using it as a stable and a tippling place, while saw-pits were made in the sacred building and carpenters plied their trade. At Chichester the pikes of the Puritans and their wild savagery reduced the interior to a ruinous desolation. The usual scenes of mad iconoclasm were enacted—stained glass windows broken, altars thrown down, lead stripped from the roof, brasses and effigies defaced and broken. A creature named " Blue Dick " was the wild leader of this savage crew of spoliators who left little but the bare walls and a mass of broken fragments strewing the pavement. We need not record similar scenes which took place almost everywhere.

The last and grievous rule of iconoclasm set in with the restorers, who worked their will upon the fabric of our cathedrals and churches and did so much to obliterate all the fragments of good architectural work which the Cromwellian soldiers and the spoliators at the time of the Reformation had left. The memory of Wyatt and his imitators is not revered when we see the results of their work on our ecclesiastical fabrics, and we need not wonder that so much of English art has vanished.

The cathedral of Bristol suffered from other causes. The darkest spot in the history of the city is the story of the Reform riots of 1831, sometimes called "the Bristol Revolution," when the dregs of the population pillaged and plundered, burnt the bishop's palace, and were guilty of the most atrocious vandalism.

The city of Bath, once the rival of Wells—the contention between the monks of St. Peter and the canons of St. Andrews at Wells being hot and fierce—has many attractions. Its minster, rebuilt by Bishop Oliver King of Wells (1495–1503), and restored in the seventeenth century, and also in modern times, is not a very interesting building, though it lacks not some striking features, and certainly contains some fine tombs and monuments of the fashionable folk who flocked to Bath in the days of its splendour. The

Fred Roe

The "Stone House," Rye, Sussex

city itself abounds in interest. It is a gem of Georgian art, with a complete homogeneous architectural character of its own which makes it singular and unique. It is full of memories of the great folks who thronged its streets, attended the Bath and Pump Room, and listened to sermons in the Octagon. It tells of the autocracy of Beau Nash, of Goldsmith, Sheridan, David Garrick, of the "First Gentleman of Europe," and many others who made Bath famous. And now it is likely that this unique little city with its memories and its charming architectural features is to be mutilated for purely commercial reasons. Every one knows Bath Street with its colonnaded loggias on each side terminated with a crescent at each end, and leading to the Cross Bath in the centre of the eastern crescent. That the original founders of Bath Street regarded it as an important architectural feature of the city is evident from the inscription in abbreviated Latin which was engraved on the first stone of the street when laid :—

PRO

VRBIS DIG : ET AMP :

HÆC PON : CVRAV :

SC :

DELEGATI

A : D : MDCCXCI.

I : HORTON, PRAET :

T : BALDWIN, ARCHITECTO.

which may be read to the effect that "for the dignity and enlargement (of the city) the delegates I. Horton, Mayor, and T. Baldwin, architect, laid this (stone) A.D. 1791."

It is actually proposed by the new proprietors of the Grand Pump Hotel to entirely destroy the beauty of this street by removing the colonnaded loggia on one side of this street and constructing a new side to the hotel two or three storeys higher, and thus to change the whole character of the street and practically destroy it. It is a sad pity, and we should have hoped that the city Council would have resisted very strongly the proposal that the proprietors of the hotel have made to their body. But we hear that the Council is lukewarm in its opposition to the scheme, and has indeed officially approved it. It is astonishing what city and borough councils will do, and this Bath Council has "the discredit of having, for purely commercial reasons, made the first move towards the destruction architecturally of the peculiar charm of their unique and beautiful city."[1]

Evesham is entirely a monastic town. It sprang up under the sheltering walls of the famous abbey—

> A pretty burgh and such as Fancy loves
> For bygone grandeurs.

This abbey shared the fate of many others which we have mentioned. The Dean of Gloucester thus muses over the "Vanished Abbey":—

"The stranger who knows nothing of its story would surely smile if he were told that beneath the grass and daisies round him were hidden the vast foundation storeys of one of the mightiest of our proud mediæval abbeys; that on the spot where he was standing were once grouped a forest of tall columns bearing up lofty fretted roofs; that all around once were altars all agleam with colour and with gold; that besides the many altars were once grouped in that sacred spot chauntries and tombs, many of them marvels of grace and beauty, placed there in the memory of men great in the service of Church and State—of men whose names were household words in the England of our fathers; that close to him were once stately cloisters, great monastic buildings, including refectories, dormitories, chapter-house, chapels, infirmary, granaries, kitchens—all the varied piles of buildings which used to make up the hive of a great monastery."

It was commenced by Bishop Egwin, of Worcester, in 702 A.D., but the era of its great prosperity set in after the battle of Evesham when Simon de Montford was slain, and his body buried in the monastic church. There was his shrine to which was great pilgrimage, crowds flocking to lay their offerings there; and riches poured into the treasury of the monks, who made great additions

[1] *The Builder*, March 6, 1909.

to their house, and reared noble buildings. Little is left of its former grandeur. You can discover part of the piers of the great central tower, the cloister arch of Decorated work of great beauty erected in 1317, and the abbey fishponds. The bell tower is one of the glories of Evesham. It was built by the last abbot, Abbot Lichfield, and was not quite completed before the destruction of the great abbey church adjacent to it. It is a grand specimen of Perpendicular architecture.

Fifteenth-century House, Market Place, Evesham

At the corner of the Market Place there is a picturesque old house with gable and carved barge-boards and timber-framed arch, and we see the old Norman gateway named Abbot Reginald's Gateway, after the name of its builder, who also erected part of the wall enclosing the monastic buildings. A timber-framed structure now stretches across the arcade, but a recent restoration has exposed the Norman columns which support the arch. The Church House, always an interesting building in old towns and villages, wherein church ales and semi-ecclesiastical functions took place, has been restored. Passing under the arch we see the two churches in one churchyard—All Saints and St. Laurence. The former has some Norman work at the inner door of the porch, but its main construction is Decorated and Perpendicular.

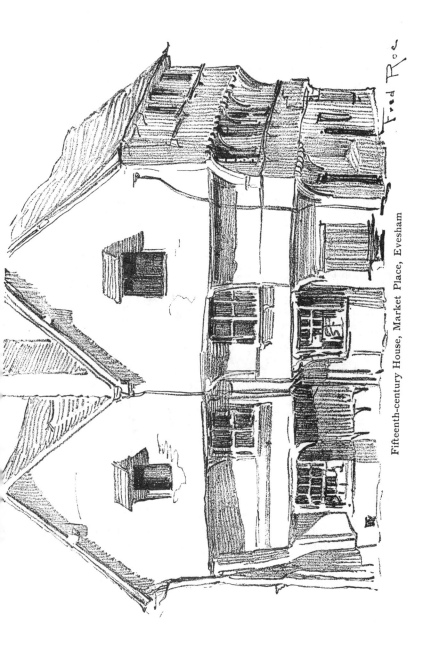

Fifteenth-century House, Market Place, Evesham

15

Its most interesting feature is the Lichfield Chapel, erected by the last abbot, whose initials and the arms of the abbey appear on escutcheons on the roof. The fan-tracery roof is especially noticeable, and the good modern glass. The church of St. Laurence is entirely Perpen-dicular, and the chantry of Abbot Lichfield, with its fan-tracery vaulting, is a gem of English architecture.

Fifteenth-century House in Cowl Street, Evesham

Amongst the remains of the abbey buildings may be seen the Almonry, the residence of the almoner, formerly used as a gaol. An interesting stone lantern of fifteenth-century work is preserved here. Another abbey gateway is near at hand, but little evidence remains of its former Gothic work. Part of the old wall built by Abbot William de Chyryton early in the fourteenth century remains. In the town there is a much-modernized town hall, and near it the old-fashioned Booth Hall, a half-timbered building, now used as shops and cottages, where formerly courts were held, including the court of

Half-timber House, Alcester, Warwick

pie-powder, the usual accompaniment of every fair.
Bridge Street is one of the most attractive streets in
the borough, with its quaint old house, and the famous
inn, "The Crown." The old house in Cowl Street was
formerly the White Hart Inn, which tells a curious
Elizabethan story about "the Fool and the Ice," an
incident supposed to be referred to by Shakespeare in
Troilus and Cressida (Act iii. sc. 3): "The fool slides
o'er the ice that you should break." The Queen Anne

Half-timber House at Alcester

house in the High Street, with its wrought-iron railings
and brackets, called Dresden House and Almswood, one
of the oldest dwelling-houses in the town, are worthy of
notice by the students of domestic architecture.

There is much in the neighbourhood of Evesham which
is worthy of note, many old-fashioned villages and
country towns, manor-houses, churches, and inns which
are refreshing to the eyes of those who have seen so much
destruction, so much of the England that is vanishing.
The old abbey tithe-barn at Littleton of the fourteenth
century, Wickhamford Manor, the home of Penelope
Washington, whose tomb is in the adjoining church,

the picturesque village of Cropthorne, Winchcombe and
its houses, Sudeley Castle, the timbered houses at Norton
and Harvington, Broadway and Campden, abounding
with beautiful houses, and the old town of Alcester,
of which some views are given—all these contain many
objects of antiquarian and artistic interest, and can easily
be reached from Evesham. In that old town we have
seen much to interest, and the historian will delight to
fight over again the battle of Evesham and study the
records of the siege of the town in the Civil War.

CHAPTER X

OLD INNS

THE trend of popular legislation is in the direction of the diminishing of the number of licensed premises and the destruction of inns. Very soon, we may suppose, the " Black Boy " and the " Red Lion " and hosts of other old signs will have vanished, and there will be a very large number of famous inns which have "retired from business." Already their number is considerable. In many towns through which in olden days the stage-coaches passed inns were almost as plentiful as blackberries ; they were needed then for the numerous passengers who journeyed along the great roads in the coaches ; they are not needed now when people rush past the places in express trains. Hence the order has gone forth that these superfluous houses shall cease to be licensed premises and must submit to the removal of their signs. Others have been so remodelled in order to provide modern comforts and conveniences that scarce a trace of their old-fashioned appearance can be found. Modern temperance legislators imagine that if they can only reduce the number of inns they will reduce drunkenness and make the English people a sober nation. This is not the place to discuss whether the destruction of inns tends to promote temperance. We may, perhaps, be permitted to doubt the truth of the legend, oft repeated on temperance platforms, of the working man, returning homewards from his toil, struggling past nineteen inns and succumbing to the syren charms of the twentieth. We may fear lest the gathering together of large numbers of men in a few public-houses may not increase rather than diminish their thirst and the love of good fellowship which in some mysterious way is stimulated by the imbibing of many pots of beer. We may, perhaps, feel some misgiving with regard to the temperate habits of the people, if instead of well-conducted hostels, duly inspected by the police, the landlords of which are liable to prosecution for improper conduct, we see arising a host of ungoverned clubs, wherein no control is exercised over the manners of the members and adequate supervision impossible. We cannot refuse to listen to the opinion of certain royal commissioners who, after much sifting of evidence, came to the conclusion that as far as the suppression of public-houses had gone, their diminution had not lessened the convictions for drunkenness.

But all this is beside our subject. We have only to record another feature of vanishing England, the gradual disappearance of many of its ancient and historic inns, and to describe some of the fortunate survivors. Many of them are very old, and cannot long contend against the fiery eloquence of the young temperance orator, the newly fledged justice of the peace, or the budding member of Parliament who tries to win votes by pulling things down.

We have, however, still some of these old hostelries left; medieval pilgrim inns redolent of the memories of the not very pious companies of men and women who wended their way to visit the shrines of St. Thomas of Canterbury or Our Lady at Walsingham; historic inns wherein some of the great events in the annals of England have occurred; inns associated with old romances or frequented by notorious highwaymen, or that recall the adventures of Mr. Pickwick and other heroes and villains of Dickensian tales. It is well that we should try to depict some of these before they altogether vanish.

There was nothing vulgar or disgraceful about an inn a century ago. From Elizabethan times to the early part of the nineteenth century they were frequented by most

of the leading spirits of each generation. Archbishop
Leighton, who died in 1684, often used to say to Bishop
Burnet that " if he were to choose a place to die in it
should be an inn ; it looked like a pilgrim's going home,
to whom this world was all as an Inn, and who was weary
of the noise and confusion of it." His desire was fulfilled. He died at the old Bell Inn in Warwick Lane,
London, an old galleried hostel which was not demolished
until 1865. Dr. Johnson, when delighting in the comfort
of the Shakespeare's Head Inn, between Worcester
and Lichfield, exclaimed : " No, sir, there is nothing
which has yet been contrived by man, by which so much
happiness is provided as by a good tavern or inn." This
oft-quoted saying the learned Doctor uttered at the Chapel
House Inn, near King's Norton ; its glory has departed ;
it is now a simple country-house by the roadside.
Shakespeare, who doubtless had many opportunities of
testing the comforts of the famous inns at Southwark,
makes Falstaff say : " Shall I not take mine ease at mine
inn ? " ; and Shenstone wrote the well-known rhymes on
a window of the old Red Lion at Henley-on-Thames :—

> Whoe'er has travelled life's dull road,
> Where'er his stages may have been,
> May sigh to think he still has found
> The warmest welcome at an inn.

Fynes Morrison tells of the comforts of English inns
even as early as the beginning of the seventeenth century. In 1617 he wrote :—

" The world affords not such inns as England hath, for
as soon as a passenger comes the servants run to him ;
one takes his horse and walks him till he be cold, then
rubs him and gives him meat ; but let the master look to
this point. Another gives the traveller his private chamber and kindles his fire, the third pulls off his boots and
makes them clean ; then the host or hostess visits him—
if he will eat with the host—or at a common table it will
be 4d. and 6d. If a gentleman has his own chamber,
his ways are consulted, and he has music, too, if he
likes."

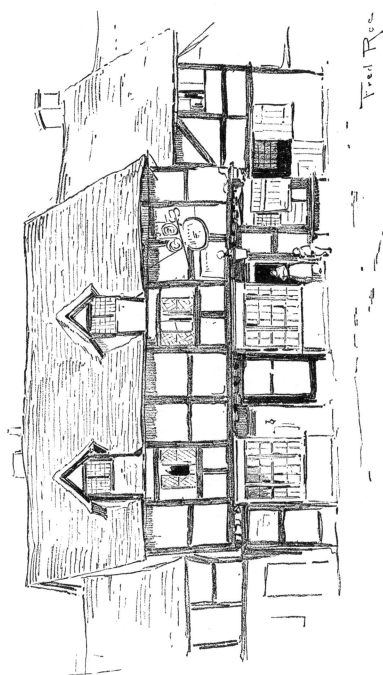

Fred Roe

The Wheelwrights' Arms, Warwick

The literature of England abounds in references to these ancient inns. If Dr. Johnson, Addison, and Goldsmith were alive now, we should find them chatting together at the Authors' Club, or the Savage, or the Athenæum. There were no literary clubs in their days, and the public parlours of the Cock Tavern or the "Cheshire Cheese" were their clubs, wherein they were quite as happy, if not quite so luxuriously housed, as if they had been members of a modern social institution. Who has not sung in praise of inns? Longfellow, in his *Hyperion*, makes Flemming say: "He who has not been at a tavern knows not what a paradise it is. O holy tavern! O miraculous tavern! Holy, because no carking cares are there, nor weariness, nor pain; and miraculous, because of the spits which of themselves turned round and round." They appealed strongly to Washington Irving, who, when recording his visit to the shrine of Shakespeare, says: "To a homeless man, who has no spot on this wide world which he can truly call his own, there is a momentary feeling of something like independence and territorial consequence, when after a weary day's travel he kicks off his boots, thrusts his feet into slippers, and stretches himself before an inn fire. Let the world without go as it may; let kingdoms rise or fall, so long as he has the wherewithal to pay his bill, he is, for the time being, the very monarch of all he surveys. . . . 'Shall I not take mine ease in mine inn?' thought I, as I gave the fire a stir, lolled back in my elbow chair, and cast a complacent look about the little parlour of the Red Horse at Stratford-on-Avon."

And again, on Christmas Eve Irving tells of his joyous long day's ride in a coach, and how he at length arrived at a village where he had determined to stay the night. As he drove into the great gateway of the inn (some of them were mighty narrow and required much skill on the part of the Jehu) he saw on one side the light of a rousing kitchen fire beaming through a window. He "entered and admired, for the hundredth time, that picture of con-

REINDEER
INN

Entrance to the Reindeer Inn, Banbury

venience, neatness, and broad honest enjoyment—the kitchen of an English inn." It was of spacious dimensions, hung round with copper and tin vessels highly polished, and decorated here and there with Christmas green. Hams, tongues, and flitches of bacon were suspended from the ceiling ; a smoke-jack made its ceaseless clanking beside the fire-place, and a clock ticked in one corner. A well-scoured deal table extended along one side of the kitchen, with a cold round of beef and other hearty viands upon it, over which two foaming tankards of ale seemed mounting guard. Travellers of inferior order were preparing to attack this stout repast, while others sat smoking and gossiping over their ale on two high-backed oaken settles beside the fire. Trim housemaids were hurrying backwards and forwards under the directions of a fresh bustling landlady ; but still seizing an occasional moment to exchange a flippant word, and have a rallying laugh with the group round the fire.

Such is the cheering picture of an old-fashioned inn in days of yore. No wonder that the writers should have thus lauded these inns ! Imagine yourself on the box-seat of an old coach travelling somewhat slowly through the night. It is cold and wet, and your fingers are frozen, and the rain drives pitilessly in your face ; and then, when you are nearly dead with misery, the coach stops at a well-known inn. A smiling host and buxom hostess greets you ; blazing fires thaw you back to life, and good cheer awaits your appetite. No wonder people loved an inn and wished to take their ease therein after the dangers and hardships of the day. Lord Beaconsfield, in his novel *Tancred*, vividly describes the busy scene at a country hostelry in the busy coaching days. The host, who is always "smiling," conveys the pleasing intelligence to the passengers : "'The coach stops here half an hour, gentlemen : dinner quite ready.' 'Tis a delightful sound. And what a dinner ! What a profusion of substantial delicacies ! What mighty and iris-tinted rounds of beef ! What vast and marble-veined ribs !

What gelatinous veal pies! What colossal hams!
These are evidently prize cheeses! And how invigorat-
ing is the perfume of those various and variegated pickles.
Then the bustle emulating the plenty; the ringing of
bells, the clash of thoroughfare, the summoning of

THE
SHOULDER
OF
MUTTON
INN

SETCH FINE ALES

The Shoulder of Mutton Inn, King's Lynn

ubiquitous waiters, and the all-pervading feeling of
omnipotence from the guests, who order what they please
to the landlord, who can produce and execute everything
they can desire. 'Tis a wondrous sight!"

And then how picturesque these old inns are, with their
swinging signs, the pump and horse-trough before the
door, a towering elm or poplar overshadowing the inn,
and round it and on each side of the entrance are

seats, with rustics sitting on them.   The old house has
picturesque gables and a tiled roof mellowed by age, with
moss and lichen growing on it, and the windows are
latticed.   A porch protects the door, and over it and up
the walls are growing old-fashioned climbing rose trees.
Morland loved to paint the exteriors of inns quite as much
as he did to frequent their interiors, and has left us many
a wondrous drawing of their beauties.   The interior is no
less picturesque, with its open ingle-nook, its high-backed
settles, its brick floor, its pots and pans, its pewter and
brass utensils.   Our artist has drawn for us many beautiful examples of old inns, which we shall visit presently
and try to learn something of their old-world charm.   He
has only just been in time to sketch them, as they are fast
disappearing.   It is astonishing how many noted inns in
London and the suburbs have vanished during the last
twenty or thirty years.

Let us glance at a few of the great Southwark inns.
The old "Tabard," from which Chaucer's pilgrims
started on their memorable journey, was destroyed by
a great fire in 1676, rebuilt in the old fashion, and continued until 1875, when it had to make way for a modern
"old Tabard" and some hop merchant's offices.   This
and many other inns had galleries running round the
yard, or at one end of it, and this yard was a busy place,
frequented not only by travellers in coach or saddle, but
by poor players and mountebanks, who set up their stage
for the entertainment of spectators who hung over the
galleries or from their rooms watched the performance.
The model of an inn-yard was the first germ of theatrical
architecture.   The "White Hart" in Southwark retained
its galleries on the north and east side of its yard until
1889, though a modern tavern replaced the south and
main portion of the building in 1865-6.   This was a noted
inn, bearing as its sign a badge of Richard II, derived
from his mother Joan of Kent.   Jack Cade stayed there
while he was trying to capture London, and another
"immortal" flits across the stage, Master Sam Weller,

of *Pickwick* fame. A galleried inn still remains at South-wark, a great coaching and carriers' hostel, the "George." It is but a fragment of its former greatness, and the present building was erected soon after the fire in 1676, and still retains its picturesqueness.

The glory has passed from most of these London inns. Formerly their yards resounded with the strains of the merry post-horn, and carriers' carts were as plentiful as omnibuses now are. In the fine yard of the "Saracen's Head," Aldgate, you can picture the busy scene, though the building has ceased to be an inn, and if you wished to travel to Norwich there you would have found your coach ready for you. The old "Bell Savage," which derives its name from one Savage who kept the "Bell on the Hoop," and not from any beautiful girl "La Belle Sauvage," was a great coaching centre, and so were the "Swan with two Necks," Lad Lane, the "Spread Eagle" and "Cross Keys" in Gracechurch Street, the "White Horse," Fetter Lane, and the "Angel," behind St. Clements. As we do not propose to linger long in London, and prefer the country towns and villages where relics of old English life survive, we will hie to one of these noted hostelries, book our seats on a Phantom coach, and haste away from the great city which has dealt so mercilessly with its ancient buildings. It is the last few years which have wrought the mischief. Many of these old inns lingered on till the 'eighties. Since then their destruction has been rapid, and the huge caravanserais, the "Cecil," the "Ritz," the "Savoy," and the "Metropole," have supplanted the old Saracen's Heads, the Bulls, the Bells, and the Boars that satisfied the needs of our forefathers in a less luxurious age.

Let us travel first along the old York road, or rather select our route, going by way of Ware, Tottenham, Edmonton, and Waltham Cross, Hatfield and Stevenage, or through Barnet, until we arrive at the Wheat Sheaf Inn on Alconbury Hill, past Little Stukeley, where the two roads conjoin and "the milestones are numbered

agreeably to that admeasurement," viz. to that from
Hicks' Hall through Barnet, as *Paterson's Roads* plainly
informs us.   Along this road you will find several of the
best specimens of old coaching inns in England.   The
famous " George " at Huntingdon, the picturesque " Fox
and Hounds " at Ware, the grand old inns at Stilton and
Grantham are some of the best inns on English roads,
and pleadingly invite a pleasant pilgrimage.   We might
follow in the wake of Dick Turpin, if his ride to York
were not a myth.   The real incident on which the story
was founded occurred about the year 1676, long before
Turpin was born.   One Nicks robbed a gentleman on
Gadshill at four o'clock in the morning, crossed the river
with his *bay* mare as soon as he could get a ferry-boat at
Gravesend, and then by Braintree, Huntingdon, and other
places reached York that evening, went to the Bowling
Green, pointedly asked the mayor the time, proved an
alibi, and got off.   This account was published as a
broadside about the time of Turpin's execution, but it
makes no allusion to him whatever.   It required the
romance of the nineteenth century to change Nicks to
Turpin and the bay mare to Black Bess.   But *revenir
à nos moutons*, or rather our inns.   The old " Fox and
Hounds " at Ware is beautiful with its swinging sign
suspended by graceful and elaborate ironwork and its
dormer windows.   The " George " at Huntingdon preserves its gallery in the inn-yard, its projecting upper
storey, its outdoor settle, and much else that is attractive.
Another " George " greets us at Stamford, an ancient
hostelry, where Charles I stayed during the Civil War
when he was journeying from Newark to Huntingdon.

And then we come to Grantham, famous for its old inns.
Foremost among them is the " Angel," which dates back
to medieval times.   It has a fine stone front with two
projecting bays, an archway with welcoming doors
on either hand, and above the arch is a beautiful little
oriel window, and carved heads and gargoyles jut out
from the stonework.   I think that this charming front

was remodelled in Tudor times, and judging from
the interior plaster-work I am of opinion that the
bays were added in the time of Henry VII, the Tudor
rose forming part of the decoration. The arch and
gateway with the oriel are the oldest parts of the front,
and on each side of the arch is a sculptured head, one
representing Edward III and the other his queen,
Philippa of Hainault. The house belonged in ancient
times to the Knights Templars, where royal and other
distinguished travellers were entertained. King John is
said to have held his court here in 1213, and the old inn
witnessed the passage of the body of Eleanor, the beloved
queen of Edward I, as it was borne to its last resting-
place at Westminster. One of the seven Eleanor crosses
stood at Grantham on St. Peter's Hill, but it shared the
fate of many other crosses and was destroyed by the
troopers of Cromwell during the Civil War. The first
floor of the " Angel " was occupied by one long room,
wherein royal courts were held. It is now divided into
three separate rooms. In this room Richard III condemned to execution the Duke of Buckingham, and probably here stayed Cromwell in the early days of his military
career and wrote his letter concerning the first action
that made him famous. We can imagine the silent
troopers assembling in the market-place late in the
evening, and then marching out twelve companies
strong to wage an unequal contest against a large body
of Royalists. The Grantham folk had much to say when
the troopers rode back with forty-five prisoners besides
divers horses and arms and colours. The " Angel "
must have seen all this and sighed for peace. Grim
troopers paced its corridors, and its stables were full of
tired horses. One owner of the inn at the beginning
of the eighteenth century, though he kept a hostel, liked
not intemperance. His name was Michael Solomon, and
he left an annual charge of 40s. to be paid to the vicar
of the parish for preaching a sermon in the parish church
against the sin of drunkenness. The interior of this

16

ancient hostelry has been modernized and fitted with the comforts which we modern folk are accustomed to expect.

Across the way is the "Angel's" rival the "George," possibly identical with the hospitium called "Le George" presented with other property by Edward IV to his mother, the Duchess of York. It lacks the appearance of age which clothes the "Angel" with dignity, and was rebuilt with red brick in the Georgian era. The coaches often called there, and Charles Dickens stayed the night and describes it as one of the best inns in England. He tells of Squeers conducting his new pupils through Grantham to Dotheboys Hall, and how after leaving the inn the luckless travellers "wrapped themselves more closely in their coats and cloaks . . . and prepared with many half-suppressed moans again to encounter the piercing blasts which swept across the open country." At the "Saracen's Head" in Westgate Isaac Newton used to stay, and there are many other inns, the majority of which rejoice in signs that are blue. We see a Blue Horse, a Blue Dog, a Blue Ram, Blue Lion, Blue Cow, Blue Sheep, and many other cerulean animals and objects, which proclaim the political colour of the great landowner. Grantham boasts of a unique inn-sign. Originally known as the "Bee-hive," a little public-house in Castlegate has earned the designation of the "Living Sign," on account of the hive of bees fixed in a tree that guards its portals. Upon the swinging sign the following lines are inscribed :—

> Stop, traveller, this wondrous sign explore,
> And say when thou hast viewed it o'er and o'er,
> Grantham, now two rarities are thine—
> A lofty steeple and a "Living Sign."

The connexion of the "George" with Charles Dickens reminds one of the numerous inns immortalized by the great novelist both in and out of London. The "Golden Cross" at Charing Cross, the "Bull" at Rochester, the "Belle Sauvage" (now demolished) near Ludgate Hill, the "Angel" at Bury St. Edmunds, the "Great White

Horse" at Ipswich, the "King's Head" at Chigwell (the
original of the "Maypole" in *Barnaby Rudge*), the
"Leather Bottle" at Cobham are only a few of those
which he by his writings made famous.

Leaving Grantham and its inns, we push along the
great North Road to Stilton, famous for its cheese, where
a choice of inns awaits us—the "Bell" and the "Angel,"
that glare at each other across the broad thoroughfare.
In the palmy days of coaching the "Angel" had stabling

A Quaint Gable. The Bell Inn, Stilton

for three hundred horses, and it was kept by Mistress
Worthington, at whose door the famous cheeses were
sold and hence called Stilton, though they were made
in distant farmsteads and villages. It is quite a modern-
looking inn as compared with the "Bell." You can see a
date inscribed on one of the gables, 1649, but this can
only mean that the inn was restored then, as the style of
architecture of "this dream in stone" shows that it must
date back to early Tudor times. It has a noble swinging
sign supported by beautifully designed ornamental ironwork, gables, bay-windows, a Tudor archway, tiled roof,
and a picturesque courtyard, the silence and dilapidation

of which are strangely contrasted with the continuous
bustle, life, and animation which must have existed there
before the era of railways.

Not far away is Southwell, where there is the historic
inn the "Saracen's Head." Here Charles I stayed, and
you can see the very room where he lodged on the left of
the entrance-gate. Here it was on May 5th, 1646, that
he gave himself up to the Scotch Commissioners, who
wrote to the Parliament from Southwell "that it made
them feel like men in a dream." The "Martyr-King"
entered this inn as a sovereign; he left it a prisoner
under the guard of his Lothian escort. Here he slept his
last night of liberty, and as he passed under the archway
of the "Saracen's Head" he started on that fatal journey
that terminated on the scaffold at Whitehall. You can
see on the front of the inn over the gateway a stone
lozenge with the royal arms engraved on it with the date
1693, commemorating this royal melancholy visit. In
later times Lord Byron was a frequent visitor.

On the high, wind-swept road between Ashbourne and
Buxton there is an inn which can defy the attacks of the
reformers. It is called the Newhaven Inn and was built
by a Duke of Devonshire for the accommodation of
visitors to Buxton. King George IV was so pleased with
it that he gave the Duke a perpetual licence, with which
no Brewster Sessions can interfere. Near Buxton is the
second highest inn in England, the "Cat and Fiddle,"
and "The Traveller's Rest" at Flash Bar, on the Leek
road, ranks as third, the highest being the Tan Hill Inn,
near Brough, on the Yorkshire moors.

Norwich is a city remarkable for its old buildings and
famous inns. A very ancient inn is the "Maid's Head"
at Norwich, a famous hostelry which can vie in interest
with any in the kingdom. Do we not see there the
identical room in which good Queen Bess is said to have
reposed on the occasion of her visit to the city in 1578?
You cannot imagine a more delightful old chamber, with
its massive beams, its wide fifteenth-century fire-place,

The Bell Inn, Stilton

and its quaint lattice, through which the moonbeams
play upon antique furniture and strange, fantastic carvings. This oak-panelled room recalls memories of the
Orfords, Walpoles, Howards, Wodehouses, and other
distinguished guests whose names live in England's
annals. The old inn was once known as the Murtel
or Molde Fish, and some have tried to connect the
change of name with the visit of Queen Elizabeth;
unfortunately for the conjecture, the inn was known as
the Maid's Head long before the days of Queen Bess.
It was built on the site of an old bishop's palace, and in
the cellars may be seen some traces of Norman masonry.
One of the most fruitful sources of information about
social life in the fifteenth century are the *Paston Letters*.
In one written by John Paston in 1472 to "Mestresse
Margret Paston," he tells her of the arrival of a visitor,
and continues: "I praye yow make hym goode cheer
. . . it were best to sette hys horse at the Maydes Hedde,
and I shall be content for ther expenses." During the
Civil War this inn was the rendezvous of the Royalists,
but alas! one day Cromwell's soldiers made an attack on
the "Maid's Head," and took for their prize the horses
of Dame Paston stabled here.

We must pass over the records of civic feasts and
aldermanic junketings, which would fill a volume, and
seek out the old "Briton's Arms," in the same city, a
thatched building of venerable appearance with its projecting upper storeys and lofty gable. It looks as if it
may not long survive the march of progress.

The parish of Heigham, now part of the city of Norwich, is noted as having been the residence of Bishop
Hall, "the English Seneca," and author of the *Medita-
tions*, on his ejection from the bishopric in 1647 till his
death in 1656 [1] The house in which he resided, now

---

[1] It is erroneously styled Bishop Hall's Palace. An episcopal palace is
the official residence of the bishop in his cathedral city. Not even a
country seat of a bishop is correctly called a palace, much less the residence of a bishop when ejected from his see.

Fred Roe

The "Briton's Arms," Norwich

known as the Dolphin Inn, still stands, and is an interesting building with its picturesque bays and mullioned windows and ingeniously devised porch. It has actually been proposed to pull down, or improve out of existence, this magnificent old house. Its front is a perfect specimen of flint and stone sixteenth-century architecture. Over the main door appears an episcopal coat of arms with the date 1587, while higher on the front appears the date of a restoration (in two bays):—

N^{AO} A^O DNI	1615

Just inside the doorway is a fine Gothic stoup into which bucolic rustics now knock the fag-ends of their pipes. The staircase newel is a fine piece of Gothic carving with an embattled moulding, a poppy-head and heraldic lion. Pillared fire-places and other tokens of departed greatness testify to the former beauty of this old dwelling-place.

We will now start back to town by the coach which leaves the "Maid's Head" (or did leave in 1762) at half-past eleven in the forenoon, and hope to arrive in London on the following day, and thence hasten southward to Canterbury. Along this Dover road are some of the best inns in England: the "Bull" at Dartford, with its galleried courtyard, once a pilgrims' hostel; the "Bull" and "Victoria" at Rochester, reminiscent of *Pickwick;* the modern "Crown" that supplants a venerable inn where Henry VIII first beheld Anne of Cleves; the "White Hart"; and the "George," where pilgrims stayed; and so on to Canterbury, a city of memories, which happily retains many features of old English life that have not altogether vanished. Its grand cathedral, its churches, St. Augustine's College, its quaint streets, like Butchery Lane, with their houses bending forward in a friendly manner to almost meet each other, as well as its old inns, like the "Falstaff" in High Street, near West Gate, stand-

Fred Roe

The Dolphin Inn, Heigham, Norwich

ing on the site of a pilgrims' inn, with its sign showing
the valiant and portly knight, and supported by elaborate
ironwork, its tiled roof and picturesque front, all combine to make Canterbury as charming a place of modern
pilgrimage as it was attractive to the pilgrims of another
sort who frequented its inns in days of yore.

Shield and Monogram on doorway
of the Dolphin Inn, Heigham

Staircase Newel at the
Dolphin Inn
From *Old Oak Furniture*, by Fred Roe

And now we will discard the cumbersome old coaches
and even the " Flying Machines," and travel by another
flying machine, an airship, landing where we will,
wherever a pleasing inn attracts us. At Glastonbury is
the famous " George," which has hardly changed its
exterior since it was built by Abbot Selwood in 1475
for the accommodation of middle-class pilgrims, those of
high degree being entertained at the abbot's lodgings.
At Gloucester we find ourselves in the midst of memories
of Roman, Saxon, and monastic days. Here too are
some famous inns, especially the quaint " New Inn," in

Northgate Street, a somewhat peculiar sign for a hostelry
built (so it is said) for the use of pilgrims frequenting the
shrine of Edward II in the cathedral. It retains all its
ancient medieval picturesqueness. Here the old gallery
which surrounded most of our inn-yards remains. Carved

The Falstaff Inn, Canterbury

beams and door-posts made of chestnut are seen everywhere, and at the corner of New Inn Lane is a very
elaborate sculpture, the lower part of which represents
the Virgin and Holy Child. Here, in Hare Lane, is also
a similar inn, the Old Raven Tavern, which has suffered much in the course of ages. It was formerly built
around a courtyard, but only one side of it is left.

There are many fine examples of old houses that are not inns in Gloucester, beautiful half-timbered black and white structures, such as Robert Raikes's house, the printer who has the credit of founding the first Sunday-school, the old Judges' House in Westgate Street, the old Deanery with its Norman room, once the Prior's Lodge of the Benedictine Abbey. Behind many a modern front there exist curious carvings and quaintly panelled rooms and elaborate ceilings. There is an interesting carved-panel room in the Tudor House, Westgate Street. The panels are of the linen-fold pattern, and at the head of each are various designs, such as the Tudor Rose and Pomegranate, the Lion of England, etc. The house originally known as the Old Blue Shop has some magnificent mantelpieces, and also St. Nicholas House can boast of a very elaborately carved example of Elizabethan sculpture.

We journey thence to Tewkesbury and visit the grand silver-grey abbey that adorns the Severn banks. Here are some good inns of great antiquity. The "Wheat-sheaf" is perhaps the most attractive, with its curious gable and ancient lights, and even the interior is not much altered. Here too is the "Bell," under the shadow of the abbey tower. It is the original of Phineas Fletcher's house in the novel *John Halifax, Gentleman.* The "Bear and the Ragged Staff" is another half-timbered house with a straggling array of buildings and curious swinging signboard, the favourite haunt of the disciples of Izaak Walton, under the over-hanging eaves of which the Avon silently flows.

The old "Seven Stars" at Manchester is said to be the most ancient in England, claiming a licence 563 years old. But it has many rivals, such as the "Fighting Cocks" at St. Albans, the "Dick Whittington" in Cloth Fair, St. Bartholomews, the "Running Horse" at Leatherhead, wherein John Skelton, the poet laureate of Henry VIII, sang the praises of its landlady, Eleanor Rumming, and several others. The "Seven Stars" has

many interesting features and historical associations.
Here came Guy Fawkes and concealed himself in " Ye
Guy Faux Chamber," as the legend over the door testifies.
What strange stories could this old inn tell us! It could
tell us of the Flemish weavers who, driven from their own
country by religious persecutions and the atrocities of
Duke Alva, settled in Manchester in 1564, and drank

The Bear and Ragged Staff Inn, Tewkesbury

many a cup of sack at the "Seven Stars," rejoicing in
their safety. It could tell us of the disputes between the
clergy of the collegiate church and the citizens in 1574,
when one of the preachers, a bachelor of divinity, on his
way to the church was stabbed three times by the dagger
of a Manchester man; and of the execution of three
popish priests, whose heads were afterwards exposed from
the tower of the church. Then there is the story of the
famous siege in 1642, when the King's forces tried to

take the town and were repulsed by the townsfolk, who
were staunch Roundheads. "A great and furious skirmish did ensue," and the "Seven Stars" was in the
centre of the fighting. Sir Thomas Fairfax made Manchester his head-quarters in 1643, and the walls of the
"Seven Stars" echoed with the carousals of the Roundheads. When Fairfax marched from Manchester to
relieve Nantwich, some dragoons had to leave hurriedly,
and secreted their mess plate in the walls of the old inn,
where it was discovered only a few years ago, and may
now be seen in the parlour of this interesting hostel. In
1745 it furnished accommodation for the soldiers of Prince
Charles Edward, the Young Pretender, and was the head-
quarters of the Manchester regiment. One of the rooms
is called "Ye Vestry," on account of its connexion with
the collegiate church. It is said that there was a secret
passage between the inn and the church, and, according
to the Court Leet Records, some of the clergy used to go
to the "Seven Stars" in sermon-time in their surplices to
refresh themselves. *O tempora! O mores!* A horse-
shoe at the foot of the stairs has a story to tell. During
the war with France in 1805 the press-gang was billeted
at the "Seven Stars." A young farmer's lad was leading
a horse to be shod which had cast a shoe. The press-
gang rushed out, seized the young man, and led him off
to serve the king. Before leaving he nailed the shoe to a
post on the stairs, saying, "Let this stay till I come from
the wars to claim it." So it remains to this day un-
claimed, a mute reminder of its owner's fate and of the
manners of our forefathers.

Another inn, the "Fighting Cocks" at St. Albans,
formerly known as "Ye Old Round House," close to the
River Ver, claims to be the oldest inhabited house in
England. It probably formed part of the monastic
buildings, but its antiquity as an inn is not, as far as
I am aware, fully established.

The antiquary must not forget the ancient inn at Bain-
bridge, in Wensleydale, which has had its licence since

1445, and plays its little part in *Drunken Barnaby's Journal*.

Many inns have played an important part in national events. There is the "Bull" at Coventry, where Henry VII stayed before the battle of Bosworth Field, where he won for himself the English crown. There Mary

Fire-place in the George Inn, Norton St. Philip, Somerset

Queen of Scots was detained by order of Elizabeth. There the conspirators of the Gunpowder Plot met to devise their scheme for blowing up the Houses of Parliament. The George Inn at Norton St. Philip, Somerset, took part in the Monmouth rebellion. There the Duke stayed, and there was much excitement in the inn when he informed his officers that it was his intention to attack Bristol. Thence he marched with his rude levies to

Keynsham, and after a defeat and a vain visit to Bath he returned to the "George" and won a victory over Faversham's advanced guard. You can still see the Monmouth room in the inn with its fine fire-place.

The Crown and Treaty Inn at Uxbridge reminds one of the meeting of the Commissioners of King and Parliament, who vainly tried to arrange a peace in 1645; and at the "Bear," Hungerford, William of Orange received the Commissioners of James II, and set out thence on his march towards London and the English throne.

The Dark Lantern Inn at Aylesbury, in a nest of poor houses, seems to tell by its unique sign of plots and conspiracies.

Aylesbury is noted for its inns. The famous "White Hart" is no more. It has vanished entirely, having disappeared in 1863. It had been modernized, but could boast of a timber balcony round the courtyard, ornamented with ancient wood carvings brought from Salden House, an old seat of the Fortescues, near Winslow. Part of the inn was built by the Earl of Rochester in 1663, and many were the great feasts and civic banquets that took place within its hospitable doors. The "King's Head" dates from the middle of the fifteenth century and is a good specimen of the domestic architecture of the Tudor period. It formerly issued its own tokens. It was probably the hall of some guild or fraternity. In a large window are the arms of England and Anjou. The George Inn has some interesting paintings which were probably brought from Eythrope House on its demolition in 1810, and the "Bull's Head" has some fine beams and panelling.

Some of the inns of Burford and Shrewsbury we have seen when we visited those old-world towns. Wymondham, once famous for its abbey, is noted for its "Green Dragon," a beautiful half-timbered house with projecting storeys, and in our wanderings we must not forget to see along the Brighton road the picturesque "Star" at Alfriston with its three oriel windows, one of the oldest in Sussex.

Fred Roe

The Green Dragon Inn, Wymondham, Norfolk

It was once a sanctuary within the jurisdiction of the Abbot of Battle for persons flying from justice. Hither came men-slayers, thieves, and rogues of every description, and if they reached this inn-door they were safe. There is a record of a horse-thief named Birrel in the days of Henry VIII seeking refuge here for a crime com-

The Star Inn
Alfriston
Sussex

mitted at Lydd, in Kent. It was intended originally as a house for the refreshment of mendicant friars. The house is very quaint with its curious carvings, including a great red lion that guards the side, the figure-head of a wrecked Dutch vessel lost in Cuckmen Haven. Alfriston was noted as a great nest of smugglers, and the "Star" was often frequented by Stanton Collins and his gang, who struck terror into their neighbours, daringly carried on their trade, and drank deep at the inn when the kegs were safely housed. Only fourteen years ago the last of his gang died in Eastbourne Workhouse. Smuggling is a vanished profession nowadays, a feature of vanished England that no one would seek to revive. Who can tell whether it may not be as prevalent as ever it was, if tariff reform and the imposition of heavy taxes on imports become articles of our political creed?

Many of the inns once famous in the annals of the road have now "retired from business" and have taken down their signs. The First and Last Inn, at Croscombe, Somerset, was once a noted coaching hostel, but since coaches ceased to run it was not wanted and has closed its doors to the public. Small towns like Hounslow, Wycombe, and Ashbourne were full of important inns which, being no longer required for the accommodation of travellers, have retired from work and converted themselves into private houses. Small villages like Little Brickhill, which happened to be a stage, abounded with hostels which the ending of the coaching age made unnecessary. The Castle Inn at Marlborough, once one of the finest in England, is now part of a great public school. The house has a noted history. It was once a nobleman's mansion, being the home of Frances Countess of Hereford, the patron of Thomson, and then of the Duke of Northumberland, who leased it to Mr. Cotterell for the purpose of an inn. Crowds of distinguished folk have thronged its rooms and corridors, including the great Lord Chatham, who was laid up here with an attack of gout for seven weeks in 1762 and made all the inn-servants wear his livery. Mr. Stanley Weyman has made it the scene of one of his charming romances. It was not until 1843 that it took down its sign, and has since patiently listened to the conjugation of Greek and Latin verbs, to classic lore, and other studies which have made Marlborough College one of the great and successful public schools. Another great inn was the fine Georgian house near one of the entrances to Kedleston Park, built by Lord Scarsdale for visitors to the medicinal waters in his park. But these waters have now ceased to cure the mildest invalid, and the inn is now a large farm-house with vast stables and barns.

It seems as if something of the foundations of history were crumbling to read that the "Star and Garter" at Richmond is to be sold at auction. That is a melancholy fate for perhaps the most famous inn in the country—a place at which princes and statesmen have stayed, and to which Louis Philippe and his Queen resorted. The "Star and Garter" has figured in the romances of some of our greatest novelists. One comes across it in Meredith and Thackeray, and it finds its way into numerous memoirs, nearly always with some comment upon its unique beauty of situation, a beauty that was never more real than at this moment when the spring foliage is just beginning to peep.

The motor and changing habits account for the evil days upon which the hostelry has fallen. Trains and trams have brought to the doors almost of the "Star and Garter" a public that has not the means to make use of its 120 bedrooms. The richer patrons of other days flash past on their motors, making for those resorts higher up the river which are filling the place in the economy of the London Sunday and week-end which Richmond occupied in times when travelling was more difficult. These changes are inevitable. The "Ship" at Greenwich has gone, and Cabinet Ministers can no longer dine there. The convalescent home, which was the undoing of certain Poplar Guardians, is housed in an hotel as famous as the "Ship," in its days once the resort of Pitt and his bosom friends. Indeed, a pathetic history might be written of the famous hostelries of the past.

Not far from Marlborough is Devizes, formerly a great coaching centre, and full of inns, of which the most noted is the "Bear," still a thriving hostel, once the home of the great artist Sir Thomas Lawrence, whose father was the landlord.

It is impossible within one chapter to record all the old

Courtyard of the George Inn, Norton St. Philip Somerset

inns of England, we have still a vast number left un-
chronicled, but perhaps a sufficient number of examples
has been given of this important feature of vanishing
England. Some of these are old and crumbling, and
may die of old age. Others will fall a prey to licensing
committees. Some have been left high and dry, deserted
by the stream of guests that flowed to them in the old
coaching days. Motor-cars have resuscitated some and
brought prosperity and life to the old guest-haunted
chambers. We cannot dwell on the curious signs that
greet us as we travel along the old highways, or strive to
interpret their origin and meaning. We are rather fond
in Berkshire of the "Five Alls," the interpretation of
which is cryptic. The Five Alls are, if I remember
right—

> "I rule all" [the king].
> "I pray for all" [the bishop].
> "I plead for all" [the barrister].
> "I fight for all" [the soldier].
> "I pay for all" [the farmer].

One of the most humorous inn signs is "The Man
Loaded with Mischief," which is found about a mile from
Cambridge, on the Madingley road. The original Mischief was designed by Hogarth for a public-house in
Oxford Street. It is needless to say that the signboard,
and even the name, have long ago disappeared from the
busy London thoroughfare, but the quaint device must
have been extensively copied by country sign-painters.
There is a "Mischief" at Wallingford, and a "Load of
Mischief" at Norwich, and another at Blewbury. The inn
on the Madingley road exhibits the sign in its original
form. Though the colours are much faded from exposure
to the weather, traces of Hogarthian humour can be
detected. A man is staggering under the weight of a
woman, who is on his back. She is holding a glass of
gin in her hand; a chain and padlock are round the man's
neck, labelled "Wedlock." On the right-hand side is the

"The Dark Lantern" Inn
Aylesbury
16 aug 1902

Fred Roe

shop of "S. Gripe, Pawnbroker," and a carpenter is just going in to pledge his tools.

The art of painting signboards is almost lost, and when they have to be renewed sorry attempts are made to imitate the old designs. Some celebrated artists have not thought it below their dignity to paint signboards. Some have done this to show their gratitude to their kindly host and hostess for favours received when they sojourned at inns during their sketching expeditions. The "George" at Wargrave has a sign painted by the distinguished painters Mr. George Leslie, R.A., and Mr. Broughton, R.A., who, when staying at the inn, kindly painted the sign, which is hung carefully within doors that it may not be exposed to the mists and rains of the Thames valley. St. George is sallying forth to slay the dragon on the one side, and on the reverse he is refreshing himself with a tankard of ale after his labours. Not a few artists in the early stages of their career have paid their bills at inns by painting for the landlord. Morland was always in difficulties and adorned many a signboard, and the art of David Cox, Herring, and Sir William Beechey has been displayed in this homely fashion. David Cox's painting of the Royal Oak at Bettws-y-Coed was the subject of prolonged litigation, the sign being valued at £1000, the case being carried to the House of Lords, and there decided in favour of the freeholder.

Sometimes strange notices appear in inns. The following rather remarkable one was seen by our artist at the "County Arms," Stone, near Aylesbury :—

"A man is specially engaged to do all the cursing and swearing that is required in this establishment. A dog is also kept to do all the barking. Our prize-fighter and chucker-out has won seventy-five prize-fights and has never been beaten, and is a splendid shot with the revolver. An undertaker calls here for orders every morning."

Motor-cars have somewhat revived the life of the old inns on the great coaching roads, but it is only the

larger and more important ones that have been aroused
into a semblance of their old life. The cars disdain the
smaller establishments, and run such long distances that
only a few houses along the road derive much benefit from
them. For many their days are numbered, and it may be
useful to describe them before, like four-wheelers and
hansom-cabs, they have quite vanished away.

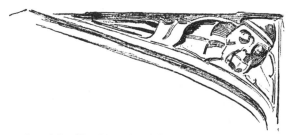

Spandril. The Marquis of Granby Inn, Colchester

CHAPTER XI

OLD MUNICIPAL BUILDINGS

NO class of buildings has suffered more than the old town halls of our country boroughs. Many of these towns have become decayed and all their ancient glories have departed. They were once flourishing places in the palmy days of the cloth trade, and could boast of fairs and markets and a considerable number of inhabitants and wealthy merchants; but the tide of trade has flowed elsewhere. The invention of steam and complex machinery necessitating proximity to coal-fields has turned its course elsewhere, to the smoky regions of Yorkshire and Lancashire, and the old town has lost its prosperity and its power. Its charter has gone; it can boast of no municipal corporation; hence the town hall is scarcely needed save for some itinerant Thespians, an occasional public meeting, or as a storehouse of rubbish. It begins to fall into decay, and the decayed town is not rich enough, or public-spirited enough, to prop its weakened timbers. For the sake of the safety of the public it has to come down.

On the other hand, an influx of prosperity often dooms the aged town hall to destruction. It vanishes before a wave of prosperity. The borough has enlarged its borders. It has become quite a great town and transacts much business. The old shops have given place to grand emporiums with large plate-glass windows, wherein are exhibited the most recent fashions of London and Paris, and motor-cars can be bought, and all is very brisk and up-to-date. The old town hall is now deemed a very poor and inadequate building. It is small, inconvenient, and unsuited to the taste of the municipal councillors, whose ideas have expanded with their trade. The Mayor and Corporation meet, and decide to build a brand-new town hall replete with every luxury and convenience. The old must vanish.

And yet, how picturesque these ancient council chambers are. They usually stand in the centre of the market-place, and have an undercroft, the upper storey resting on pillars. Beneath this shelter the market women display their wares and fix their stalls on market days, and there you will perhaps see the fire-engine, at least the old primitive one which was in use before a grand steam fire-engine had been purchased and housed in a station of its own. The building has high pointed gables and mullioned windows, a tiled roof mellowed with age, and a finely wrought vane, which is a credit to the skill of the local blacksmith. It is a sad pity that this "thing of beauty" should have to be pulled down and be replaced by a modern building which is not always creditable to the architectural taste of the age. A law should be passed that no old town halls should be pulled down, and that all new ones should be erected on a different site. No more fitting place could be found for the storage of the antiquities of the town, the relics of its old municipal life, sketches of its old buildings that have vanished, and portraits of its worthies, than the ancient building which has for so long kept watch and ward over its destinies and been the scene of most of the chief events connected with its history.

Happily several have been spared, and they speak to us of the old methods of municipal government; of the merchant guilds, composed of rich merchants and clothiers, who met therein to transact their common business. The guild hall was the centre of the trade of the town and of its social and commercial life. An amazing amount of business was transacted therein. If you study the records of any ancient borough you will discover that the pulse of life beat fast in the old guild hall. There the merchants

met to talk over their affairs and "drink their guild."
There the Mayor came with the Recorder or "Stiward" to
hold his courts and to issue all "processes as attache-
mentes, summons, distresses, precepts, warantes, sub-
sideas, recognissaunces, etc." The guild hall was like
a living thing. It held property, had a treasury, received
the payments of freemen, levied fines on "foreigners"
who were "not of the guild," administered justice, settled
quarrels between the brethren of the guild, made loans to
merchants, heard the complaints of the aggrieved, held
feasts, promoted loyalty to the sovereign, and insisted
strongly on every burgess that he should do his best to
promote the "comyn weele and prophite of ye saide
gylde." It required loyalty and secrecy from the members of the common council assembled within its walls,
and no one was allowed to disclose to the public its
decisions and decrees. This guild hall was a living thing.
Like the Brook it sang :—

> Men may come and men may go,
> But I flow on for ever."

Mayor succeeded mayor, and burgess followed burgess,
but the old guild hall lived on, the central mainspring of
the borough's life. Therein were stored the archives of
the town, the charters won, bargained for, and granted
by kings and queens, which gave them privileges of
trade, authority to hold fairs and markets, liberty to
convey and sell their goods in other towns. Therein were
preserved the civic plate, the maces that gave dignity to
their proceedings, the cups bestowed by royal or noble
personages or by the affluent members of the guild in
token of their affection for their town and fellowship.
Therein they assembled to don their robes to march in
procession to the town church to hear Mass, or in later
times a sermon, and then refreshed themselves with a
feast at the charge of the hall. The portraits of the
worthies of the town, of royal and distinguished patrons,
adorned the walls, and the old guild hall preached daily

Fred Roe

The Town Hall, Shrewsbury

lessons to the townsfolk to uphold the dignity and promote the welfare of the borough, and good feeling and
the sense of brotherhood among themselves.

We give an illustration of the town hall of Shrewsbury,
a notable building and well worthy of study as a specimen
of a municipal building erected at the close of the sixteenth
century.   The style is that of the Renaissance with the
usual mixture of debased Gothic and classic details, but
the general effect is imposing ; the arches and parapet are
especially characteristic.   An inscription over the arch at
the north end records :—

"The xv^{th} day of June was this building begonne,
William Jones and Thomas Charlton, Gent, then Bailiffes,
and was erected and covered in their time, 1595."

A full description of this building is given in Canon
Auden's history of the town.   He states that "under
the clock is the statue of Richard Duke of York, father
of Edward IV, which was removed from the old Welsh
Bridge at its demolition in 1791.   This is flanked by an
inscription recording this fact on the one side, and on the
other by the three leopards' heads which are the arms of
the town.   On the other end of the building is a sun-dial,
and also a sculptured angel holding a shield on which are
the arms of England and France.   This was removed
from the gate of the town, which stood at the foot of the
castle, on its demolition in 1825.   The principal entrance
is on the west, and over this are the arms of Queen
Elizabeth and the date 1596.   It will be noticed that one
of the supporters is not the unicorn, but the red dragon
of Wales.   The interior is now partly devoted to various
municipal offices, and partly used as the Mayor's Court,
the roof of which still retains its old character."   It was
formerly known as the Old Market Hall, but the business
of the market has been transferred to the huge but
tasteless building of brick erected at the top of Mardol in
1869, the erection of which caused the destruction of
several picturesque old houses which can ill be spared.

Cirencester possesses a magnificent town hall, a stately

Perpendicular building, which stands out well against the noble church tower of the same period. It has a gateway flanked by buttresses and arcades on each side and two upper storeys with pierced battlements at the top which are adorned with richly floriated pinnacles. A great charm of the building are the three oriel windows extending from the top of the ground-floor division to the foot of the battlements. The surface of the wall of the façade is cut into panels, and niches for statues adorn the faces of the four buttresses. The whole forms a most elaborate piece of Perpendicular work of unusual character. We understand that it needs repair and is in some danger. The aid of the Society for the Protection of Ancient Buildings has been called in, and their report has been sent to the civic authorities, who will, we hope, adopt their recommendations and deal kindly and tenderly with this most interesting structure.

Another famous guild hall is in danger, that at Norwich. It has even been suggested that it should be pulled down and a new one erected, but happily this wild scheme has been abandoned. Old buildings like not new inventions, just as old people fear to cross the road lest they should be run over by a motor-car. Norwich Guildhall does not approve of electric tram-cars, which run close to its north side and cause its old bones to vibrate in a most uncomfortable fashion. You can perceive how much it objects to these horrid cars by feeling the vibration of the walls when you are standing on the level of the street or on the parapet. You will not therefore be surprised to find ominous cracks in the old walls, and the roof is none too safe, the large span having tried severely the strength of the old oak beams. It is a very ancient building, the crypt under the east end, vaulted in brickwork, probably dating from the thirteenth century, while the main building was erected in the fifteenth century. The walls are well built, three feet in thickness, and constructed of uncut flints ; the east end is enriched with diaper-work in chequers of stone and knapped flint.

Some new buildings have been added on the south side
within the last century. There is a clock turret at the
east end, erected in 1850 at the cost of the then Mayor.
Evidently the roof was giving the citizens anxiety at that
time, as the good donor presented the clock tower on
condition that the roof of the council chamber should be
repaired. This famous old building has witnessed many
strange scenes, such as the burning of old dames who
were supposed to be witches, the execution of criminals
and conspirators, the savage conflicts of citizens and
soldiers in days of rioting and unrest. These good
citizens of Norwich used to add considerably to the
excitement of the place by their turbulence and eagerness for fighting. The crypt of the Town Hall is just old
enough to have heard of the burning of the cathedral and
monastery by the citizens in 1272, and to have seen the
ringleaders executed. Often was there fighting in the
city, and this same old building witnessed in 1549 a great
riot, chiefly directed against the religious reforms and
change of worship introduced by the first Prayer Book of
Edward VI. It was rather amusing to see Parker, afterwards Archbishop of Canterbury, addressing the rioters
from a platform, under which stood the spearmen of Kett,
the leader of the riot, who took delight in pricking the
feet of the orator with their spears as he poured forth his
impassioned eloquence. In an important city like Norwich the guild hall has played an important part in the
making of England, and is worthy in its old age of
the tenderest and most reverent treatment, and even
of the removal from its proximity of the objectionable
electric tram-cars.

As we are at Norwich it would be well to visit another old
house, which though not a municipal building, is a unique
specimen of the domestic architecture of a Norwich citizen
in days when, as Dr. Jessop remarks, "there was no coal
to burn in the grate, no gas to enlighten the darkness
of the night, no potatoes to eat, no tea to drink, and when
men believed that the sun moved round the earth once in

365 days, and would have been ready to burn the culprit who should dare to maintain the contrary." It is called Strangers' Hall, a most interesting medieval mansion which had never ceased to be an inhabited house for at least 500 years, till it was purchased in 1899 by Mr. Leonard Bolingbroke, who rescued it from decay, and permits the public to inspect its beauties. The crypt and cellars, and possibly the kitchen and buttery, were portions of the original house owned in 1358 by Robert Herdegrey, Burgess in Parliament and Bailiff of the City, and the present hall, with its groined porch and oriel window, was erected later over the original fourteenth-century cellars. It was inhabited by a succession of merchants and chief men of Norwich, and at the beginning of the sixteenth century passed into the family of Sotherton. The merchant's mark of Nicholas Sotherton is painted on the roof of the hall. You can see this fine hall with its screen and gallery and beautifully-carved woodwork. The present Jacobean staircase and gallery, big oak window, and doorways leading into the garden are later additions made by Francis Cook, grocer of Norwich, who was mayor of the city in 1627. The house probably took its name from the family of Le Strange, who settled in Norwich in the sixteenth century. In 1610 the Sothertons conveyed the property to Sir le Strange Mordant, who sold it to the above-mentioned Francis Cook. Sir Joseph Paine came into possession just before the Restoration, and we see his initials, with those of his wife Emma, and the date 1659, in the spandrels of the fire-places in some of the rooms. This beautiful memorial of the merchant princes of Norwich, like many other old houses, fell into decay. It is most pleasant to find that it has now fallen into such tender hands, that its old timbers have been saved and preserved by the generous care of its present owner, who has thus earned the gratitude of all who love antiquity.

Sometimes buildings erected for quite different purposes have been used as guild halls. There was one at

18

Reading, a guild hall near the holy brook in which the women washed their clothes, and made so much noise by "beating their battledores" (the usual style of washing in those days) that the mayor and his worthy brethren were often disturbed in their deliberations, so they petitioned the King to grant them the use of the deserted church of the Greyfriars' Monastery lately dissolved in the town. This request was granted, and in the place where the friars sang their services and preached, the mayor and burgesses "drank their guild" and held their banquets. When they got tired of that building they filched part of the old grammar school from the boys, making an upper storey, wherein they held their council meetings. The old church then was turned into a prison, but now happily it is a church again. At last the corporation had a town hall of their own, which they decorated with the initials s.p.q.r., Romanus and Readingensis conveniently beginning with the same letter. Now they have a grand new town hall, which provides every accommodation for this growing town.

The Newbury town hall, a Georgian structure, has just been demolished. It was erected in 1740–1742, taking the place of an ancient and interesting guild hall built in 1611 in the centre of the market-place. The councillors were startled one day by the collapse of the ceiling of the hall, and when we last saw the chamber tons of heavy plaster were lying on the floor. The roof was unsound; the adjoining street too narrow for the hundred motors that raced past the dangerous corners in twenty minutes on the day of the Newbury races; so there was no help for the old building; its fate was sealed, and it was bound to come down. But the town possesses a very charming Cloth Hall, which tells of the palmy days of the Newbury cloth-makers, or clothiers, as they were called; of Jack of Newbury, the famous John Winchcombe, or Smallwoode, whose story is told in Deloney's humorous old black-letter pamphlet, entitled *The Most Pleasant and Delectable Historie of John Winchcombe, otherwise called Jacke of*

The Greenland Fishery House, King's Lynn. An old Guild House of the time of James I

Fred Roe

Newberie, published in 1596. He is said to have furnished one hundred men fully equipped for the King's
service at Flodden Field, and mightily pleased Queen
Catherine, who gave him a "riche chain of gold," and
wished that God would give the King many such clothiers.
You can see part of the house of this worthy, who died in
1519. Fuller stated in the seventeenth century that this
brick and timber residence had been converted into sixteen clothiers' houses. It is now partly occupied by the
Jack of Newbury Inn. A fifteenth-century gable with
an oriel window and carved barge-board still remains,
and you can see a massive stone chimney-piece in one of
the original chambers where Jack used to sit and receive
his friends. Some carvings also have been discovered in
an old house showing what is thought to be a carved portrait of the clothier. It bears the initials J. W., and
another panel has a raised shield suspended by strap and
buckle with a monogram I. S., presumably John Smallwoode. He was married twice, and the portrait busts
on each side are supposed to represent his two wives.
Another carving represents the Blessed Trinity under the
figure of a single head with three faces within a wreath of
oak-leaves with floriated spandrels.[1] We should like to
pursue the subject of these Newbury clothiers and see
Thomas Dolman's house, which is so fine and large and
cost so much money that his workpeople used to sing a
doggerel ditty :—

Lord have mercy upon us miserable sinners,
Thomas Dolman has built a new house and turned away all his spinners.

The old Cloth Hall which has led to this digression has
been recently restored, and is now a museum.

The ancient town of Wallingford, famous for its castle,
had a guild hall with selds under it, the earliest mention
of which dates back to the reign of Edward II, and
occurs constantly as the place wherein the burghmotes
were held. The present town hall was erected in 1670—

[1] *History of Newbury*, by Walter Money, F.S.A.

a picturesque building on stone pillars. This open space beneath the town hall was formerly used as a corn-market, and so continued until the present corn-exchange was erected half a century ago. The slated roof is gracefully curved, is crowned by a good vane, and a neat dormer window juts out on the side facing the market-place. Below this is a large Renaissance window opening on to a balcony whence orators can address the crowds assembled in the market-place at election times. The walls of the hall are hung with portraits of the worthies and benefactors of the town, including one of Archbishop Laud. A mayor's feast was, before the passing of the Municipal Corporations Act, a great occasion in most of our boroughs, the expenses of which were defrayed by the rates. The upper chamber in the Wallingford town hall was formerly a kitchen, with a huge fire-place, where mighty joints and fat capons were roasted for the banquet. Outside you can see a ring of light-coloured stones, called the bull-ring, where bulls, provided at the cost of the Corporation, were baited. Until 1840 our Berkshire town of Wokingham was famous for its annual bull-baiting on St. Thomas's Day. A good man, one George Staverton, was once gored by a bull; so he vented his rage upon the whole bovine race, and left a charity for the providing of bulls to be baited on the festival of this saint, the meat afterwards to be given to the poor of the town. The meat is still distributed, but the bulls are no longer baited. Here at Wokingham there was a picturesque old town hall with an open undercroft, supported on pillars; but the townsfolk must needs pull it down and erect an unsightly brick building in its stead. It contains some interesting portraits of royal and distinguished folk dating from the time of Charles I, but how the town became possessed of these paintings no man knoweth.

Another of our Berkshire towns can boast of a fine town hall that has not been pulled down like so many of its fellows. It is not so old as some, but is in itself a memorial of some vandalism, as it occupies the site of the old Market Cross, a thing of rare beauty, beautifully carved and erected in Mary's reign, but ruthlessly destroyed by Waller and his troopers during the Civil War period. Upon the ground on which it stood thirty-four years later—in 1677—the Abingdon folk reared their fine town hall; its style resembles that of Inigo Jones, and it has an open undercroft—a kindly shelter from the weather for market women. Tall and graceful it dominates the market-place, and it is crowned with a pretty cupola and a fine vane. You can find a still more interesting hall in the town, part of the old abbey, the gateway with its adjoining rooms, now used as the County Hall, and there you will see as fine a collection of plate and as choice an array of royal portraits as ever fell to the lot of a provincial county town. One of these is a Gainsborough. One of the reasons why Abingdon has such a good store of silver plate is that according to their charter the Corporation has to pay a small sum yearly to their High Stewards, and these gentlemen—the Bowyers of Radley and the Earls of Abingdon—have been accustomed to restore their fees to the town in the shape of a gift of plate.

We might proceed to examine many other of these interesting buildings, but a volume would be needed for the purpose of recording them all. Too many of the ancient ones have disappeared and their places taken by modern, unsightly, though more convenient buildings. We may mention the salvage of the old market-house at Winster, in Derbyshire, which has been rescued by that admirable National Trust for Places of Historic Interest or Natural Beauty, which descends like an angel of mercy on many a threatened and abandoned building and preserves it for future generations. The Winster market-house is of great age ; the lower part is doubtless as old as the thirteenth century, and the upper part was added in the seventeenth. Winster was at one time an important place ; its markets were famous, and this building

Fred Roe

The Market House, Wymondham, Norfolk

must for very many years have been the centre of the commercial life of a large district. But as the market has diminished in importance, the old market-house has fallen out of repair, and its condition has caused anxiety to antiquaries for some time past. Local help has been forthcoming under the auspices of the National Trust, in which it is now vested for future preservation.

Though not a town hall, we may here record the saving of a very interesting old building, the Palace Gatehouse at Maidstone, the entire demolition of which was proposed. It is part of the old residence of the Archbishops of Canterbury, near the Perpendicular church of All Saints, on the banks of the Medway, whose house at Maidstone added dignity to the town and helped to make it the important place it was. The Palace was originally the residence of the Rector of Maidstone, but was given up in the thirteenth century to the Archbishop. The oldest part of the existing building is at the north end, where some fifteenth-century windows remain. Some of the rooms have good old panelling and open stone fire-places of the fifteenth-century date. But decay has fallen on the old building. Ivy is allowed to grow over it unchecked, its main stems clinging to the walls and disturbing the stones. Wet has begun to soak into the walls through the decayed stone sills. Happily the gate-house has been saved, and we doubt not that the en-lightened Town Council will do its best to preserve this interesting building from further decay.

The finest Early Renaissance municipal building is the picturesque guild hall at Exeter, with its richly ornamented front projecting over the pavement and carried on arches. The market-house at Rothwell is a beautifully designed building erected by Sir Thomas Tresham in 1577. Being a Recusant, he was much persecuted for his religion, and never succeeded in finishing the work. We give an illustration of the quaint little market-house at Wymond-ham, with its open space beneath, and the upper storey supported by stout posts and brackets. It is entirely built of timber and plaster. Stout posts support the upper floor, beneath which is a covered market. The upper chamber is reached by a quaint rude wooden staircase. Chipping Campden can boast of a handsome oblong market-house, built of stone, having five arches with three gables on the long sides, and two arches with gables over each on the short sides. There are mullioned windows under each gable.

The city of Salisbury could at one time boast of several halls of the old guilds which flourished there. There was a charming island of old houses near the cattle-

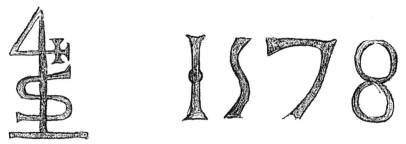

Guild Mark and Date on doorway, Burford, Oxon

market, which have all disappeared. They were most picturesque and interesting buildings, and we regret to have to record that new half-timbered structures have been erected in their place with sham beams, and boards nailed on to the walls to represent beams, one of the monstrosities of modern architectural art. The old Joiners' Hall has happily been saved by the National Trust. It has a very attractive sixteenth-century façade, though the interior has been much altered. Until the early years of the nineteenth century it was the hall of the guild or company of the joiners of the city of New Sarum.

Such are some of the old municipal buildings of England. There are many others which might have been mentioned. It is a sad pity that so many have disappeared and been replaced by modern and uninteresting structures.

If a new town hall be required in order to keep pace with the increasing dignity of an important borough, the Corporation can at least preserve their ancient municipal hall which has so long watched over the fortunes of the town and shared in its joys and sorrows, and seek a fresh site for their new home without destroying the old.

CHAPTER XII

CROSSES

A CAREFUL study of the ordnance maps of certain counties of England reveals the extraordinary number of ancient crosses which are scattered over the length and breadth of the district. Local names often suggest the existence of an ancient cross, such as Blackrod, or Black-rood, Oakenrod, Crosby, Cross Hall, Cross Hillock. But if the student sally forth to seek this sacred symbol of the Christian faith, he will often be disappointed. The cross has vanished, and even the recollection of its existence has completely passed away. Happily not all have disappeared, and in our travels we shall be able to discover many of these interesting specimens of ancient art, but not a tithe of those that once existed are now to be discovered.

Many causes have contributed to their disappearance. The Puritans waged insensate war against the cross. It was in their eyes an idol which must be destroyed. They regarded them as popish superstitions, and objected greatly to the custom of "carrying the corse towards the church all garnished with crosses, which they set down by the way at every cross, and there all of them devoutly on their knees make prayers for the dead."[1] Iconoclastic mobs tore down the sacred symbol in blind fury. In the summer of 1643 Parliament ordered that all crucifixes, crosses, images, and pictures should be obliterated or otherwise destroyed, and during the same year the two Houses passed a resolution for the destruction of all

[1] Report of the State of Lancashire in 1590 (Chetham Society, Vol. XCVI, p. 5).

crosses throughout the kingdom. They ordered Sir Robert Harlow to superintend the levelling to the ground of St. Paul's Cross, Charing Cross, and that in Cheapside, and a contemporary print shows the populace busily engaged in tearing down the last. Ladders are placed against the structure, workmen are busy hammering the figures, and a strong rope is attached to the actual cross on the summit and eager hands are dragging it down. Similar scenes were enacted in many other towns, villages, and cities of England, and the wonder is that any crosses should have been left. But a vast number did remain in order to provide further opportunities for vandalism and wanton mischief, and probably quite as many have disappeared during the eighteenth and nineteenth centuries as those which were destroyed by Puritan iconoclasts. When trade and commerce developed, and villages grew into towns, and sleepy hollows became hives of industry, the old market-places became inconveniently small, and market crosses with their usually accompanying stocks and pillories were swept away as useless obstructions to traffic.[1] Thus complaints were made with regard to the market-place at Colne. There was no room for the coaches to turn. Idlers congregated on the steps of the cross and interfered with the business of the place. It was pronounced a nuisance, and in 1882 was swept away. Manchester market cross existed until 1816, when for the sake of utility and increased space it was removed. A stately Jacobean Proclamation cross remained at Salford until 1824. The Preston Cross, or rather obelisk, consisting of a clustered Gothic column, thirty-one feet high, standing on a lofty pedestal which rested on three steps, was taken down by an act of vandalism in 1853. The Covell Cross at Lancaster shared its fate, being destroyed in 1826 by the justices when they purchased the house now used as the judges' lodgings. A few years ago it was rebuilt as a memorial of the accession of King Edward VII.

[1] *Ancient Crosses of Lancashire*, by Henry Taylor.

Individuals too, as well as corporations, have taken a hand in the overthrow of crosses. There was a wretch named Wilkinson, vicar of Goosnargh, Lancashire, who delighted in their destruction. He was a zealous Protestant, and on account of his fame as a prophet of evil his deeds were not interfered with by his neighbours. He used to foretell the deaths of persons obnoxious to him, and unfortunately several of his prophecies were fulfilled, and he earned the dreaded character of a wizard. No one dared to prevent him, and with his own hands he pulled down several of these venerable monuments. Some drunken men in the early years of the nineteenth century pulled down the old market cross at Rochdale. There was a cross on the bowling-green at Whalley in the seventeenth century, the fall of which is described by a cavalier, William Blundell, in 1642. When some gentlemen came to use the bowling-green they found their game interfered with by the fallen cross. A strong, powerful man was induced to remove it. He reared it, and tried to take it away by wresting it from edge to edge, but his foot slipped; down he fell, and the cross falling upon him crushed him to death. A neighbour immediately he heard the news was filled with apprehension of a similar fate, and confessed that he and the deceased had thrown down the cross. It was considered a dangerous act to remove a cross, though the hope of discovering treasure beneath it often urged men to essay the task. A farmer once removed an old boundary stone, thinking it would make a good " buttery stone." But the results were dire. Pots and pans, kettles and crockery placed upon it danced a clattering dance the livelong night, and spilled their contents, disturbed the farmer's rest, and worried the family. The stone had to be conveyed back to its former resting-place, and the farm again was undisturbed by tumultuous spirits. Some of these crosses have been used for gate-posts. Vandals have sometimes wanted a sun-dial in their churchyards, and have ruthlessly knocked off the head and upper part of the shaft of a cross, as they did at Halton, Lancashire, in order to provide a base for their dial. In these and countless other ways have these crosses suffered, and certainly, from the æsthetic and architectural point of view, we have to bewail the loss of many of the most lovely monuments of the piety and taste of our fore-fathers.

We will now gather up the fragments of the ancient crosses of England ere these also vanish from our country. They served many purposes and were of divers kinds. There were preaching-crosses, on the steps of which the early missionary or Saxon priest stood when he pro-claimed the message of the gospel, ere churches were built for worship. These wandering clerics used to set up crosses in the villages, and beneath their shade preached, baptized, and said Mass. The pagan Saxons worshipped stone pillars ; so in order to wean them from their super-stition the Christian missionaries erected these stone crosses and carved upon them the figures of the Saviour and His Apostles, displaying before the eyes of their hearers the story of the Cross written in stone. The north of England has many examples of these crosses, some of which were fashioned by St. Wilfrid, Archbishop of York, in the eighth century. When he travelled about his diocese a large number of monks and workmen attended him, and amongst these were the cutters in stone, who made the crosses and erected them on the spots which Wilfrid consecrated to the worship of God. St. Paulinus and others did the same. Hence arose a large number of these Saxon works of art, which we pro-pose to examine and to try to discover the meaning of some of the strange sculptures found upon them.

In spite of iconoclasm and vandalism there remains in England a vast number of pre-Norman crosses, and it will be possible to refer only to the most noted and curious examples. These belong chiefly to four main schools of art—the Celtic, Saxon, Roman, and Scandi-navian. These various streams of northern and classical

Fred Roe

Stretham Cross
Isle of Ely.

ideas met and were blended together, just as the wild sagas of the Vikings and the teaching of the gospel showed themselves together in sculptured representations and symbolized the victory of the Crucified One over the legends of heathendom. The age and period of these crosses, the greater influence of one or other of these schools have wrought differences; the beauty and delicacy of the carving is in most cases remarkable, and we stand amazed at the superabundance of the inventive faculty that could produce such wondrous work. A great characteristic of these early sculptures is the curious interlacing scroll-work, consisting of knotted and interlaced cords of divers patterns and designs. There is an immense variety in this carving of these early artists. Examples are shown of geometrical designs, of floriated ornament, of which the conventional vine pattern is the most frequent, and of rope-work and other interlacing ornament. We can find space to describe only a few of the most remarkable.

The famous Bewcastle Cross stands in the most northern corner of the county of Cumberland. Only the shaft remains. In its complete condition it must have been at least twenty-one feet high. A runic inscription on the west side records that it was erected "in memory of Alchfrith lately king" of Northumbria. He was the son of Oswy, the friend and patron of St. Wilfrid, who loved art so much that he brought workmen from Italy to build churches and carve stone, and he decided in favour of the Roman party at the famous Synod of Whitby. On the south side the runes tell that the cross was erected in "the first year of Ecgfrith, King of this realm," who began to reign 670 A.D. On the west side are three panels containing deeply incised figures, the lowest one of which has on his wrist a hawk, an emblem of nobility; the other three sides are filled with interlacing, floriated, and geometrical ornament. Bishop Browne believes that these scrolls and interlacings had their origin in Lombardy and not in Ireland, that they were Italian and not Celtic, and that the same sort of designs were used in the southern land early in the seventh century, whence they were brought by Wilfrid to this country.

Another remarkable cross is that of Ruthwell, now sheltered from wind and weather in the Durham Cathedral Museum.   It is very similar to that at Bewcastle, though probably not wrought by the same hands.   In the panels are sculptures representing events in the life of our Lord. The lowest panel is too defaced for us to determine the subject; on the second we see the flight into Egypt; on the third figures of Paul, the first hermit, and Anthony, the first monk, are carved; on the fourth is a representa- tion of our Lord treading under foot the heads of swine; and on the highest there is the figure of St. John the Baptist with the lamb.   On the reverse side are the Annunciation, the Salutation, and other scenes of gospel history, and the other sides are covered with floral and other decoration.   In addition to the figures there are five stanzas of an Anglo-Saxon poem of singular beauty expressed in runes.   It is the story of the Cruci- fixion told in touching words by the cross itself, which narrates its own sad tale from the time when it was a growing tree by the woodside until at length, after the body of the Lord had been taken down—

> The warriors left me there
> Standing defiled with blood.

On the head of the cross are inscribed the words "Cædmon made me"—Cædmon the first of English poets who poured forth his songs in praise of Almighty God and told in Saxon poetry the story of the Creation and of the life of our Lord.

Another famous cross is that at Gosforth, which is of a much later date and of a totally different character from those which we have described.   The carvings show that it is not Anglian, but that it is connected with Viking thought and work.   On it is inscribed the story of

19

one of the sagas, the wild legends of the Norsemen, preserved by their scalds or bards, and handed down from generation to generation as the precious traditions of their race.   On the west side we see Heimdal, the brave watchman of the gods, with his sword withstanding the powers of evil, and holding in his left hand the Gialla horn, the terrible blast of which shook the world.   He is overthrowing Hel, the grim goddess of the shades of death, who is riding on the pale horse.   Below we see Loki, the murderer of the holy Baldur, the blasphemer of the gods, bound by strong chains to the sharp edges of a rock, while as a punishment for his crimes a snake drops poison upon his face, making him yell with pain, and the earth quakes with his convulsive tremblings.   His faithful wife Sigyn catches the poison in a cup, but when the vessel is full she is obliged to empty it, and then a drop falls on the forehead of Loki, the destroyer, and the earth shakes on account of his writhings.   The continual conflict between good and evil is wonderfully described in these old Norse legends.   On the reverse side we see the triumph of Christianity, a representation of the Crucifixion, and beneath this the woman bruising the serpent's head.   In the former sculptures the monster is shown with two heads ; here it has only one, and that is being destroyed.   Christ is conquering the powers of evil on the cross.   In another fragment at Gosforth we see Thor fishing for the Midgard worm, the offspring of Loki, a serpent cast into the sea which grows continually and threatens the world with destruction.   A bull's head is the bait which Thor uses, but fearing for the safety of his boat, he has cut the fishing-line and released the monstrous worm ; giant whales sport in the sea which afford pastime to the mighty Thor.   Such are some of the strange tales which these crosses tell.

There is an old Viking legend inscribed on the cross at Leeds.   Volund, who is the same mysterious person as our Wayland Smith, is seen carrying off a swan-maiden.   At his feet are his hammer, anvil, bellows, and pincers. The cross was broken to pieces in order to make way for the building of the old Leeds church hundreds of years ago, but the fragments have been pieced together, and we can see the swan-maiden carried above the head of Volund, her wings hanging down and held by two ropes that encircle her waist. The smith holds her by her back hair and by the tail of her dress. There were formerly several other crosses which have been broken up and used as building material.

At Halton, Lancashire, there is a curious cross of inferior workmanship, but it records the curious mingling of Pagan and Christian ideas and the triumph of the latter over the Viking deities. On one side we see emblems of the Four Evangelists and the figures of saints; on the other are scenes from the Sigurd legend. Sigurd sits at the anvil with hammer and tongs and bellows, forging a sword. Above him is shown the magic blade completed, with hammer and tongs, while Fafni writhes in the knotted throes that everywhere signify his death. Sigurd is seen toasting Fafni's heart on a spit. He has placed the spit on a rest, and is turning it with one hand, while flames ascend from the faggots beneath. He has burnt his finger and is putting it to his lips. Above are the interlacing boughs of a sacred tree, and sharp eyes may detect the talking pies that perch thereon, to which Sigurd is listening. On one side we see the noble horse Grani coming riderless home to tell the tale of Sigurd's death, and above is the pit with its crawling snakes that yawns for Gunnar and for all the wicked whose fate is to be turned into hell. On the south side are panels filled with a floriated design representing the vine and twisted knot-work rope ornamentation. On the west is a tall Resurrection cross with figures on each side, and above a winged and seated figure with two others in a kneeling posture. Possibly these represent the two Marys kneeling before the angel seated on the stone of the holy sepulchre on the morning of the Resurrection of our Lord.

A curious cross has at last found safety after many vicissitudes in Hornby Church, Lancashire. It is one of the most beautiful fragments of Anglian work that has come down to modern times. One panel shows a representation of the miracle of the loaves and fishes. At the foot are shown the two fishes and the five loaves carved in bold relief. A conventional tree springs from the central loaf, and on each side is a nimbed figure. The carving is still so sharp and crisp that it is difficult to realize that more than a thousand years have elapsed since the sculptor finished his task.

It would be a pleasant task to wander through all the English counties and note all pre-Norman crosses that remain in many a lonely churchyard; but such a lengthy journey and careful study are too extended for our present purpose. Some of them were memorials of deceased persons; others, as we have seen, were erected by the early missionaries; but preaching crosses were erected and used in much later times; and we will now examine some of the medieval examples which time has spared, and note the various uses to which they were adapted. The making of graves has often caused the undermining and premature fall of crosses and monuments; hence early examples of churchyard crosses have often passed away and medieval ones been erected in their place. Churchyard crosses were always placed at the south side of the church, and always faced the east. The carving and ornamentation naturally follow the style of architecture prevalent at the period of their erection. They had their uses for ceremonial and liturgical purposes, processions being made to them on Palm Sunday, and it is stated in Young's *History of Whitby* that "devotees creeped towards them and kissed them on Good Fridays, so that a cross was considered as a necessary appendage to every cemetery." Preaching crosses were also erected in distant parts of large parishes in the days when churches were few, and sometimes market crosses were used for this purpose.

WAYSIDE OR WEEPING CROSSES

Along the roads of England stood in ancient times many a roadside or weeping cross. Their purpose is well set forth in the work *Dives et Pauper*, printed at Westminster in 1496. Therein it is stated: "For this reason ben ye crosses by ye way, that when folk passynge see the crosses, they sholde thynke on Hym that deyed on the crosse, and worshyppe Hym above all things." Along the pilgrim ways doubtless there were many, and near villages and towns formerly they stood, but unhappily they made such convenient gate-posts when the head was knocked off. Fortunately several have been rescued and restored. It was a very general custom to erect these wayside crosses along the roads leading to an old parish church for the convenience of funerals. There were no hearses in those days; hence the coffin had to be carried a long way, and the roads were bad, and bodies heavy, and the bearers were not sorry to find frequent resting-places, and the mourners' hearts were comforted by constant prayer as they passed along the long, sad road with their dear ones for the last time. These wayside crosses, or weeping crosses, were therefore of great practical utility. Many of the old churches in Lancashire were surrounded by a group of crosses, arranged in radiating lines along the converging roads, and at suitable distances for rest. You will find such ranges of crosses in the parishes of Aughton, Ormskirk, and Burscough Priory, and at each a prayer for the soul of the departed was offered or the *De profundis* sung. Every one is familiar with the famous Eleanor crosses erected by King Edward I to mark the spots where the body of his beloved Queen rested when it was being borne on its last sad pilgrimage to Westminster Abbey.

MARKET CROSSES

Market crosses form an important section of our subject, and are an interesting feature of the old market-places wherein they stand. Mr. Gomme contends that

they were the ancient meeting-places of the local assem-
blies, and we know that for centuries in many towns they
have been the rallying-points for the inhabitants.   Here
fairs were proclaimed, and are still in some old-fashioned
places, beginning with the quaint formula "O yes,
O yes, O yes!" a strange corruption of the old Norman-
French word *oyez*, meaning "Hear ye."   I have printed
in my book *English Villages* a very curious proclamation
of a fair and market which was read a few years ago at
Broughton-in-Furness by the steward of the lord of the
manor from the steps of the old market cross.   Very
comely and attractive structures are many of these ancient
crosses.   They vary very much in different parts of
the country and according to the period in which they
were erected.   The earliest are simple crosses with steps.
Later on they had niches for sculptured figures, and then
in the southern shires a kind of penthouse, usually
octagonal in shape, enclosed the cross, in order to provide shelter from the weather for the market-folk.   In the
north the hardy Yorkshiremen and Lancastrians recked
not for rain and storms, and few covered-in crosses can be
found.   You will find some beautiful specimens of these
at Malmesbury, Chichester, Somerton, Shepton Mallet,
Cheddar, Axbridge, Nether Stowey, Dunster, South
Petherton, Banwell, and other places.

Salisbury market cross, of which we give an illustration, is remarkable for its fine and elaborate Gothic
architectural features, its numerous niches and foliated
pinnacles.   At one time a sun-dial and ball crowned the
structure, but these have been replaced by a cross.   It is
usually called the Poultry Cross.   Near it and in other
parts of the city are quaint overhanging houses.   Though
the Guildhall has vanished, destroyed in the eighteenth
century, the Joiners' Hall, the Tailors' Hall, the meeting-
places of the old guilds, the Hall of John Halle, and the
Old George are still standing with some of their features
modified, but not sufficiently altered to deprive them of
interest.

The Market Cross
Salisbury.
Wilts

Fred Roe
Oct 1908

Sometimes you will find above a cross an overhead chamber, which was used for the storing of market appurtenances. The reeve of the lord of the manor, or if the town was owned by a monastery, or the market and fair had been granted to a religious house, the abbot's official sat in this covered place to receive dues from the merchants or stall-holders.

There are no less than two hundred old crosses in Somerset, many of them fifteenth-century work. Saxon crosses exist at Rowberrow and Kelston ; a twelfth-century cross at Harptree ; Early English crosses at Chilton Trinity, Dunster, and Broomfield ; Decorated crosses at Williton, Wiveliscombe, Bishops-Lydeard, Chewton Mendip, and those at Sutton Bingham and Wraghall are fifteenth century. But not all these are market crosses. The south-west district of England is particularly rich in these relics of ancient piety, but many have been allowed to disappear. Glastonbury market cross, a fine Perpendicular structure with a roof, was taken down in 1808, and a new one with no surrounding arcade was erected in 1846. The old one bore the arms of Richard Bere, abbot of Glastonbury, who died in 1524. The wall of an adjacent house has a piece of stone carving representing a man and a woman clasping hands, and tradition asserts that this formed part of the original cross. Together with the cross was an old conduit, which frequently accompanied the market cross. Cheddar Cross is surrounded by its battlemented arcade with grotesque gargoyles, a later erection, the shaft going through the roof. Taunton market cross was erected in 1867 in place of a fifteenth-century structure destroyed in 1780. On its steps the Duke of Monmouth was proclaimed king, and from the window of the Old Angel Inn Judge Jeffreys watched with pleasure the hanging of the deluded followers of the duke from the tie-beams of the Market Arcade. Dunster market cross is known as the Yarn Market, and was erected in 1600 by George Luttrell, sheriff of the county of Somerset. The town

was famous for its kersey cloths, sometimes called
"Dunsters," which were sold under the shade of this
structure.

Wymondham, in the county of Norfolk, standing on
the high road between Norwich and London, has a fine
market cross erected in 1617. A great fire raged here in
1615, when three hundred houses were destroyed, and
probably the old cross vanished with them, and this one
was erected to supply its place.

The old cross at Wells, built by William Knight,
bishop of Bath in 1542, was taken down in 1783. Leland
states that it was "a right sumptuous Peace of worke."
Over the vaulted roof was the *Domus Civica* or town hall.
The tolls of the market were devoted to the support of
the choristers of Wells Cathedral. Leland also records
a market cross at Bruton which had six arches and a
pillar in the middle "for market folkes to stande yn."
It was built by the last abbot of Bruton in 1533, and was
destroyed in 1790. Bridgwater Cross was removed in
1820, and Milverton in 1850. Happily the inhabitants of
some towns and villages were not so easily deprived
of their ancient crosses, and the people of Croscombe,
Somerset, deserve great credit for the spirited manner in
which they opposed the demolition of their cross about
thirty years ago.

Witney Butter Cross, Oxon, the town whence blankets
come, has a central pillar which stands on three
steps, the superstructure being supported on thirteen
circular pillars. An inscription on the lantern above
records the following :—

GULIEIMUS BLAKE

Armiger de Coggs

1683

Restored 1860

1889

1894

It has a steep roof, gabled and stone-slated, which is

not improved by the pseudo-Gothic barge-boards, added
during the restorations.

Many historical events of great importance have taken
place at these market crosses which have been so hardly
used.   Kings were always proclaimed here at their
accession, and would-be kings have also shared that
honour.   Thus at Lancaster in 1715 the Pretender was
proclaimed king as James III, and, as we have stated,
the Duke of Monmouth was proclaimed king at Taunton
and Bridgwater.   Charles II received that honour at
Lancaster market cross in 1651, nine years before he
ruled.   Banns of marriage were published here in Cromwell's time, and these crosses have witnessed all the cruel
punishments which were inflicted on delinquents in the
" good old days."   The last step of the cross was often
well worn, as it was the seat of the culprits who sat in
the stocks.   Stocks, whipping-posts, and pillories, of
which we shall have much to say, always stood nigh
the cross, and as late as 1822 a poor wretch was tied
to a cart-wheel at the Colne Cross, Lancashire, and
whipped.

Sometimes the cross is only a cross in name, and an
obelisk has supplanted the Christian symbol.   The change
is deemed to be attributable to the ideas of some of the
Reformers who desired to assert the supremacy of the
Crown over the Church.   Hence they placed an orb on
the top of the obelisk surmounted by a small, plain Latin
cross, and later on a large crown took the place of the
orb and cross.   At Grantham the Earl of Dysart erected
an obelisk which has an inscription stating that it occupies the site of the Grantham Eleanor cross.   This is
a strange error, as this cross stood on an entirely different
site on St. Peter's Hill and was destroyed by Cromwell's
troopers.   The obelisk replaced the old market cross,
which was regarded with much affection and reverence
by the inhabitants, who in 1779, when it was taken down
by the lord of the manor, immediately obtained a manda-
mus for its restoration.   The Mayor and Corporation still

Under the old Butter Cross
Witney Oxon

Fred Roe
23 May
1908

proclaim the Lent Fair in quaint and archaic language at this poor substitute for the old cross.

One of the uses of the market cross was to inculcate the sacredness of bargains. There is a curious stone erection in the market-place at Middleham, Yorkshire, which seems to have taken the place of the market cross and to have taught the same truth. It consists of a platform on which are two pillars; one carries the effigy of some animal in a kneeling posture, resembling a sheep or a cow, the other supports an octagonal object traditionally supposed to represent a cheese. The farmers used to walk up the opposing flights of steps when concluding a bargain and shake hands over the sculptures.[1]

BOUNDARY CROSSES

Crosses marked in medieval times the boundaries of ecclesiastical properties, which by this sacred symbol were thus protected from encroachment and spoliation. County boundaries were also marked by crosses and meare stones. The seven crosses of Oldham marked the estate owned by the Hospital of St. John of Jerusalem.

CROSSES AT CROSS-ROADS AND HOLY WELLS

Where roads meet and many travellers passed a cross was often erected. It was a wayside or weeping cross. There pilgrims knelt to implore divine aid for their journey and protection from outlaws and robbers, from accidents and sudden death. At holy wells the cross was set in order to remind the frequenters of the sacredness of the springs and to wean them from all superstitious thoughts and pagan customs. Sir Walter Scott alludes to this connexion of the cross and well in *Marmion*, when he tells of "a little fountain cell" bearing the legend :—

> Drink, weary pilgrim, drink and pray
> For the kind soul of Sybil Grey,
> Who built this cross and well.

[1] *Ancient Crosses and Holy Wells of Lancashire*, by Henry Taylor, F.S.A.

"In the corner of a field on the Billington Hall Farm, just outside the parish of Haughton, there lies the base, with a portion of the shaft, of a fourteenth-century wayside cross. It stands within ten feet of an old disused lane leading from Billington to Bradley. Common report pronounced it to be an old font. Report states that it was said to be a stone dropped out of a cart as the stones from Billington Chapel were being conveyed to Bradley to be used in building its churchyard wall. A superstitious veneration has always attached to it. A former owner of the property wrote as follows: 'The late Mr. Jackson, who was a very superstitious man, once told me that a former tenant of the farm, whilst ploughing the field, pulled up the stone, and the same day his team of wagon-horses was all drowned. He then put it into the same place again, and all went on right; and that he himself would not have it disturbed upon any account.' A similar legend is attached to another cross. Cross Llywydd, near Raglan, called The White Cross, which is still complete, and has evidently been whitewashed, was moved by a man from its base at some cross-roads to his garden. From that time he had no luck and all his animals died. He attributed this to his sacrilegious act and removed it to a piece of waste ground. The next owner afterwards enclosed the waste with the cross standing in it.

"The Haughton Cross is only a fragment—almost precisely similar to a fragment at Butleigh, in Somerset, of early fourteenth-century date. The remaining part is clearly the top stone of the base, measuring 2 ft. 1½ in. square by 1 ft. 6 in. high, and the lowest portion of the shaft sunk into it, and measuring 1 ft. 1 in. square by 10½ in. high. Careful excavation showed that the stone is probably still standing on its original site."[1]

"There is in the same parish, where there are four cross-roads, a place known as 'The White Cross.' Not a vestige of a stone remains. But on a slight mound at the crossing stands a venerable oak, now dying. In Monmouthshire oaks have often been so planted on the sites of crosses; and in some cases the bases of the crosses still remain. There are in that county about thirty sites of such crosses, and in seventeen some stones still exist; and probably there are many more unknown

[1] A paper read before the Penkside Clerical Society, by G. T. Royds, Rector of Haughton and Rural Dean of Stafford.

to the antiquary, but hidden away in corners of old paths, and in field-ways, and in ditches that used to serve as roads. A question of great interest arises. What were the origin and use of these wayside crosses? and why were so many of them, especially at cross-roads, known as 'The White Cross'? At Abergavenny a cross stood at cross-roads. There is a White Cross Street in London and one in Monmouth, where a cross stood. Were these planted by the White Cross Knights (the Knights of Malta, or of S. John of Jerusalem)? Or are they the work of the Carmelite, or White, Friars? There is good authority for the general idea that they were often used as preaching stations, or as praying stations, as is so frequently the case in Brittany. But did they at cross-roads in any way serve the purpose of the modern sign-post? They are certainly of very early origin. The author of *Ecclesiastical Polity* says that the erection of way-side crosses was a very ancient practice. Chrysostom says that they were common in his time. Eusebius says that their building was begun by Constantine the Great to eradicate paganism. Juvenal states that a shapeless post, with a marble head of Mercury on it, was erected at cross-roads to point out the way; and Eusebius says that wherever Constantine found a statue of Bivialia (the Roman goddess who delivered from straying from the path), or of Mercurius Triceps (who served the same kind purpose for the Greeks), he pulled it down and had a cross placed upon the site. If, then, these cross-road crosses of later medieval times also had something to do with directions for the way, another source of the designa-tion 'White Cross' is by no means to be laughed out of court, viz. that they were whitewashed, and thus more prominent objects by day, and especially by night. It is quite certain that many of them were whitewashed, for the remains of this may still be seen on them. And the use of whitewash or plaister was far more usual in England than is generally known. There is no doubt that the whole of the outside of the abbey church of St. Albans, and of White Castle, from top to base, were coated with whitewash." [1]

Whether they were whitened or not, or whether they served as guide-posts or stations for prayer, it is well that they should be carefully preserved and restored as

[1] *Ibid.*

memorials of the faith of our forefathers, and for the purpose of raising the heart of the modern pilgrim to Christ, the Saviour of men.

SANCTUARY CROSSES

When criminals sought refuge in ancient sanctuaries, such as Durham, Beverley, Ripon, Manchester, and other places which provided the privilege, having claimed sanctuary and been provided with a distinctive dress, they were allowed to wander within certain prescribed limits. At Beverley Minster the fugitive from justice could wander with no fear of capture to a distance extending a mile from the church in all directions. Richly carved crosses marked the limit of the sanctuary. A peculiar reverence for the cross protected the fugitives from violence if they kept within the bounds. In Cheshire, in the wild region of Delamere Forest, there are several ancient crosses erected for the convenience of travellers; and under their shadows they were safe from robbery and violence at the hands of outlaws, who always respected the reverence attached to these symbols of Christianity.

CROSSES AS GUIDE-POSTS

In wild moorland and desolate hills travellers often lost their way. Hence crosses were set up to guide them along the trackless heaths. They were as useful as sign-posts, and conveyed an additional lesson. You will find such crosses in the desolate country on the borderland of Yorkshire and Lancashire. They were usually placed on the summit of hills. In Buckinghamshire there are two crosses cut in the turf on a spur of the Chilterns, White-leaf and Bledlow crosses, which were probably marks for the direction of travellers through the wild and dangerous woodlands, though popular tradition connects them with the memorials of ancient battles between the Saxons and Danes.

From time out of mind crosses have been the rallying point for the discussion of urgent public affairs. It was so in London.   Paul's Cross was the constant meeting-place of the citizens of London whenever they were excited by oppressive laws, the troublesome competition of "foreigners," or any attempt to interfere with their privileges and liberties.   The meetings of the shire or hundred moots took place often at crosses, or other conspicuous or well-known objects.   Hundreds were named after them, such as the hundred of Faircross in Berkshire, of Singlecross in Sussex, Normancross in Huntingdonshire, and Brothercross and Guiltcross, or Gyldecross, in Norfolk.

Stories and legends have clustered around them.   There is the famous Stump Cross in Cheshire, the subject of one of Nixon's prophecies.   It is supposed to be sinking into the ground.   When it reaches the level of the earth the end of the world will come.   A romantic story is associated with Mab's Cross, in Wigan, Lancashire.   Sir William Bradshaigh was a great warrior, and went crusading for ten years, leaving his beautiful wife, Mabel, alone at Haigh Hall.   A dastard Welsh knight compelled her to marry him, telling her that her husband was dead, and treated her cruelly ; but Sir William came back to the hall disguised as a palmer.   Mabel, seeing in him some resemblance to her former husband, wept sore, and was beaten by the Welshman.   Sir William made himself known to his tenants, and raising a troop, marched to the hall. The Welsh knight fled, but Sir William followed him and slew him at Newton, for which act he was outlawed a year and a day.   The lady was enjoined by her confessor to do penance by going once a week, bare-footed and bare-legged, to a cross near Wigan, two miles from the hall, and it is called Mab's Cross to this day.   You can see in Wigan Church the monument of Sir William and his lady, which tells this sad story, and also the cross—at least, all that remains of it—the steps, a pedestal, and part of the shaft—in Standisgate, "to witness if I lie." It is true that Sir William was born ten years after the last of the crusades had ended ; but what does that matter? He was probably fighting for his king, Edward II, against the Scots, or he was languishing a prisoner in some dungeon. There was plenty of fighting in those days for those who loved it, and where was the Englishman then who did not love to fight for his king and country, or seek for martial glory in other lands, if an ungrateful country did not provide him with enough work for his good sword and ponderous lance?

Such are some of the stories that cluster round these crosses. It is a sad pity that so many should have been allowed to disappear. More have fallen owing to the indifference and apathy of the people of England in the eighteenth and nineteenth centuries than to the wanton and iconoclastic destruction of the Puritans. They are holy relics of primitive Christianity. On the lonely mountainsides the tired traveller found in them a guide and friend, a director of his ways and an uplifter of his soul. In the busy market-place they reminded the trader of the sacredness of bargains and of the duty of honest dealing. Holy truths were proclaimed from their steps. They connected by a close and visible bond religious duties with daily life ; and not only as objects of antiquarian interest, but as memorials of the religious feelings, habits, and customs of our forefathers, are they worthy of careful preservation.

CHAPTER XIII

STOCKS, WHIPPING-POSTS, AND OLD-TIME PUNISHMENTS

NEAR the village cross almost invariably stood the parish stocks, instruments of rude justice, the use of which has only just passed away. The "oldest inhabitant" can remember well the old stocks standing in the village green and can tell of the men who suffered in them. Many of these instruments of torture still remain, silent witnesses of old-time ways. You can find them in multitudes of remote villages in all parts of the country, and vastly uncomfortable it must have been to have one's "feet set in the stocks." A well-known artist who delights in painting monks a few years ago placed the portly model who usually "sat" for him in the village stocks of Sulham, Berkshire, and painted a picture of the monk in disgrace. The model declared that he was never so uncomfortable in his life and his legs and back ached for weeks afterwards. To make the penalty more realistic the artist might have prevailed upon some village urchins to torment the sufferer by throwing stones, refuse, or garbage at him, some village maids to mock and jeer at him, and some mischievous men to distract his ears with inharmonious sounds. In an old print of two men in the stocks I have seen a malicious wretch scraping piercing noises out of a fiddle and the victims trying to drown the hideous sounds by putting their fingers into their ears. A few hours in the stocks was no light penalty.

These stocks have a venerable history. They date

back to Saxon times and appear in drawings of that
period. It is a pity that they should be destroyed; but
borough corporations decide that they interfere with the
traffic of a utilitarian age and relegate them to a museum
or doom them to be cut up as faggots. Country folk
think nothing of antiquities, and a local estate agent or
the village publican will make away with this relic of
antiquity and give the "old rubbish" to Widow Smith
for firing. Hence a large number have disappeared,
and it is wonderful that so many have hitherto escaped.
Let the eyes of squires and local antiquaries be ever
on the watch lest those that remain are allowed to vanish.

By ancient law[1] every town or village was bound to
provide a pair of stocks. It was a sign of dignity, and if
the village had this seat for malefactors, a constable, and
a pound for stray cattle, it could not be mistaken for
a mere hamlet. The stocks have left their mark on English literature. Shakespeare frequently alludes to them.
Falstaff, in *The Merry Wives of Windsor*, says that but
for his "admirable dexterity of wit the knave constable had
set me i' the stocks, i' the common stocks." "What needs
all that and a pair of stocks in the town," says Luce in the
Comedy of Errors. "Like silly beggars, who sitting in
stocks refuge their shame," occurs in *Richard II ;* and in
King Lear Cornwall exclaims—

> " Fetch forth the stocks !
> You stubborn ancient knave."

Who were the culprits who thus suffered? Falstaff
states that he only just escaped the punishment of being
set in the stocks for a witch. Witches usually received
severer justice, but stocks were often used for keeping
prisoners safe until they were tried and condemned, and
possibly Shakespeare alludes in this passage only to the
preliminaries of a harsher ordeal. Drunkards were the
common defaulters who appeared in the stocks, and by an
Act of 2 James I they were required to endure six hours'

---

[1] Act of Parliament, 1405.

incarceration with a fine of five shillings. Vagrants always received harsh treatment unless they had a licence, and the corporation records of Hungerford reveal the fact that they were always placed in the pillory and whipped. The stocks, pillory, and whipping-post were three different implements of punishment, but, as was the case at Wallingford, Berkshire, they were sometimes allied and combined. The stocks secured the feet, the pillory "held in durance vile" the head and the hands, while the whipping-post imprisoned the hands only by clamps on the sides of the post. In the constable's accounts of Hungerford we find such items as :—

> " Pd for cheeke and brace for the pillory   00,02,00
> Pd for mending the pillory   .   .   00,00,06
> Pd the Widow Tanner for iron geare for
>   the whipping post .   .   .   00,03,06 "

Whipping was a very favourite pastime at this old Berkshire town ; this entry will suffice :—

> " Pd to John Savidge for his extra-
>   ordinary paines this yeare and
>   whipping of severall persons   .   00,05,00 "

John Savidge was worthy of his name, but the good folks of Hungerford tempered mercy with justice and usually gave a monetary consolation to those who suffered from the lash. Thus we read :—

> " Gave a poore man that was whipped
>   and sent from Tythinge to Tyth-
>   inge   .   .   .   .   00,00,04 "

Women were whipped at Hungerford, as we find that the same John Savidge received 2d. for whipping Dorothy Millar. All this was according to law. The first Whipping Act was passed in 1530 when Henry VIII reigned, and according to this barbarous piece of legislation the victim was stripped naked and tied to a cart-tail, dragged through the streets of the town, and whipped "till his body was bloody." In Elizabeth's time the cart-tail went out of fashion and a whipping-post was substituted, and only the upper part of the body was exposed. The tramp question was as troublesome in the seventeenth century as it is to-day. We confine them in workhouse-cells and make them break stones or pick oakum ; whipping was the solution adopted by our forefathers. We have seen John Savidge wielding his whip, which still exists among the curiosities at Hungerford. At Barnsley in 1632 Edward Wood was paid iiijd. "for whiping of three wanderers." Ten years earlier Richard White received only iid. for performing the like service for six wanderers. Mr. W. Andrews has collected a vast store of curious anecdotes on the subject of whippings, recorded in his *Bygone Punishments*, to which the interested reader is referred. The story he tells of the brutality of Judge Jeffreys may be repeated. This infamous and inhuman judge sentenced a woman to be whipped, and said, "Hangman, I charge you to pay particular attention to this lady. Scourge her soundly, man ; scourge her till her blood runs down ! It is Christmas, a cold time for madam to strip. See that you warm her shoulders thoroughly." It was not until 1791 that the whipping of female vagrants was expressly forbidden by Act of Parliament.

Stocks have been used in quite recent times. So late as 1872, at Newbury, one Mark Tuck, a devoted disciple of John Barleycorn, suffered this penalty for his misdeeds.[1] He was a rag and bone dealer, and knew well the inside of Reading jail. *Notes and Queries*[2] contains an account of the proceedings, and states that he was "fixed in the stocks for drunkenness and disorderly conduct in the Parish Church on Monday evening." Twenty-six years had elapsed since the stocks were last used, and their reappearance created no little sensation and amusement, several hundreds of persons being attracted to the spot where they were fixed. Tuck was seated on a stool, and his legs were secured in the stocks at a few minutes past

---

[1] *History of Hungerford*, by W. Money, p. 38.
[2] *Notes and Queries*, 4th series, X, p. 6.

one o'clock, and as the church clock, immediately facing him, chimed each quarter, he uttered expressions of thankfulness, and seemed anything but pleased at the laughter and derision of the crowd. Four hours having passed, Tuck was released, and by a little stratagem on the part of the police he escaped without being interfered with by the crowd.

Sunday drinking during divine service provided in many places victims for the stocks. So late as half a century ago it was the custom for the churchwardens to go out of church during the morning service on Sundays and visit the public-houses to see if any persons were tippling there, and those found *in flagrante delicto* were immediately placed in the stocks. So arduous did the churchwardens find this duty that they felt obliged to regale themselves at the alehouses while they made their tour of inspection, and thus rendered themselves liable to the punishment which they inflicted on others. Mr. Rigbye, postmaster at Croston, Lancashire, who was seventy-three years of age in 1899, remembered these Sunday-morning searches, and had seen drunkards sitting in the stocks, which were fixed near the southern step of the village cross. Mr. Rigbye, when a boy, helped to pull down the stocks, which were then much dilapidated. A certain Richard Cottam, called " Cockle Dick," was the last man seen in them.[1]

The same morning perambulating of ale-houses was carried on at Skipton, the churchwardens being headed by the old beadle, an imposing personage, who wore a cocked hat and an official coat trimmed with gold, and carried in majestic style a trident staff, a terror to evil-doers, at least to those of tender years.[2] At Beverley the stocks still preserved in the minster were used as late as 1853; Jim Brigham, guilty of Sunday tippling, and dis-

[1] *Ancient Crosses and Holy Wells of Lancashire*, by H. Taylor, F.S A., p. 37.
[2] *History of Skipton*, W. H. Dawson, quoted in *Bygone Punishments*, p. 199.

covered by the churchwardens in their rounds, was the last victim. Some sympathizer placed in his mouth a lighted pipe of tobacco, but the constable in charge hastily snatched it away. James Gambles, for gambling on Sunday, was confined in the Stanningley stocks, Yorkshire, for six hours in 1860. The stocks and village well remain still at Standish, near the cross, and also the stone cheeks of those at Eccleston Green bearing the date 1656. At Shore Cross, near Birkdale, the stocks remain, also the iron ones at Thornton, Lancashire, described in Mrs. Blundell's novel *In a North Country Village;* also at Formby they exist, though somewhat dilapidated.

Whether by accident or design, the stocks frequently stand close to the principal inn in a village. As they were often used for the correction of the intemperate their presence was doubtless intended as a warning to the frequenters of the hostelry not to indulge too freely. Indeed, the sight of the stocks, pillory, and whipping-post must have been a useful deterrent to vice. An old writer states that he knew of the case of a young man who was about to annex a silver spoon, but on looking round and seeing the whipping-post he relinquished his design. The writer asserts that though it lay immediately in the high road to the gallows, it had stopped many an adventurous young man in his progress thither.

The ancient Lancashire town of Poulton-in-the-Fylde has a fairly complete set of primitive punishment implements. Close to the cross stand the stocks with massive ironwork, the criminals, as usual, having been accustomed to sit on the lowest step of the cross, and on the other side of the cross is the rogue's whipping-post, a stone pillar about eight feet high, on the sides of which are hooks to which the culprit was fastened. Between this and the cross stands another useful feature of a Lancashire market-place, the fish stones, an oblong raised slab for the display and sale of fish.

In several places we find that movable stocks were in use, which could be brought out whenever occasion required. A set of these exists at Garstang, Lancashire. The quotation already given from *King Lear*, "Fetch forth the stocks," seems to imply that in Shakespeare's time they were movable. Beverley stocks were movable, and in *Notes and Queries* we find an account of a mob at Shrewsbury dragging around the town in the stocks an incorrigible rogue one Samuel Tisdale in the year 1851.

The Rochdale stocks remain, but they are now in the churchyard, having been removed from the place where the markets were formerly held at Church Stile. When these kind of objects have once disappeared it is rarely that they are ever restored. However, at West Derby this unusual event has occurred, and five years ago the restoration was made. It appears that in the village there was an ancient pound or pinfold which had degenerated into an unsightly dust-heap, and the old stocks had passed into private hands. The inhabitants resolved to turn the untidy corner into a garden, and the lady gave back the stocks to the village. An inscription records: "To commemorate the long and happy reign of Queen Victoria and the coronation of King Edward VII, the site of the ancient pound of the Dukes of Lancaster and other lords of the manor of West Derby was enclosed and planted, and the village stocks set therein. Easter, 1904."

This inscription records another item of vanishing England. Before the Inclosure Acts at the beginning of the last century there were in all parts of the country large stretches of unfenced land, and cattle often strayed far from their homes and presumed to graze on the open common lands of other villages. Each village had its pound-keeper, who, when he saw these estrays, as the lawyers term the valuable animals that were found wandering in any manor or lordship, immediately drove them into the pound. If the owner claimed them, he had certain fees to pay to the pound-keeper and the cost of the keep. If they were not claimed they became the property of the lord of the manor, but it was required that they should be proclaimed in the church and two market towns next adjoining the place where they were found, and a year and a day must have elapsed before they became the actual property of the lord. The possession of a pound was a sign of dignity for the village. Now that commons have been enclosed and waste lands reclaimed, stray cattle no longer cause excitement in the village, the pound-keeper has gone, and too often the pound itself has disappeared. We had one in our village twenty years ago, but suddenly, before he could be remonstrated with, an estate agent, not caring for the trouble and cost of keeping it in repair, cleared it away, and its place knows it no more. In very many other villages similar happenings have occurred. Sometimes the old pound has been utilized by road surveyors as a convenient place for storing gravel for mending roads, and its original purpose is forgotten.

It would be a pleasant task to go through the towns and villages of England to discover and to describe traces of these primitive implements of torture, but such a record would require a volume instead of a single chapter. In Berkshire we have several left to us. There is a very complete set at Wallingford, pillory, stocks, and whipping-post, now stored in the museum belonging to Miss Hedges in the castle, but in western Berkshire they have nearly all disappeared. The last pair of stocks that I can remember stood at the entrance to the town of Wantage. They have only disappeared within the last few years. The whipping-post still exists at the old Town Hall at Faringdon, the staples being affixed to the side of the ancient "lock-up," known as the Black Hole.

At Lymm, Cheshire, there are some good stocks by the cross in that village, and many others may be discovered by the wandering antiquary, though their existence is little known and usually escapes the attention of the writers on local antiquities. As relics of primitive modes of administering justice, it is advisable that they should be preserved.

Yet another implement of rude justice was the cucking or ducking stool, which exists in a few places. It was used principally for the purpose of correcting scolding women. Mr. Andrews, who knows all that can be known about old-time punishments, draws a distinction between the cucking and ducking stool, and states that the former originally was a chair of infamy where immoral women and scolds were condemned to sit with bare feet and head to endure the derision of the populace, and had no relation to any ducking in water. But it appears that later on the terms were synonymous, and several of these implements remain. This machine for quieting intemperate scolds was quite simple. A plank with a chair at one end was attached by an axle to a post which was fixed on the bank of a river or pond, or on wheels, so that it could be run thither; the culprit was tied to the chair, and the other end of the plank was alternately raised or lowered so as to cause the immersion of the scold in the chilly water. A very effectual punishment! The form of the chair varies. The Leominster ducking-stool is still preserved, and this implement was the latest in use, having been employed in 1809 for the ducking of Jenny Pipes, *alias* Jane Corran, a common scold, by order of the magistrates, and also as late as 1817; but in this case the victim, one Sarah Leeke, was only wheeled round the town in the chair, and not ducked, as the water in the Kenwater stream was too shallow for the purpose. The cost of making the stool appears in many corporation accounts. That at Hungerford must have been in pretty frequent use, as there are several entries for repairs in the constable's accounts.[1] Thus we find the item under the year 1669 :—

"Pd for the Cucking stoole .   . 01,10,00"

[1] The corporation of Hungerford is peculiar, the head official being termed the constable, who corresponded with the mayor in less original boroughs.

and in 1676 :—

> "Pd for nailes and workmanship about
> the stocks and cucking stoole   .   00,07,00"

At Kingston-upon-Thames in 1572 the accounts show
the expenditure :—

> " The making of the cucking-stool   .   8s.   od.
> Iron work for the same   .   .   3s.   od.
> Timber for the same   .   .   .   7s.   6d.
> Three brasses for the same and three
>   wheels   .   .   .   .   4s.   1od.
>   £1   3s.   4d."

We need not record similar items shown in the accounts
of other boroughs. You will still find examples of this
fearsome implement at Leicester in the museum, Wootton
Bassett, the wheels of one in the church of St. Mary,
Warwick; two at Plymouth, one of which was used in
1808 ; King's Lynn, Norfolk, in the museum ; Ipswich,
Scarborough, Sandwich, Fordwich, and possibly some
other places of which we have no record.

We find in museums, but not in common use, another
terrible implement for the curbing of the rebellious
tongues of scolding women. It was called the brank or
scold's bridle, and probably came to us from Scotland
with the Solomon of the North, whither the idea of it had
been conveyed through the intercourse of that region
with France. It is a sort of iron cage or framework
helmet, which was fastened on the head, having a flat
tongue of iron that was placed on the tongue of the
victim and effectually restrained her from using it. Sometimes the iron tongue was embellished with spikes so as
to make the movement of the human tongue impossible
except with the greatest agony. Imagine the poor
wretch with her head so encaged, her mouth cut and
bleeding by this sharp iron tongue, none too gently
fitted by her rough torturers, and then being dragged
about the town amid the jeers of the populace, or chained
to the pillory in the market-place, an object of ridicule

and contempt.   Happily this scene has vanished from
vanishing England.   Perhaps she was a loud-voiced
termagant ; perhaps merely the ill-used wife of a drunken
wretch, who well deserved her scolding ; or the daring
teller of home truths to some jack-in-office, who thus
revenged himself.   We have shrews and scolds still ;
happily they are restrained in a less barbarous fashion.
You may still see some fearsome branks in museums.
Reading, Leeds, York, Walton-on-Thames, Congleton,
Stockport, Macclesfield, Warrington, Morpeth, Ham-
stall Ridware, in Staffordshire, Lichfield, Chesterfield
(now in possession of the Walsham family), Leicester, Dod-
dington Park, Lincolnshire (a very grotesque example),
the Ashmolean Museum at Oxford, Ludlow, Shrewsbury,
Oswestry, Whitchurch, Market Drayton, are some of the
places which still possess scolds' bridles.   Perhaps it is
wrong to infer from the fact that most of these are to be
found in the counties of Cheshire, Staffordshire, and
Shropshire, that the women of those shires were especially
addicted to strong and abusive language.   It may be
only that antiquaries in those counties have been more
industrious in unearthing and preserving these curious
relics of a barbarous age.   The latest recorded occasion
of its use was at Congleton in 1824, when a woman
named Ann Runcorn was condemned to endure the bridle
for abusing and slandering the churchwardens when they
made their tour of inspection of the alehouses during the
Sunday-morning service.   There are some excellent drawings of branks, and full descriptions of their use, in Mr.
Andrews's *Bygone Punishments*.

Another relic of old-time punishments most gruesome
of all are the gibbet-irons wherein the bones of some
wretched breaker of the laws hung and rattled as the
irons creaked and groaned when stirred by the breeze.
Pour l'encouragement des autres, our wise forefathers
enacted that the bodies of executed criminals should be
hanged in chains.   At least this was a common practice
that dated from medieval times, though it was not

actually legalized until 1752.[1] This Act remained in force until 1834, and during the interval thousands of bodies were gibbeted and left creaking in the wind at Hangman's Corner or Gibbet Common, near the scene of some murder or outrage. It must have been ghostly and ghastly to walk along our country lanes and hear the dreadful noise, especially if the tradition were true

> That the wretch in his chains, each night took the pains,
> To come down from the gibbet—and walk.

In order to act as a warning to others the bodies were kept up as long as possible, and for this purpose were saturated with tar. On one occasion the gibbet was fired and the tar helped the conflagration, and a rapid and effectual cremation ensued. In many museums gibbet-irons are preserved.

Punishments in olden times were usually çruel. Did they act as deterrents to vice? Modern judges have found the use of the lash a cure for robbery from the person with violence. The sight of whipping-posts and stocks, we learn, has stayed young men from becoming topers and drunkards. A brank certainly in one recorded case cured a woman from coarse invective and abuse. But what effect had the sight of the infliction of cruel punishments upon those who took part in them or witnessed them? It could only have tended to make cruel natures more brutal. Barbarous punishments, public hangings, cruel sports such as bull-baiting, dog-fighting, bear-baiting, prize-fighting and the like could not fail to exercise a bad influence on the populace ; and where one was deterred from vice, thousands were brutalized and their hearts and natures hardened, wherein vicious pleasures, crime, and lust found a congenial soil. But we can still see our stocks on the village greens, our branks, ducking-stools, and pillories in museums, and remind ourselves of the customs of former days which have not so very long ago passed away.

[1] Act of Parliament 25 George II.

CHAPTER XIV

OLD BRIDGES

THE passing away of the old bridges is a deplorable feature of vanishing England. Since the introduction of those terrible traction-engines, monstrous machines that drag behind them a whole train of heavily laden trucks, few of these old structures that have survived centuries of ordinary use are safe from destruction. The immense weight of these road-trains are enough to break the back of any of the old-fashioned bridges. Constantly notices have to be set up stating : "This bridge is only sufficient to carry the ordinary traffic of the district, and traction-engines are not allowed to proceed over it." Then comes an outcry from the proprietors of locomotives demanding bridges suitable for their convenience. County councils and district councils are worried by their importunities, and soon the venerable structures are doomed, and an iron-girder bridge hideous in every particular replaces one of the most beautiful features of our village.

When the Sonning bridges that span the Thames were threatened a few years ago, English artists, such as Mr. Leslie and Mr. Holman-Hunt, strove manfully for their defence. The latter wrote :—

"The nation, without doubt, is in serious danger of losing faith in the testimony of our poets and painters to the exceptional beauty of the land which has inspired them. The poets, from Chaucer to the last of his true British successors, with one voice enlarge on the overflowing sweetness of England, her hills and dales, her pastures with sweet flowers, and the loveliness of her

318

silver streams. It is the cherishing of the wholesome enjoyments of daily life that has implanted in the sons of England love of home, goodness of nature, and sweet reasonableness, and has given strength to the thews and sinews of her children, enabling them to defend her land, her principles, and her prosperity. With regard to the three Sonning bridges, parts of them have been already rebuilt with iron fittings in recent years, and no disinterested reasonable person can see why they could not be easily made sufficient to carry all existing traffic. If the bridges were to be widened in the service of some disproportionate vehicles it is obvious that the traffic such enlarged bridges are intended to carry would be put forward as an argument for demolishing the exquisite old bridge over the main river which is the glory of this exceptionally picturesque and well-ordered village; and this is a matter of which even the most utilitarian would soon see the evil in the diminished attraction of the river not only to Englishmen, but to Colonials and Americans who have across the sea read widely of its beauty. Remonstrances must look ahead, and can only now be of avail in recognition of future further danger. We are called upon to plead the cause for the whole of the beauty-loving England, and of all river-loving people in particular."

Gallantly does the great painter express the views of artists, and such vandalism is as obnoxious to antiquaries as it is to artists and lovers of the picturesque. Many of these old bridges date from medieval times, and are relics of antiquity that can ill be spared. Brick is a material as nearly imperishable as any that man can build with. There is hardly any limit to the life of a brick or stone bridge, whereas an iron or steel bridge requires constant supervision. The oldest iron bridge in this country—at Coalbrookdale, in Shropshire—has failed after 123 years of life. It was worn out by old age, whereas the Roman bridge at Rimini, and the medieval ones at St. Ives, Bradford-on-Avon, and countless other places in this country and abroad, are in daily use and are likely to remain serviceable for many years to come, unless these ponderous trains break them down.

The interesting bridge which crosses the River Conway at Llanrwst was built in 1636 by Sir Richard Wynn, then the owner of Gwydir Castle, from the designs of Inigo Jones. Like many others, it is being injured by traction-trains carrying unlimited weights. Happily the Society for the Protection of Ancient Buildings heard the plaint of the old bridge that groaned under its heavy burdens and cried aloud for pity. The society listened to its pleading, and carried its petition to the Carmarthen County Council, with excellent results. This enlightened Council decided to protect the bridge and save it from further harm.

The building of bridges was anciently regarded as a charitable and religious act, and guilds and brother-hoods existed for their maintenance and reparation. At Maidenhead there was a notable bridge, for the sustenance of which the Guild of St. Andrew and St. Mary Magdalene was established by Henry VI in 1452. An early bridge existed here in the thirteenth century, a grant having been made in 1298 for its repair. A bridge-master was one of the officials of the corporation, according to the charter granted to the town by James II. The old bridge was built of wood and supported by piles. No wonder that people were terrified at the thought of passing over such structures in dark nights and stormy weather. There was often a bridge-chapel, as on the old Caversham bridge, wherein they said their prayers, and perhaps made their wills, before they ventured to cross.

Some towns owe their existence to the making of bridges. It was so at Maidenhead. It was quite a small place, a cluster of cottages, but Camden tells us that after the erection of the bridge the town began to have inns and to be so frequented as to outvie its " neighbouring mother, Bray, a much more ancient place," where the famous " Vicar " lived. The old bridge gave place in 1772 to a grand new one with very graceful arches, which was designed by Sir Roland Taylor.

Abingdon, another of our Berkshire towns, has a famous

bridge that dates back to the fifteenth century, when it was erected by some good merchants of the town, John Brett and John Huchyns and Geoffrey Barbour, with the aid of Sir Peter Besils of Besselsleigh, who supplied the stone from his quarries. It is an extremely graceful structure, well worthy of the skill of the medieval builders. It is some hundreds of yards in length, spanning the Thames and meadows that are often flooded, the main stream being spanned by six arches. Henry V is credited with its construction, but he only graciously bestowed his royal licence. In fact these merchants built two bridges, one called Burford Bridge and the other across the ford at Culham. The name Burford has nothing to do with the beautiful old town which we have already visited, but is a corruption of Borough-ford, the town ford at Abingdon. Two poets have sung their praises, one in atrocious Latin and the other in quaint, old-fashioned English. The first poet made a bad shot at the name of the king, calling him Henry IV instead of Henry V, though it is a matter of little importance, as neither monarch had anything to do with founding the structure. The Latin poet sings, if we may call it singing :—

> Henricus Quartus quarto fundaverat anno
> Rex pontem Burford super undas atque Culham-ford.

The English poet fixes the date of the bridge, 4 Henry V (1416) and thus tells its story :—

> King Henry the fyft, in his fourthe yere
> He hath i-founde for his folke a brige in Berkshire
> For cartis with cariage may goo and come clere,
> That many wynters afore were marred in the myre.
>
> Now is Culham hithe[1] i-come to an ende
> And al the contre the better and no man the worse,
> Few folke there were coude that way mende,
> But they waged a cold or payed of ther purse ;
> An if it were a beggar had breed in his bagge,
> He schulde be right soone i-bid to goo aboute ;

[1] Ferry.

21

And if the pore penyless the hireward would have,
A hood or a girdle and let him goo aboute.
Culham hithe hath caused many a curse
I' blyssed be our helpers we have a better waye,
Without any peny for cart and horse.

Another blyssed besiness is brigges to make
That there the pepul may not passe after great schowres,
Dole it is to draw a dead body out of a lake
That was fulled in a fount stoon and felow of owres.

The poet was grateful for the mercies conveyed to him
by the bridge. "Fulled in a fount stoon," of course,
means "washed or baptized in a stone font." He
reveals the misery and danger of passing through a
ford "after great showers," and the sad deaths which
befell adventurous passengers when the river was swollen
by rains and the ford well-nigh impassable. No wonder
the builders of bridges earned the gratitude of their
fellows. Moreover, this Abingdon Bridge was free to
all persons, rich and poor alike, and no toll or pontage
was demanded from those who would cross it.

Within the memory of man there was a beautiful old
bridge between Reading and Caversham. It was built
of brick, and had ten arches, some constructed of stone.
About the time of the Restoration some of these were
ruinous, and obstructed the passage by penning up the
water above the bridge so that boats could not pass without the use of a winch, and in the time of James II the
barge-masters of Oxford appealed to Courts of Exchequer,
asserting that the charges of pontage exacted on all
barges passing under the bridge were unlawful, claiming exemption from all tolls by reason of a charter
granted to the citizens of Oxford by Richard II. They
won their case. This bridge is mentioned in the Close
Rolls of the early years of Edward I as a place where
assizes were held. The bridge at Cromarsh and Grand-
pont outside Oxford were frequently used for the same
purpose. So narrow was it that two vehicles could not
pass. For the safety of the foot passenger little angles
were provided at intervals into which he could step in

order to avoid being run over by carts or coaches. The chapel on the bridge was a noted feature of the bridge. It was very ancient. In 1239 Engelard de Cyngny was ordered to let William, chaplain of the chapel of Caversham, have an oak out of Windsor Forest with which to make shingles for the roofing of the chapel. Passengers made offerings in the chapel to the priest in charge of it for the repair of the bridge and the maintenance of the chapel and priest. It contained many relics of saints, which at the Dissolution were eagerly seized by Dr. London, the King's Commissioner. About the year 1870 the old bridge was pulled down and the present hideous iron-girder erection substituted for it. It is extremely ugly, but is certainly more convenient than the old narrow bridge, which required passengers to retire into the angle to avoid the danger of being run over.

These bridges can tell many tales of battle and bloodshed. There was a great skirmish on Caversham Bridge in the Civil War in a vain attempt on the part of the Royalists to relieve the siege of Reading. When Wallingford was threatened in the same period of the Great Rebellion, one part of the bridge was cut in order to prevent the enemy riding into the town. And you can still detect the part that was severed. There is a very interesting old bridge across the upper Thames between Bampton and Faringdon. It is called Radcot Bridge; probably built in the thirteenth century, with its three arches and a heavy buttress in the middle niched for a figure of the Virgin, and a cross formerly stood in the centre. A "cut" has diverted the course of the river to another channel, but the bridge remains, and on this bridge a sharp skirmish took place between Robert de Vere, Earl of Oxford, Marquis of Dublin, and Duke of Ireland, a favourite of Richard II, upon whom the King delighted to bestow titles and honours. The rebellious lords met the favourite's forces at Radcot, where a fierce fight ensued. De Vere was taken in the rear, and surrounded by the forces of the Duke of Gloucester and the Earl of Derby, and being hard pressed, he plunged into the icy river (it was on the 20th day of December, 1387) with his armour on, and swimming down-stream with difficulty saved his life.   Of this exploit a poet sings :—

> Here Oxford's hero, famous for his boar,
> While clashing swords upon his target sound,
> And showers of arrows from his breast rebound,
> Prepared for worst of fates, undaunted stood,
> And urged his heart into the rapid flood.
> The waves in triumph bore him, and were proud
> To sink beneath their honourable load.

Religious communities, monasteries and priories, often constructed bridges.   There is a very curious one at Croyland, probably erected by one of the abbots of the famous abbey of Croyland or Crowland.   This bridge is regarded as one of the greatest curiosities in the kingdom. It is triangular in shape, and has been supposed to be emblematical of the Trinity.   The rivers Welland, Nene, and a drain called Catwater flow under it.   The ascent is very steep, so that carriages go under it.   The triangular bridge of Croyland is mentioned in a charter of King Edred about the year 941, but the present bridge is probably not earlier than the fourteenth century.   However, there is a rude statue said to be that of King Ethelbald, and may have been taken from the earlier structure and built into the present bridge.   It is in a sitting posture at the end of the south-west wall of the bridge.   The figure has a crown on the head, behind which are two wings, the arms bound together, round the shoulders a kind of mantle, in the left hand a sceptre and in the right a globe.   The bridge consists of three piers, whence spring three pointed arches which unite their groins in the centre.   Croyland is an instance of a decayed town, the tide of its prosperity having flowed elsewhere.   Though nominally a market-town, it is only a village, with little more than the ruins of its former splendour remaining, when the great abbey attracted

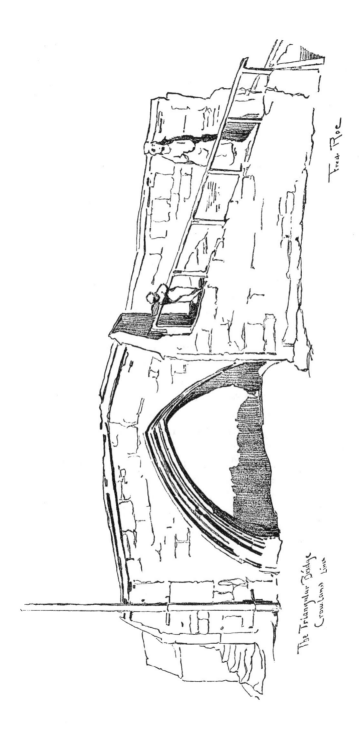

The Triangular Bridge
Crowland Lincs

Fred. Roe

to it crowds of the nobles and gentry of England, and employed vast numbers of labourers, masons, and craftsmen on the works of the abbey and in the supply of its needs.

All over the country we find beautiful old bridges, though the opening years of the present century, with the increase of heavy traction-engines, have seen many disappear. At Coleshill, Warwickshire, there is a graceful old bridge leading to the town with its six arches and massive cutwaters. Kent is a county of bridges, picturesque medieval structures which have survived the lapse of time and the storms and floods of centuries. You can find several of these that span the Medway far from the busy railway lines and the great roads. There is a fine medieval fifteenth-century bridge at Yalding across the Beult, long, fairly level, with deeply embayed cutwaters of rough ragstone. Twyford Bridge belongs to the same period, and Lodingford Bridge, with its two arches and single-buttressed cutwater, is very picturesque. Teston Bridge across the Medway has five arches of carefully wrought stonework and belongs to the fifteenth century, and East Farleigh is a fine example of the same period with four ribbed and pointed arches and four bold cutwaters of wrought stones, one of the best in the country. Aylesford Bridge is a very graceful structure, though it has been altered by the insertion of a wide span arch in the centre for the improvement of river navigation. Its existence has been long threatened, and the Society for the Protection of Ancient Buildings has done its utmost to save the bridge from destruction. Its efforts are at length crowned with success, and the Kent County Council has decided that there are not sufficient grounds to justify the demolition of the bridge and that it shall remain. The attack upon this venerable structure will probably be renewed some day, and its friends will watch over it carefully and be prepared to defend it again when the next onslaught is made. It is certainly one of the most beautiful bridges in Kent. Little known and seldom seen by the world, and unappreciated even by the antiquary or the motorist, these Medway bridges continue their placid existence and proclaim the enduring work of the English masons of nearly five centuries ago.

Many of our bridges are of great antiquity. The Eashing bridges over the Wey near Godalming date from the time of King John and are of singular charm and beauty. Like many others they have been threatened, the Rural District Council having proposed to widen and strengthen them, and completely to alter their character and picturesqueness. Happily the bridges were private property, and by the action of the Old Guildford Society

Fred Roe

Huntingdon Bridge

and the National Trust they have been placed under the guardianship of the Trust, and are now secure from molestation.

We give an illustration of the Crane Bridge, Salisbury, a small Gothic bridge near the Church House, and seen in conjunction with that venerable building it forms a very beautiful object. Another illustration shows the huge bridge at Huntingdon spanning the Ouse with six arches. It is in good preservation, and has an arcade of Early Gothic arches, and over it the coaches used to run along the great North Road, the scene of the mythical ride of Dick Turpin, and doubtless the youthful feet of Oliver Cromwell, who was born at Huntingdon, often traversed it. There is another fine bridge at St. Neots with a watch-tower in the centre.

The little town of Bradford-on-Avon has managed to preserve almost more than any other place in England the old features which are fast vanishing elsewhere. We have already seen that most interesting untouched specimen of Saxon architecture the little Saxon church, which we should like to think is the actual church built by St. Aldhelm, but we are compelled to believe on the authority of experts that it is not earlier than the tenth century. In all probability a church was built by St. Aldhelm at Bradford, probably of wood, and was afterwards rebuilt in stone when the land had rest and the raids of the Danes had ceased, and King Canute ruled and encouraged the building of churches, and Bishops Dunstan and Æthelwold of Winchester were specially prominent in the work. Bradford, too, has its noble church, parts of which date back to Norman times; its famous fourteenth-century barn at Barton Farm, which has a fifteenth-century porch and gatehouse; many fine examples of the humbler specimens of domestic architecture; and the very interesting Kingston House of the seventeenth century, built by one of the rich clothiers of Bradford, when the little town (like Abingdon) "stondeth by clothing," and all the houses in the place were figuratively "built upon wool-packs." But we are thinking of bridges, and Bradford has two, the earlier one being a little footbridge by the abbey grange, now called Barton Farm. Miss Alice Dryden tells the story of the town bridge in her *Memorials of Old Wiltshire*. It was originally only wide enough for a string of packhorses to pass along it. The ribbed portions of the southernmost arches and the piers for the chapel are early fourteenth century, the other arches were built later. Bradford became so prosperous, and the stream of traffic so much increased, and wains took the place of packhorses, that the narrow bridge was not sufficient for it; so the good clothiers built in the time of James I a second bridge alongside the first. Orders were issued in 1617 and 1621 for "the repair of the very fair bridge consisting of many

The Crane Bridge
Salisbury.
Fred Roe.

goodly arches of freestone," which had fallen into decay.
The cost of repairing it was estimated at 200 marks.
There is a building on the bridge corbelled out on a
specially built pier of the bridge, the use of which is not
at first sight evident. Some people call it the watch-
house, and it has been used as a lock-up ; but Miss
Dryden tells us that it was a chapel, similar to those
which we have seen on many other medieval bridges.
It belonged to the Hospital of St. Margaret, which stood
at the southern end of the bridge, where the Great
Western Railway crosses the road. This chapel retains
little of its original work, and was rebuilt when the bridge
was widened in the time of James I. Formerly there
was a niche for a figure looking up the stream, but this
has gone with much else during the drastic restoration.
That a bridge-chapel existed here is proved by Aubrey,
who mentions "the chapel for masse in the middest of
the bridge" at Bradford.

Sometimes bridges owe their origin to curious circumstances. There was an old bridge at Olney, Buckinghamshire, of which Cowper wrote when he sang :—

> That with its wearisome but needful length
> Bestrides the flood.

The present bridge that spans the Ouse with three arches
and a causeway has taken the place of the long bridge
of Cowper's time. This long bridge was built in the
days of Queen Anne by two squires, Sir Robert Throckmorton of Weston Underwood and William Lowndes of
Astwood Manor. These two gentlemen were sometimes
prevented from paying visits to one another by floods, as
they lived on opposite sides of the Ouse. They accord-
ingly built the long bridge in continuation of an older
one, of which only a small portion remains at the north
end. Sir Robert found the material and Mr. Lowndes
the labour. This story reminds one of a certain road in
Berks and Bucks, the milestones along which record the
distance between Hatfield and Bath? Why Hatfield? It

Fred Roe
8 Octr 1908

Watch House
On The Bridge
Bradford on Avon
Wilts.

is not a place of great resort or an important centre of population. But when we gather that a certain Marquis of Salisbury was troubled with gout, and had frequently to resort to Bath for the "cure," and constructed the road for his special convenience at his own expense, we begin to understand the cause of the carving of Hatfield on the milestones.

The study of the bridges of England seems to have been somewhat neglected by antiquaries. You will often find some good account of a town or village in guide-books or topographical works, but the story of the bridges is passed over in silence. Owing to the reasons we have already stated, old bridges are fast disappearing and are being substituted by the hideous erections of iron and steel. It is well that we should attempt to record those that are left, photograph them and paint them, ere the march of modern progress, evinced by the traction-engine and the motor-car, has quite removed and destroyed them.

CHAPTER XV

OLD HOSPITALS AND ALMSHOUSES

THERE are in many towns and villages hospitals —not the large modern and usually unsightly buildings wherein the sick are cured, with wards all spick and span and up to date—but beautiful old buildings mellowed with age wherein men and women, on whom the snows of life have begun to fall thickly, may rest and recruit and take their ease before they start on the long, dark journey from which no traveller returns to tell to those he left behind how he fared.

Almshouses we usually call them now, but our forefathers preferred to call them hospitals, God's hostels, "God huis," as the Germans call their beautiful house of pity at Lübeck, where the tired-out and moneyless folk might find harbourage. The older hospitals were often called "bede-houses," because the inmates were bound to pray for their founder and benefactors. Some medieval hospitals, memorials of the charity of pre-Reformation Englishmen, remain, but many were suppressed during the age of spoliation ; and others have been so rebuilt and restored that there is little left of the early foundation.

We may notice three classes of these foundations. First, there are the pre-Reformation bede-houses or hospitals ; the second group is composed of those which were built during the spacious days of Queen Elizabeth, James I, and Charles I. The Civil War put a stop to the foundation of almshouses. The principal landowners were impoverished by the war or despoiled by the Puritans, and could not build ; the charity of the latter was

devoted to other purposes.   With the Restoration of the
Church and the Monarchy another era of the building
of almshouses set in, and to this period very many of our
existing institutions belong.

Of the earliest group we have several examples left.
There is the noble hospital of St. Cross at Winchester,

Gateway of St. John's Hospital, Canterbury

founded in the days of anarchy during the contest between
Stephen and Matilda for the English throne.   Its hospitable door is still open.   Bishop Henry of Blois was
its founder, and he made provision for thirteen poor men
to be housed, boarded, and clothed, and for a hundred
others to have a meal every day.   He placed the hospital
under the care of the Master of the Knights Hospitallers.
Fortunately it was never connected with a monastery.

Hence it escaped pillage and destruction at the dissolution of monastic houses. Bishop Henry was a great builder, and the church of the hospital is an interesting example of a structure of the Transition Norman period, when the round arch was giving way to the Early English pointed arch. To this foundation was added in 1443 by Cardinal Beaufort an extension called the " Almshouse of Noble Poverty," and it is believed that the present domestic buildings were erected by him.[1] The visitor can still obtain the dole of bread and ale at the gate of St. Cross. Winchester is well provided with old hospitals : St. John's was founded in 931 and refounded in 1289 ; St. Mary Magdalen, by Bishop Toclyve in 1173–88 for nine lepers ; and Christ's Hospital in 1607.

We will visit some less magnificent foundations. Some are of a very simple type, resembling a church with nave and chancel. The nave part was a large hall divided by partitions on each side of an alley into little cells in which the bedesmen lived. Daily Mass was celebrated in the chancel, the chapel of hospital, whither the inmates resorted ; but the sick and infirm who could not leave their cells were able to join in the service. St. Mary's Hospital, at Chichester, is an excellent example, as it retains its wooden cells, which are still used by the inmates. It was formerly a nunnery, but in 1229 the nuns departed and the almswomen took their place. It is of wide span with low side-walls, and the roof is borne by wooden pillars. There are eight cells of two rooms each, and beyond the screen is a little chapel, which is still used by the hospitallers.[2]

Archbishop Chichele founded a fine hospital at Higham Ferrers in Northamptonshire, which saw his lowly birth, together with a school and college, about the year 1475. The building is still in existence and shows a good roof

---

[1] Mr. Nisbett gives a good account of the hospital in *Memorials of Old Hampshire*, and Mr. Champneys fully describes the buildings in the *Architectural Review*, October, 1903, and April, 1904.

[2] The *Treasury*, November, 1907, an article on hospitals by Dr. Hermitage Day.

and fine Perpendicular window, but the twelve bedesmen and the one sister, who was to be chosen for her plainness, no longer use the structure.

Stamford can boast of a fine medieval hospital, the foundation of Thomas Browne in 1480 for the accommodation of ten old men and two women. A new quadrangle has been built for the inmates, but you can still see the old edifice with its nave of two storeys, its fifteenth-century stained glass, and its chapel with its screen and stalls and altar.

Stamford has another hospital which belongs to our second group. Owing to the destruction of monasteries, which had been great benefactors to the poor and centres of vast schemes of charity, there was sore need for almshouses and other schemes for the relief of the aged and destitute. The *nouveaux riches*, who had fattened on the spoils of the monasteries, sought to salve their consciences by providing for the wants of the poor, building grammar schools, and doing some good with their wealth. Hence many almshouses arose during this period. This Stamford home was founded by the great Lord Burghley in 1597. It is a picturesque group of buildings with tall chimneys, mullioned and dormer windows, on the bank of the Welland stream, and occupies the site of a much more ancient foundation.

There is the college at Cobham, in Kent, the buildings forming a pleasant quadrangle south of the church. Flagged pathways cross the greensward of the court, and there is a fine hall wherein the inmates used to dine together.

As we traverse the village streets we often meet with these grey piles of sixteenth-century almshouses, often low, one-storeyed buildings, picturesque and impressive, each house having a welcoming porch with a seat on each side and a small garden full of old-fashioned flowers. The roof is tiled, on which moss and lichen grow, and the chimney-stacks are tall and graceful. An inscription records the date and name of the generous founder with his arms and motto. Such a home of peace you will find at Quainton, in Buckinghamshire, founded, as an inscription records, "Anno Dom. 1687. These almshouses were then erected and endow'd by Richard Winwood, son and heir of Right Honble Sir Ralph Winwood, Bart., Principal Secretary of State to King James ye First." Within these walls dwell (according to the rules drawn up by Sir Ralph Verney in 1695) "three poor men— widowers,—to be called Brothers, and three poor women— widows,—to be called Sisters." Very strict were these rules for the government of the almshouses, as to erroneous opinions in any principle of religion, the rector of Quainton being the judge, the visiting of alehouses, the good conduct of the inmates, who were to be "no whisperers, quarrelers, evil speakers or contentious."

These houses at Quainton are very humble abodes; other almshouses are large and beautiful buildings erected by some rich merchant, or great noble, or London City company, for a large scheme of charity. Such are the beautiful almshouses in the Kingsland Road, Shoreditch, founded in the early part of the eighteenth century under the terms of the will of Sir Robert Geffery. They stand in a garden about an acre in extent, a beautiful oasis in the surrounding desert of warehouses, reminding the passer-by of the piety and loyal patriotism of the great citizens of London, and affording a peaceful home for many aged folk. This noble building, of great architectural dignity, with the figure of the founder over the porch and its garden with fine trees, has only just escaped the hands of the destroyer and been numbered among the bygone treasures of vanished England. It was seriously proposed to pull down this peaceful home of poor people and sell the valuable site to the Peabody Donation Fund for the erection of working-class dwellings. The almshouses are governed by the Ironmongers' Company, and this proposal was made; but, happily, the friends of ancient buildings made their protest to the Charity Commissioners, who have refused their sanction

to the sale, and the Geffery Almshouses will continue to
exist, continue their useful mission, and remain the chief
architectural ornament in a district that sorely needs
" sweetness and light."

City magnates who desired to build and endow hospitals for the aged nearly always showed their confidence
in and affection for the Livery Companies to which they
belonged by placing in their care these charitable foundations. Thus Sir Richard Whittington, of famous memory,
bequeathed to the Mercers' Company all his houses and
tenements in London, which were to be sold and the
proceeds distributed in various charitable works. With
this sum they founded a College of Priests, called
Whittington College, which was suppressed at the
Reformation, and the almshouses adjoining the old
church of St. Michael Paternoster, for thirteen poor folk,
of whom one should be principal or tutor. The Great
Fire destroyed the buildings ; they were rebuilt on the
same site, but in 1835 they were fallen into decay, and
the company re-erected them at Islington, where you will
find Whittington College, providing accommodation for
twenty-eight poor women. Besides this the Mercers have
charge of Lady Mico's Almshouses at Stepney, founded
in 1692 and rebuilt in 1857, and the Trinity Hospital at
Greenwich, founded in 1615 by Henry Howard, Earl of
Northampton. This earl was of a very charitable disposition, and founded other hospitals at Castle Rising in
Norfolk and Clun in Shropshire. The Mercers continue
to manage the property and have built a new hospital at
Shottisham, besides making grants to the others created
by the founder. It is often the custom of the companies
to expend out of their private income far more than they
receive from the funds of the charities which they administer.

The Grocers' Company have almshouses and a Free
Grammar School at Oundle in Northamptonshire, founded
by Sir William Laxton in 1556, upon which they have
expended vast sums of money. The Drapers administer

Inmate of the Trinity Bede House at Castle Rising, Norfolk

the Mile End Almshouses and school founded in 1728 by Francis Bancroft, Sir John Jolles's almshouses at Tottenham, founded in 1618, and very many others. They have two hundred in the neighbourhood of London alone, and many others in different parts of the country. Near where I am writing is Lucas's Hospital at Wokingham, founded by Henry Lucas in 1663, which he placed in the charge of the company. It is a beautiful Carolian house with a central portion and two wings, graceful and pleasing in every detail. The chapel is situated in one wing and the master's house in the other, and there are sets of rooms for twelve poor men chosen from the parishes in the neighbourhood. The Fishmongers have the management of three important hospitals. At Bray, in Berkshire, famous for its notable vicar, there stands the ancient Jesus Hospital, founded in 1616 under the will of William Goddard, who directed that there should be built rooms with chimneys in the said hospital, fit and convenient for forty poor people to dwell and inhabit it, and that there should be one chapel or place convenient to serve Almighty God in for ever with public and divine prayers and other exercises of religion, and also one kitchen and bakehouse common to all the people of the said hospital. Jesus Hospital is a quadrangular building, containing forty almshouses surrounding a court which is divided into gardens, one of which is attached to each house. It has a pleasing entrance through a gabled brick porch which has over the Tudor-shaped doorway a statue of the founder and mullioned latticed windows. The old people live happy and contented lives, and find in the eventide of their existence a cheerful home in peaceful and beautiful surroundings. The Fishmongers also have almshouses at Harrietsham, in Kent, founded by Mark Quested, citizen and fishmonger of London, in 1642, which they rebuilt in 1772, and St. Peter's Hospital, Wandsworth, formerly called the Fishmongers' Almshouses. The Goldsmiths have a very palatial pile of almshouses at Acton Park, called Perryn's Almshouses, with a grand

The Hospital
for Ancient Fishermen
Great Yarmouth
Aug 1908

Fred Roe.

entrance portico, and most of the London companies provide in this way homes for their decayed members, so
that they may pass their closing years in peace and
freedom from care.

Fishermen, who pass their lives in storm and danger
reaping the harvest of the sea, have not been forgotten
by pious benefactors.   One of the most picturesque
buildings in Great Yarmouth is the Fishermen's Hospital, of which we give some illustrations. It was founded
by the corporation of the town in 1702 for the reception
of twenty old fishermen and their wives. It is a charming house of rest, with its gables and dormer windows
and its general air of peace and repose.   The old men
look very comfortable after battling for so many years
with the storms of the North Sea.   Charles II granted to
the hospital an annuity of £160 for its support, which was
paid out of the excise on beer, but when the duty was
repealed the annuity naturally ceased.

The old hospital at King's Lynn was destroyed during
the siege, as this quaint inscription tells :—

> THIS HOSPITAL WAS
> BURNT DOWN AT LIN
> SEGE AND REBULT
> 1649 NATH MAXEY
> MAYOR AND EDW
> ROBINSON ALDMAN
> TREASURER PRO TEM
> P.R.O.

Norwich had several important hospitals.   Outside the
Magdalen gates stood the Magdalen Hospital, founded
by Bishop Herbert, the first bishop.   It was a house for
lepers, and some portions of the Norman chapel still
exist in a farm-building by the roadside.   The far-famed
St. Giles's Hospital in Bishopsgate Street is an ancient
foundation, erected by Bishop Walter Suffield in 1249
for poor chaplains and other poor persons.   It nearly
vanished at the Reformation era, like so many other
kindred institutions, but Henry VIII and Edward VI
granted it a new charter.   The poor clergy were, how-

ever, left out in the cold, and the benefits were confined
to secular folk. For the accommodation of its inmates
the chancel of the church was divided by a floor into an
upper and a lower storey, and this arrangement still exists,
and you can still admire the picturesque ivy-clad tower,
the wards with cosy ingle-nooks at either end and
cubicles down the middle, the roof decorated with eagles,
deemed to be the cognizance of Queen Anne of Bohemia,
wife of Richard II, the quaint little cloister, and above
all, the excellent management of this grand institution,

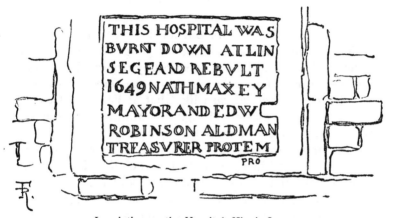

Inscription on the Hospital, King's Lynn

the "Old Man's Hospital," as it is called, which provides
for the necessities of 150 old folk, whose wants are cared
for by a master and twelve nurses.

Let us travel far and visit another charming almshouse,
Abbot's Hospital, at Guildford, which is an architectural
gem and worthy of the closest inspection. It was founded
by Archbishop Abbot in 1619, and is a noble building of
mellowed brick with finely carved oak doors, graceful
chimneys with their curious "crow-rests," noble staircases, interesting portraits, and rare books, amongst
which is a Vinegar Bible. The chapel with its Flemish
windows showing the story of Jacob and Esau, and oak
carvings and almsbox dated 1619, is especially attractive.

Here the founder retired in sadness and sorrow after his unfortunate day's hunting in Bramshill Park, where he accidentally shot a keeper, an incident which gave occasion to his enemies to blaspheme and deride him. Here the Duke of Monmouth was confined on his way to London after the battle of Sedgemoor. The details of the building are worthy of attention, especially the ornamented doors and doorways, the elaborate latches, beautifully designed and furnished with a spring, and elegant casement-fasteners. Guildford must have had a school of great artists of these window-fasteners. Near the hospital there is a very interesting house, No. 25 High Street, now a shop, but formerly the town clerk's residence and the lodgings of the judges of assize ; no better series in England of beautifully designed window-fasteners can be found than in this house, erected in 1683 ; it also has a fine staircase like that at Farnham Castle, and some good plaster ceilings resembling Inigo Jones's work and probably done by his workmen.

The good town of Abingdon has a very celebrated hospital founded in 1446 by the Guild of the Holy Cross, a fraternity composed of "good men and true," wealthy merchants and others, which built the bridge, repaired roads, maintained a bridge priest and a rood priest, and held a great annual feast at which the brethren consumed as much as 6 calves, 16 lambs, 80 capons, 80 geese, and 800 eggs. It was a very munificent and beneficent corporation, and erected these almshouses for thirteen poor men and the same number of poor women. That hospital founded so long ago still exists. It is a curious and ancient structure in one storey, and is denoted Christ's Hospital. One of our recent writers on Berkshire topography, whose historical accuracy is a little open to criticism, gives a good description of the building :—

"It is a long range of chambers built of mellow brick and immemorial oak, having in their centre a small hall, darkly wainscoted, the very table in which makes a collector sinfully covetous. In front of the modest doors of the chambers inhabited by almsmen and almswomen runs a tiny cloister with oak pillars, so that the inmates may visit one another dryshod in any weather. Each door, too, bears a text from the Old or New Testament. A more typical relic of the old world, a more sequestered haven of rest, than this row of lowly buildings, looking up to the great church in front, and with its windows opening on to green turf bordered with flowers in the rear, it could not enter into the heart of man to imagine."[1]

We could spend endless time in visiting the old alms-houses in many parts of the country. There is the Ford's Hospital in Coventry, erected in 1529, an extremely good specimen of late Gothic work, another example of which is found in St. John's Hospital at Rye. The Corsham Almshouses in Wiltshire, erected in 1663, are most picturesque without, and contain some splendid woodwork within, including a fine old reading-desk with carved seat in front. There is a large porch with an immense coat-of-arms over the door. In the region of the Cotswolds, where building-stone is plentiful, we find a noble set of almshouses at Chipping Campden in Gloucestershire, a gabled structure near the church with tall, graceful chimneys and mullioned windows, having a raised causeway in front protected by a low wall. Ewelme, in Oxfordshire, is a very attractive village with a row of cottages half a mile long, which have before their doors a sparkling stream dammed here and there into watercress beds. At the top of the street on a steep knoll stand church and school and almshouses of the mellowest fifteenth-century bricks, as beautiful and structurally sound as the pious founders left them. These founders were the unhappy William de la Pole, first Duke of Suffolk, and his good wife the Duchess Alice. The Duke inherited Ewelme through his wife Alice Chaucer, a kinswoman of the poet, and "for love of her and the commoditie of her landes fell much to dwell in Oxfordshire," and in 1430–40 was busy building

---

[1] *Highways and Byways in Berkshire.*

a manor-place of "brick and Tymbre and set within a fayre mote," a church, an almshouse, and a school. The manor-place, or "Palace," as it was called, has disappeared, but the almshouse and school remain, witnesses of the munificence of the founders. The poor Duke, favourite minister of Henry VI, was exiled by the Yorkist faction, and beheaded by the sailors on his way to banishment. Twenty-five years of widowhood fell to the bereaved duchess, who finished her husband's buildings, called the almshouses "God's House," and then reposed beneath one of the finest monuments in England in the church hard by. The almshouses at Audley End, Essex, are amongst the most picturesque in the country. Such are some of these charming homes of rest that time has spared.

The old people who dwell in them are often as picturesque as their habitations. Here you will find an old woman with her lace-pillow and bobbins, spectacles on nose, and white bonnet with strings, engaged in working out some intricate lace pattern. In others you will see the inmates clad in their ancient liveries. The dwellers in the Coningsby Hospital at Hereford, founded in 1614 for old soldiers and aged servants, had a quaint livery consisting of "a fustian suit of ginger colour, of a soldier-like fashion, and seemly laced; a cloak of red cloth lined with red baize and reaching to the knees, to be worn in walks and journeys, and a gown of red cloth, reaching to the ankle, lined also with baize, to be worn within the hospital." They are, therefore, known as Red Coats. The almsmen of Ely and Rochester have cloaks. The inmates of the Hospital of St. Cross wear as a badge a silver cross potent. At Bottesford they have blue coats and blue "beef-eater" hats, and a silver badge on the left arm bearing the arms of the Rutland family—a peacock in its pride, surmounted by a coronet and surrounded by a garter.

It is not now the fashion to found almshouses. We build workhouses instead, vast ugly barracks wherein

Fred Roe

Ancient Inmates of the Fishermen's Hospital, Great Yarmouth

the poor people are governed by all the harsh rules of the
Poor Law, where husband and wife are separated from
each other, and "those whom God hath joined together
are," by man and the Poor Law, "put asunder"; where
the industrious labourer is housed with the lazy and
ne'er-do-weel. The old almshouses were better homes
for the aged poor, homes of rest after the struggle for
existence, and harbours of refuge for the tired and weary
till they embark on their last voyage.

Cottages at Evesham

CHAPTER XVI

VANISHING FAIRS

THE " oldest inhabitants " of our villages can remember many changes in the social conditions of country life. They can remember the hard time of the Crimean war when bread was two shillings and eightpence a gallon, when food and work were both scarce, and starvation wages were doled out. They can remember the " machine riots," and tumultuous scenes at election times, and scores of interesting facts, if only you can get them to talk and tell you their recollections. The changed condition of education puzzles them. They can most of them read, and perhaps write a little, but they prefer to make their mark and get you to attest it with the formula, "the mark of J—N." Their schooling was soon over. When they were nine years of age they were ploughboys, and had a rough time with a cantankerous ploughman who often used to ply his whip on his lad or on his horses quite indiscriminately. They have seen many changes, and do not always " hold with " modern notions ; and one of the greatest changes they have seen is in the fairs. They are not what they were. Some, indeed, maintain some of their usefulness, but most of them have degenerated into a form of mild Saturnalia, if not into a scandal and a nuisance ; and for that reason have been suppressed.

Formerly quite small villages had their fairs. If you look at an old almanac you will see a list of fair-days with the names of the villages which, when the appointed days come round, cannot now boast of the presence of a single stall or merry-go-round. The day of the fair was nearly

always on or near the festival of the patron saint to whom
the church of that village is dedicated.   There is, of course,
a reason for this.   The word "fair" is derived from the
Latin word *feria*, which means a festival, the parish feast
day.   On the festival of the patron saint of a village
church crowds of neighbours from adjoining villages
would flock to the place, the inhabitants of which used to

Stalls at Banbury Fair

keep open house, and entertain all their relations and
friends who came from a distance.   They used to make
booths and tents with boughs of trees near the church,
and celebrated the festival with much thanksgiving and
prayer.   By degrees they began to forget their prayers
and remembered only the feasting; country people flocked
from far and near; the pedlars and hawkers came to find
a market for their wares.   Their stalls began to multiply,
and thus the germ of a fair was formed.

In such primitive fairs the traders paid no toll or rent
for their stalls, but by degrees the right of granting per-

mission to hold a fair was vested in the King, who for various considerations bestowed this favour on nobles, merchant guilds, bishops, or monasteries. Great profits arose from these gatherings. The traders had to pay toll on all the goods which they brought to the fair, in addition to the payment of stallage or rent for the ground on which they displayed their merchandise, and also a charge on all the goods they sold. Moreover, the trades-folk of the town were obliged to close their shops during the days of the fair, and to bring their goods to the fair, so that the toll-owner might gain good profit withal.

We can imagine, or try to imagine, the roads and streets leading to the market-place thronged with traders and chapmen, the sellers of ribbons and cakes, minstrels and morris-dancers, smock-frocked peasants and sombre-clad monks and friars. Then a horn was sounded, and the lord of the manor, or the bishop's bailiff, or the mayor of the town proclaimed the fair ; and then the cries of the traders, the music of the minstrels, the jingling of the bells of the morris-dancers, filled the air and added animation to the spectacle.

There is a curious old gateway, opposite the fair-ground at Smithfield, which has just recently narrowly escaped destruction, and very nearly became part of the vanished glories of England. Happily the donations of the public poured in so well that the building was saved. This Smithfield gateway dates back to the middle of the thirteenth century, the entrance to the Priory of St. Bartholomew, founded by Rahere, the court jester of Henry I, a century earlier. Every one knows the story of the building of this Priory, and has followed its extraordinary vicissitudes, the destruction of its nave at the dissolution of monasteries, the establishment of a fringe factory in the Lady Chapel, and the splendid and continuous work of restoration which has been going on during the last forty years. We are thankful that this choir of St. Bartholomew's Church should have been preserved for future generations as an example of the earliest and most important ecclesiastical buildings in London. But we are concerned now with this gateway, the beauty of which is partially concealed by the neighbouring shops and dwellings that surround it, as a poor and vulgar frame may disfigure some matchless gem of artistic painting. Its old stones know more about fairs than do most things. It shall tell its own history. You can still admire the work of the Early English builders, the receding orders with exquisite mouldings and dog-tooth ornament—the hall-mark of the early Gothic artists. It looks upon the Smithfield market, and how many strange scenes of London history has this gateway witnessed! Under its arch possibly stood London's first chronicler, Fitzstephen, the monk, when he saw the famous horse fairs that took place in Smithfield every Friday, which he described so graphically. Thither flocked earls, barons, knights, and citizens to look on or buy. The monk admired the nags with their sleek and shining coats, smoothly ambling along, the young blood colts not yet accustomed to the bridle, the horses for burden, strong and stout-limbed, and the valuable chargers of elegant shape and noble height, with nimbly moving ears, erect necks, and plump haunches. He waxes eloquent over the races, the expert jockeys, the eager horses, the shouting crowds. "The riders, inspired with the love of praise and the hope of victory, clap spurs to their flying horses, lashing them with their whips, and inciting them by their shouts"; so wrote the worthy monk Fitzstephen. He evidently loved a horse-race, but he need not have given us the startling information, "their chief aim is to prevent a competitor getting before them." That surely would be obvious even to a monk. He also examined the goods of the peasants, the implements of husbandry, swine with their long sides, cows with distended udders, *Corpora magna boum, lanigerumque pecus*, mares fitted for the plough or cart, some with frolicsome colts running by their sides. A very animated scene, which must have

delighted the young eyes of the stone arch in the days of
its youth, as it did the heart of the monk.

Still gayer scenes the old gate has witnessed. Smithfield was the principal spot in London for jousts, tournaments, and military exercises, and many a grand display
of knightly arms has taken place before this priory gate.
"In 1357 great and royal jousts were then holden in
Smithfield; there being present the Kings of England,
France, and Scotland, with many other nobles and great
estates of divers lands," writes Stow. Gay must have
been the scene in the forty-eighth year of Edward III,
when Dame Alice Perrers, the King's mistress, as Lady
of the Sun, rode from the Tower of London to Smithfield
accompanied by many lords and ladies, every lady
leading a lord by his horse-bridle, and there began a
great joust which endured seven days after. The lists
were set in the great open space with tiers of seats around,
a great central canopy for the Queen of Beauty, the royal
party, and divers tents and pavilions for the contending
knights and esquires. It was a grand spectacle, adorned
with all the pomp and magnificence of medieval chivalry.
Froissart describes with consummate detail the jousts in
the fourteenth year of Richard II, before a grand company, when sixty coursers gaily apparelled for the jousts
issued from the Tower of London ridden by esquires of
honour, and then sixty ladies of honour mounted on
palfreys, each lady leading a knight with a chain of gold,
with a great number of trumpets and other instruments
of music with them. On arriving at Smithfield the ladies
dismounted, the esquires led the coursers which the
knights mounted, and after their helmets were set on
their heads proclamation was made by the heralds, the
jousts began, "to the great pleasure of the beholders."
But it was not all pomp and pageantry. Many and
deadly were the fights fought in front of the old gate,
when men lost their lives or were borne from the field
mortally wounded, or contended for honour and life
against unjust accusers. That must have been a sorry

23

scene in 1446, when a rascally servant, John David, accused
his master, William Catur, of treason, and had to face
the wager of battle in Smithfield. The master was well
beloved, and inconsiderate friends plied him with wine
so that he was not in a condition to fight, and was slain
by his servant. But Stow reminds us that the prosperity
of the wicked is frail. Not long after David was hanged
at Tyburn for felony, and the chronicler concludes : " Let
such false accusers note this for example, and look for
no better end without speedy repentance." He omits to
draw any moral from the intemperance of the master and
the danger of drunkenness.

But let this suffice for the jousts in Smithfield. The
old gateway heard on one occasion strange noises in the
church, Archbishop Boniface raging with oaths not to be
recited, and sounds of strife and shrieks and angry cries.
This foreigner, Archbishop of Canterbury, had dared to
come with his armed retainers from Provence to hold
a visitation of the priory. The canons received him with
solemn pomp, but respectfully declined to be visited by
him, as they had their own proper visitor, a learned man,
the Bishop of London, and did not care for another
inspector. Boniface lost his temper, struck the sub-prior,
saying, " Indeed, doth it become you English traitors so to
answer me ? " He tore in pieces the rich cope of the sub-
prior ; the canons rushed to their brother's rescue and
knocked the Archbishop down ; but his men fell upon the
canons and beat them and trod them under foot. The
old gateway was shocked and grieved to see the reverend
canons running beneath the arch bloody and miry, rent
and torn, carrying their complaint to the Bishop and then
to the King at Westminster. After which there was
much contention, and the whole city rose and would have
torn the Archbishop into small pieces, shouting, "Where
is this ruffian ? that cruel smiter ! " and much else that
must have frightened and astonished Master Boniface and
made him wish that he had never set foot in England,
but stayed quietly in peaceful Provence.

But this gateway loved to look upon the great fair that took place on the Feast of St. Bartholomew. This was granted to Rahere the Prior and to the canons and continued for seven centuries, until the abuses of modern days destroyed its character and ended its career. The scene of the actual fair was within the priory gates in the churchyard, and there during the three days of its continuance stood the booths and standings of the clothiers and drapers of London and of all England, of pewterers, and leather-sellers, and without in the open space before the priory were tents and booths and a noisy crowd of traders, pleasure-seekers, friars, jesters, tumblers, and stilt-walkers. This open space was just outside the turreted north wall of the city, and was girt by tall elms, and near it was a sheet of water whereon the London boys loved to skate when the frost came. It was the city playground, and the city gallows were placed there before they were removed to Tyburn. This dread implement of punishment stood under the elms where Cow Lane now runs: and one fair day brave William Wallace was dragged there in chains at the tails of horses, bruised and bleeding, and foully done to death after the cruel fashion of the age. All this must have aged the heart of the old gateway, and especially the sad sight of the countless burials that took place in the year of the Plague, 1349, when fifty thousand were interred in the burial ground of the Carthusians, and few dared to attend the fair for fear of the pestilence.

Other terrible things the gateway saw: the burning of heretics. Not infrequently did these fires of persecution rage. One of the first of these martyrs was John Bedley, a tailor, burnt in Smithfield in 1410. In Fox's *Book of Martyrs* you can see a woodcut of the burning of Anne Ascue and others, showing a view of the Priory and the crowd of spectators who watched the poor lady die. Not many days afterwards the fair-folk assembled, while the ground was still black with her ashes, and dogs danced and women tumbled and the devil jeered in the miracle play on the spot where martyrs died.

We should need a volume to describe all the sights of this wondrous fair, the church crowded with worshippers, the halt and sick praying for healing, the churchyard full of traders, the sheriff proclaiming new laws, the young men bowling at ninepins, pedlars shouting their wares,

An Old English Fair

players performing the miracle play on a movable stage, bands of pipers, lowing oxen, neighing horses, and bleating sheep. It was a merry sight that medieval Bartholomew Fair.

We still have Cloth Fair, a street so named, with a remarkable group of timber houses with over-sailing storeys and picturesque gables. It is a very dark and narrow thoroughfare, and in spite of many changes it remains a veritable "bit" of old London, as it was in the seventeenth century. These houses have sprung up where in olden days the merchants' booths stood for the sale of cloth. It was one of the great annual markets of the nation, the chief cloth fair in England that had no rival. Hither came the officials of the Merchant Tailors' Company bearing a silver yard measure, to try the measures of the clothiers and drapers to see if they were correct. And so each year the great fair went on, and priors and canons lived and died and were buried in the church or beneath the grass of the churchyard. But at length the days of the Priory were numbered, and it changed masters. The old gateway wept to see the cowled Black Canons depart when Henry VIII dissolved the monastery; its heart nearly broke when it heard the sounds of axes and hammers, crowbars and saws, at work on the fabric of the church pulling down the grand nave, and it scowled at the new owner, Sir Richard Rich, a prosperous political adventurer, who bought the whole estate for £1064 11s. 3d., and made a good bargain.

The monks, a colony of Black Friars, came in again with Queen Mary, but they were driven out again when Elizabeth reigned, and Lord Rich again resumed possession of the estate, which passed to his heirs, the Earls of Warwick and Holland. Each Sunday, however, the old gate welcomed devout worshippers on their way to the church, the choir having been converted into the parish church of the district, and was not sorry to see in Charles's day a brick tower rising at the west end.

In spite of the changes of ownership the fair went on increasing with the increase of the city. But the scene has changed. In the time of James I the last elm tree had gone, and rows of houses, fair and comely buildings, had sprung up. The old muddy plain had been drained and paved, and the traders and pleasure-seekers could no longer dread the wading through a sea of mud. We should like to follow the fair through the centuries, and see the sights and shows. The puppet shows were always attractive, and the wild beasts, the first animal ever exhibited being "a large and beautiful young camel from Grand Cairo in Egypt. This creature is twenty-three years old, his head and neck like those of a deer." One Flockton during the last half of the eighteenth century was the prince of puppet showmen, and he called his puppets the Italian Fantocinni. He made his figures work in a most lifelike style. He was a conjurer too, and the inventor of a wonderful clock which showed nine hundred figures at work upon a variety of trades. "Punch and Judy" always attracted crowds, and we notice the handbills of Mr. Robinson, conjurer to the Queen, and of Mr. Lane, who sings:

> It will make you to laugh, it will drive away gloom,
> To see how the eggs will dance round the room;
> And from another egg a bird there will fly,
> Which makes all the company all for to cry, etc.

The booths for actors were a notable feature of the fair. We read of Fielding's booth at the George Inn, of the performance of the *Beggar's Opera* in 1728, of Penketh-man's theatrical booth when *Wat Taylor and Jack Straw* was acted, of the new opera called *The Generous Free Mason or the Constant Lady*, of *Jephthah's Rash Vow*, and countless other plays that saw the light at Bartholomew Fair. The audience included not only the usual frequenters of fairs, but even royal visitors, noblemen, and great ladies flocked to the booths for amusement, and during its continuance the play-houses of London were closed.

I must not omit to mention the other attractions, the fireproof lady, Madam Giradelli, who put melted lead in her mouth, passed red-hot iron over her body, thrust her arm into fire, and washed her hands in boiling oil; Mr. Simon Paap, the Dutch dwarf, twenty-eight inches high; bear-dancing, the learned pig, the "beautiful spotted negro boy," peep-shows, Wombell's royal menagerie, the learned cats, and a female child with two perfect heads.

But it is time to ring down the curtain. The last days of the fair were not edifying. Scenes of riot and debauch, of violence and lawlessness disgraced the assembly. Its

usefulness as a gathering for trade purposes had passed
away. It became a nuisance and a disgrace to London.
In older days the Lord Mayor used to ride in his grand
coach to our old gateway, and there proclaim it with a
great flourish of trumpets. In 1850 his worship walked

An Ancient Maker of Nets in a Kentish Fair

quietly to the accustomed place, and found that there was
no fair to proclaim, and five years later the formality was
entirely dispensed with, and silence reigned over the historic ground over which century after century the hearts of
our forefathers throbbed with the outspoken joys of life.
The old gateway, like many aged folk, has much on
which to meditate in its advanced age.

Many other fairs have been suppressed in recent years, but some survive and thrive with even greater vigour than ever. Some are hiring fairs, where you may see young men with whipcord in their caps standing in front of inns ready to be hired by the farmers who come to seek labourers. Women and girls too come to be hired, but their number decreases every year. Such is the Abingdon fair, which no rustic in the adjoining villages ever thinks of missing. We believe that the Nottingham Goose Fair, which is attended by very large crowds, is also a hiring fair. "Pleasure fairs" in several towns and cities show no sign of diminished popularity. The famous St. Giles's Fair at Oxford is attended by thousands, and excursion trains from London, Cardiff, Reading, and other large towns bring crowds to join in the humours of the gathering, the shows covering all the broad space between St. Giles's Church and George Street. Reading Michaelmas Pleasure Fair is always a great attraction. The fair-ground is filled from end to end with roundabouts driven by steam, which also plays a hideous organ that grinds out popular tunes, swings, stalls, shows, menageries, and all "the fun of the fair." You can see biographs, hear phonographs, and a penny-in-the-slot will introduce you to wonderful sights, and have your fortune told, or shy at coco-nuts or Aunt Sally, or witness displays of boxing, or have a photograph taken of yourself, or watch weird melodramas, and all for a penny or two. No wonder the fair is popular.

There is no reverence paid in these modern gatherings to old-fashioned ways and ancient picturesque customs, but in some places these are still observed with punctilious exactness. The quaint custom of "proclaiming the fair" at Honiton, in Devonshire, is observed every year, the town having obtained the grant of a fair from the lord of the manor so long ago as 1257. The fair still retains some of the picturesque characteristics of bygone days. The town crier, dressed in old-world uniform, and carrying a pole decorated with gay flowers and surmounted by

Fred Roe.
Outside the "Lamb Inn"
Burford, Oxon

a large gilt model of a gloved hand, publicly announces the opening of the fair as follows: "Oyez! Oyez! Oyez! The fair's begun, the glove is up. No man can be arrested till the glove is taken down." Hot coins are then thrown amongst the children. The pole and glove remain displayed until the end of the fair.

Nor have all the practical uses of fairs vanished. On the Berkshire downs is the little village of West Ilsley; there from time immemorial great sheep fairs are held, and flocks are brought thither from districts far and wide. Every year herds of Welsh ponies congregate at Blackwater, in Hampshire, driven thither by inveterate custom. Every year in an open field near Cambridge the once great Stourbridge fair is held, first granted by King John to the Hospital for Lepers, and formerly proclaimed with great state by the Vice-Chancellor of the University and the Mayor of Cambridge. This was one of the largest fairs in Europe. Merchants of all nations attended it. The booths were planted in a cornfield, and the circuit of the fair, which was like a well-governed city, was about three miles. All offences committed therein were tried, as at other fairs, before a special court of *pie-poudre*, the derivation of which word has been much disputed, and I shall not attempt to conjecture or to decide. The shops were built in rows, having each a name, such as Garlick Row, Booksellers' Row, or Cooks' Row; there were the cheese fair, hop fair, wood fair; every trade was represented, and there were taverns, eating-houses, and in later years playhouses of various descriptions. As late as the eighteenth century it is said that one hundred thousand pounds' worth of woollen goods were sold in a week in one row alone. But the glories of Stourbridge fair have all departed, and it is only a ghost now of its former greatness.

The Stow Green pleasure fair, in Lincolnshire, which has been held annually for upwards of eight hundred years, having been established in the reign of Henry III, has practically ceased to exist. Held on an isolated

common two miles from Billingborough, it was formerly
one of the largest fairs in England for merchandise, and
originally lasted for three weeks. Now it is limited to
two days, and when it opened last year there were but few
attractions.

Fairs have enriched our language with at least one
word. There is a fair at Ely founded in connexion with
the abbey built by St. Etheldreda, and at this fair a
famous "fairing" was "St. Audrey's laces." St. Audrey,
or Etheldreda, in the days of her youthful vanity was very
fond of wearing necklaces and jewels. "St. Audrey's
laces" became corrupted into "Tawdry laces"; hence the
adjective has come to be applied to all cheap and showy
pieces of female ornament.

Trade now finds its way by means of other channels
than fairs. Railways and telegrams have changed the
old methods of conducting the commerce of the country.
But, as we have said, many fairs have contrived to survive, and unless they degenerate into a scandal and a
nuisance it is well that they should be continued. Education and the increasing sobriety of the nation may deprive
them of their more objectionable features, and it would be
a pity to prevent the rustic from having some amusements
which do not often fall to his lot, and to forbid him from
enjoying once a year "all the fun of the fair."

CHAPTER XVII

THE DISAPPEARANCE OF OLD DOCUMENTS

THE history of England is enshrined in its ancient documents. Some of it may be read in its stone walls and earthworks. The builders of our churches stamped its story on their stones, and by the shape of arch and design of window, by porch and doorway, tower and buttress you can read the history of the building and tell its age and the dates of its additions and alterations. Inscriptions, monuments, and brasses help to fill in the details; but all would be in vain if we had no documentary evidence, no deeds and charters, registers and wills, to help us to build up the history of each town and monastery, castle and manor. Even after the most careful searches in the Record Office and the British Museum it is very difficult oftentimes to trace a manorial descent. You spend time and labour, eyesight and midnight oil in trying to discover missing links, and very often it is all in vain; the chain remains broken, and you cannot piece it together. Some of us whose fate it is to have to try and solve some of these genealogical problems, and spend hours over a manorial descent, are inclined to envy other writers who fill their pages *currente calamo* and are ignorant of the joys and disappointments of research work.

In the making of the history of England patient research and the examination of documents are, of course, all-important. In the parish chest, in the municipal charters and records, in court rolls, in the muniment-rooms of guilds and city companies, of squire and noble, in the Record Office, Pipe Rolls, Close Rolls, royal letters and papers, etc., the real history of the country is contained. Masses of Rolls and documents of all kinds have in these late years been arranged, printed, and indexed, enabling the historical student to avail himself of vast stores of information which were denied to the historian of an earlier age, or could only be acquired by the expenditure of immense toil.

Nevertheless, we have to deplore the disappearance of large numbers of priceless manuscripts, the value of which was not recognized by their custodians. Owing to the ignorance and carelessness of these keepers of historic documents vast stores have been hopelessly lost or destroyed, and have vanished with much else of the England that is vanishing. We know of a Corporation —that of Abingdon, in Berkshire, the oldest town in the royal county and anciently its most important—which possessed an immense store of municipal archives. These manuscript books would throw light upon the history of the borough ; but in their wisdom the members of the Corporation decided that they should be sold for waste paper ! A few gentlemen were deputed to examine the papers in order to see if anything was worth preserving. They spent a few hours on the task, which would have required months for even a cursory inspection, and much expert knowledge, which these gentlemen did not possess, and reported that there was nothing in the documents of interest or importance, and the books and papers were sold to a dealer. Happily a private gentleman purchased the "waste paper," which remains in his hands, and was not destroyed : but this example only shows the insecurity of much of the material upon which local and municipal history depends.

Court rolls, valuable wills and deeds are often placed by noble owners and squires in the custody of their solicitors. They repose in peace in safes or tin boxes with the name of the client printed on them. Recent legislation has made it possible to prove a title without reference

to all the old deeds. Hence the contents of these boxes
are regarded only as old lumber and of no value. A
change is made in the office. The old family solicitor
dies, and the new man proceeds with the permission of
his clients to burn all these musty papers, which are of
immense value in tracing the history of a manor or of
a family. Some years ago a leading family solicitor
became bankrupt. His office was full of old family deeds
and municipal archives. What happened? A fire was
kindled in the garden, and for a whole fortnight it was
fed with parchment deeds and rolls, many of them of
immense value to the genealogist and the antiquary. It
was all done very speedily, and no one had a chance to
interfere. This is only one instance of what we fear has
taken place in many offices, the speedy disappearance of
documents which can never be replaced.

From the contents of the parish chests, from churchwardens' account-books, we learn much concerning the
economic history of the country, and the methods of the
administration of local and parochial government. As
a rule persons interested in such matters have to content
themselves with the statements of the ecclesiastical law
books on the subject of the repair of churches, the law of
church rates, the duties of churchwardens, and the con-
stitution and power of vestries. And yet there has always
existed a variety of customs and practices which have
stood for ages on their prescriptive usage with many
complications and minute differentiations. These old
account-books and minute-books of the churchwardens
in town and country are a very large but a very perish-
able and rapidly perishing treasury of information on
matters the very remembrance of which is passing away.
Yet little care is taken of these books. An old book is
finished and filled up with entries ; a new book is begun.
No one takes any care of the old book. It is too bulky
for the little iron register safe. A farmer takes charge
of it ; his children tear out pages on which to make their
drawings ; it is torn, mutilated, and forgotten, and the

record perishes. All honour to those who have transcribed these documents with much labour and endless pains and printed them. They will have gained no money for their toil. The public do not show their gratitude to such laborious students by purchasing many copies, but the transcribers know that they have fitted another stone in the Temple of Knowledge, and enabled antiquaries, genealogists, economists, and historical inquirers to find material for their pursuits.

The churchwardens' accounts of St. Mary's, Thame, and some of the most interesting in the kingdom, are being printed in the *Berks, Bucks, and Oxon Archæological Journal.* The originals were nearly lost. Somehow they came into the possession of the Buckinghamshire Archæological Society. The volume was lent to the late Rev. F. Lee, in whose library it remained and could not be recovered. At his death it was sold with his other books, and found its way to the Bodleian Library at Oxford. There it was transcribed by Mr. Patterson Ellis, and then went back to the Buckinghamshire Society after its many wanderings. It dates back to the fifteenth century, and records many curious items of pre-Reformation manners and customs.

From these churchwardens' accounts we learn how our forefathers raised money for the expenses of the church and of the parish. Provision for the poor, mending of roads, the improvement of agriculture by the killing of sparrows, all came within the province of the vestry, as well as the care of the church and churchyard. We learn about such things as "Gatherings" at Hocktide, Mayday, All Hallow-day, Christmas, and Whitsuntide, the men stopping the women on one day and demanding money, while on the next day the women retaliated, and always gained more for the parish fund than those of the opposite sex: Church Ales, the Holy Loaf, Paschal Money, Watching the Sepulchre, the duties of clerks and clergymen, and much else, besides the general principles of local self-government, which the vestrymen carried on until quite recent times. There are few books that provide greater information or more absorbing interest than these wonderful books of accounts. It is a sad pity that so many have vanished.

The parish register books have suffered less than the churchwardens' accounts, but there has been terrible neglect and irreparable loss. Their custody has been frequently committed to ignorant parish clerks, who had no idea of their utility beyond their being occasionally the means of putting a shilling into their pockets for furnishing extracts. Sometimes they were in the care of an incumbent who was forgetful, careless, or negligent. Hence they were indifferently kept, and baptisms, burials, and marriages were not entered as they ought to have been. In one of my own register books an indignant parson writes in the year 1768: "There does not appear any one entry of a Baptism, Marriage, or Burial in the old Register for nine successive years, viz. from the year 1732 till the year 1741, when this Register commences." The fact was that the old parchment book beginning A.D. 1553 was quite full and crowded with names, and the rector never troubled to provide himself with a new one. Fortunately this sad business took place long before our present septuagenarians were born, or there would be much confusion and uncertainty with regard to old-age pensions.

The disastrous period of the Civil War and the Commonwealth caused great confusion and many defects in the registers. Very often the rector was turned out of his parish; the intruding minister, often an ignorant mechanic, cared naught for registers. Registrars were appointed in each parish who could scarcely sign their names, much less enter a baptism. Hence we find very frequent gaps in the books from 1643 to 1660. At Tarporley, Cheshire, there is a break from 1643 to 1648, upon which a sorrowful vicar remarks :—

"This Intermission hapned by reason of the great wars obliterating memorials, wasting fortunes, and slaughtering persons of all sorts."

The Parliamentary soldiers amused themselves by tearing out the leaves in the registers for the years 1604 to the end of 1616 in the parish of Wimpole, Cambridgeshire.

There is a curious note in the register of Tunstall, Kent. There seems to have been a superfluity of members of the family of Pottman in this parish, and the clergyman appears to have been tired of recording their names in his books, and thus resolves :—

> " 1557   Mary Pottman nat. & bapt. 15 Apr.
>   Mary Pottman n. & b. 29 Jan.
>   Mary Pottman sep. 22 Aug.
>   1567
>   From henceforw^d I omitt the Pottmans."

Fire has played havoc with parish registers. The old register of Arborfield, Berkshire, was destroyed by a fire at the rectory. Those at Cottenham, Cambridgeshire, were burnt in a fire which consumed two-thirds of the town in 1676, and many others have shared the same fate. The Spaniards raided the coast of Cornwall in 1595 and burnt the church at Paul, when the registers perished in the conflagration.

Wanton destruction has caused the disappearance of many parish books. There was a parish clerk at Plungar in Leicestershire who combined his ecclesiastical duties with those of a grocer. He found the pages of the parish register very useful for wrapping up his groceries. The episcopal registry of Ely seems to have been plundered at some time of its treasures, as some one purchased a book entitled *Registrum causarum Consistorii Eliensis de Tempore Domini Thome de Arundele Episcopi Eliensis*, a large quarto, written on vellum, containing 162 double pages, which was purchased as waste paper at a grocer's shop at Cambridge together with forty or fifty old books belonging to the registry of Ely. The early registers at Christ Church, Hampshire, were destroyed by a curate's wife who had made kettle-holders of them, and would perhaps have consumed the whole parish archives in this homely fashion, had not the parish clerk, by a timely interference, rescued the remainder. One clergyman, being unable to transcribe certain entries which were required from his registers, cut them out and sent them by post; and an Essex clerk, not having ink and paper at hand for copying out an extract, calmly took out his pocket-knife and cut out two leaves, handing them to the applicant. Sixteen leaves of another old register were cut out by the clerk, who happened to be a tailor, in order to supply himself with measures. Tradesmen seem to have found these books very useful. The marriage register of Hanney, Berkshire, from 1754 to 1760 was lost, but later on discovered in a grocer's shop.

Deplorable has been the fate of these old books, so valuable to the genealogist. Upon the records contained there the possession of much valuable property may depend. The father of the present writer was engaged in proving his title to an estate, and required certificates of all the births, deaths, and marriages that had occurred in the family during a hundred years. All was complete save the record of one marriage. He discovered that his ancestor had eloped with a young lady, and the couple had married in London at a City church. The name of the church where the wedding was said to have taken place was suggested to him, but he discovered that it had been pulled down. However, the old parish clerk was discovered, who had preserved the books ; the entry was found, and all went well and the title to the estate established. How many have failed to obtain their rights and just claims through the gross neglect of the keepers or custodians of parochial documents?

An old register was kept in the drawer of an old table, together with rusty iron and endless rubbish, by a parish clerk who was a poor labouring man. Another was said to be so old and "out of date" and so difficult to read by the parson and his neighbours, that it had been tossed about the church and finally carried off by children and torn to pieces. The leaves of an old parchment register were discovered sewed together as a covering for the tester of a bedstead, and the daughters of a parish clerk, who were lace-makers, cut up the pages of a register for a supply of parchment to make patterns for their lace manufacture. Two Leicestershire registers were rescued, one from the shop of a bookseller, the other from the corner cupboard of a blacksmith, where it had lain perishing and unheard of more than thirty years. The following extract from *Notes and Queries* tells of the sad fate of other books :—

"On visiting the village school of Colton it was discovered that the 'Psalters' of the children were covered with the leaves of the Parish Register ; some of them were recovered, and replaced in the parish chest, but many were totally obliterated and cut away. This discovery led to further investigation, which brought to light a practice of the Parish Clerk and Schoolmaster of the day, who to certain 'goodies' of the village, gave the parchment leaves for hutkins for their knitting pins."

Still greater desecration has taken place. The registers of South Otterington, containing several entries of the great families of Talbot, Herbert, and Falconer, were kept in the cottage of the parish clerk, who used all those preceding the eighteenth century for waste paper, and devoted not a few to the utilitarian employment of singeing a goose. At Appledore the books were lost through having been kept in a public-house for the delectation of its frequenters.

But many parsons have kept their registers with consummate care. The name of the Rev. John Yate, rector of Rodmarton, Gloucestershire, in 1630, should be mentioned as a worthy and careful custodian on account of his quaint directions for the preservation of his registers. He wrote in the volume :—

"If you will have this Book last, bee sure to aire it att the fier or in the Sunne three or foure times a yeare—els it will grow dankish and rott, therefore look to it. It will not be amisse when you finde it dankish to wipe over the

leaves with a dry woollen cloth.   This place is very much
subject to dankishness, therefore I say looke to it."

Sometimes the parsons adorned their books with their
poetical effusions either in Latin or English.   Here are two
examples, the first from Cherry Hinton, Cambridgeshire ;
the second from Ruyton, Salop :—

> Hic puer ætatem, his Vir sponsalia noscat.
> Hic decessorum funera quisque sciat.
>
> No Flatt'ry here, where to be born and die
> Of rich and poor is all the history.
> Enough, if virtue fill'd the space between,
> Prov'd, by the ends of being, to have been.

Bishop Kennet urged his clergy to enter in their registers
not only every christening, wedding, or burial, which
entries have proved some of the best helps for the preserving of history, but also any notable events that may
have occurred in the parish or neighbourhood, such
as "storms and lightning, contagion and mortality,
droughts, scarcity, plenty, longevity, robbery, murders,
or the like casualties.   If such memorable things were
fairly entered, your parish registers would become
chronicles of many strange occurrences that would not
otherwise be known and would be of great use and
service for posterity to know."

The clergy have often acted upon this suggestion.   In
the registers of Cranbrook, Kent, we find a long account
of the great plague that raged there in 1558, with certain
moral reflections on the vice of "drunkeness which
abounded here," on the base characters of the persons
in whose houses the Plague began and ended, on the
vehemence of the infection in "the Inns and Suckling
houses of the town, places of much disorder," and tells
how great dearth followed the Plague "with much wail-
ing and sorrow," and how the judgment of God seemed
but to harden the people in their sin.

The Eastwell register contains copies of the Protesta-
tion of 1642, the Vow and Covenant of 1643, and the
Solemn League and Covenant of the same year, all

signed by sundry parishioners, and of the death of the
last of the Plantagenets, Richard by name, a bricklayer
by trade, in 1550, whom Richard III acknowledged to be
his son on the eve of the battle of Bosworth. At St.
Oswalds, Durham, there is the record of the hanging
and quartering in 1590 of "Duke, Hyll, Hogge and
Holyday, iiij Semynaryes, Papysts, Tretors and Rebels
for their horrible offences." "Burials, 1687 April 17th
Georges Vilaus Lord dooke of bookingham," is the
illiterate description of the Duke who was assassinated
by Felton and buried at Helmsley. It is impossible to
mention all the gleanings from parish registers; each
parish tells its tale, its trades, its belief in witchcraft, its
burials of soldiers killed in war, its stories of persecution,
riot, sudden deaths, amazing virtues, and terrible sins.
The edicts of the laws of England, wise and foolish, are
reflected in these pages, e.g. the enforced burial in
woollen; the relatives of those who desired to be buried
in linen were obliged to pay fifty shillings to the informer
and the same sum to the poor of the parish. The tax on
marriages, births, and burials, levied by the Government
on the estates of gentlemen in 1693, is also recorded in
such entries as the following :—

"1700. Mr. Thomas Cullum buried 27 Dec. As
the said Mr. Cullum was a gentleman, there is 24s.
to be paid for his buriall." The practice of heart-burial is
also frequently demonstrated in our books. Extraordinary
superstitions and strong beliefs, the use of talismans,
amulets, and charms, astrological observations, the black
art, scandals, barbarous punishments, weird customs that
prevailed at man's most important ceremonies, his
baptism, marriage and burial, the binding of apprentice-
ships, obsolete trades, such as that of the person who is
styled "aquavity man" or the "saltpetre man," the
mode of settling quarrels and disputes, duels, sports,
games, brawls, the expenses of supplying a queen's
household, local customs and observances—all these find
a place in these amazing records. In short, there is

scarcely any feature of the social life of our forefathers which is not abundantly set forth in our parish registers. The loss of them would indeed be great and overwhelming.

As we have said, many of them have been lost by fire and other casualties, by neglect and carelessness. The guarding of the safety of those that remain is an anxious problem. Many of us would regret to part with our registers and to allow them to leave the church or town or village wherein they have reposed so long. They are part of the story of the place, and when American ladies and gentlemen come to find traces of their ancestors they love to see these records in the village where their forefathers lived, and to carry away with them a photograph of the church, some ivy from the tower, some flowers from the rectory garden, to preserve in their western homes as memorials of the place whence their family came. It would not be the same thing if they were to be referred to a dusty office in a distant town. Some wise people say that all registers should be sent to London, to the Record Office or the British Museum. That would be an impossibility. The officials of those institutions would tremble at the thought, and the glut of valuable books would make reference a toil that few could undertake. The real solution of the difficulty is that county councils should provide accommodation for all deeds and documents, that all registers should be transcribed, that copies should be deposited in the county council depository, and that the originals should still remain in the parish chest where they have lain for three centuries and a half.

CHAPTER XVIII

OLD CUSTOMS THAT ARE VANISHING

M ANY writers have mourned over the decay of our ancient customs which the restlessness of modern life has effectually killed. New manners are ever pushing out the old, and the lover of antiquity may perhaps be pardoned if he prefers the more ancient modes. The death of the old social customs which added such diversity to the lives of our forefathers tends to render the countryman's life one continuous round of labour unrelieved by pleasant pastime, and if innocent pleasures are not indulged in, the tendency is to seek for gratification in amusements that are not innocent or wholesome.

The causes of the decline and fall of many old customs are not far to seek. Agricultural depression has killed many. The deserted farmsteads no longer echo with the sounds of rural revelry; the cheerful log-fires no longer glow in the farmer's kitchen; the harvest-home song has died away; and "largess" no longer rewards the mummers and the morris-dancers. Moreover, the labourer himself has changed; he has lost his simplicity. His lot is far better than it was half a century ago, and he no longer takes pleasure in the simple joys that delighted his ancestors in days of yore. Railways and cheap excursions have made him despise the old games and pastimes which once pleased his unenlightened soul. The old labourer is dead, and his successor is a very "up-to-date" person, who reads the newspapers and has his ideas upon politics and social questions that would have startled his less cultivated sire. The modern system of

elementary education also has much to do with the decay
of old customs.

Still we have some left. We can only here record a few
that survive. Some years ago I wrote a volume on the
subject, and searched diligently to find existing customs
in the remote corners of old England.[1] My book proved
useful to Sir Benjamin Stone, M.P., the expert photo-
grapher of the House of Commons, who went about with
his camera to many of the places indicated, and by his art
produced permanent presentments of the scenes which
I had tried to describe. He was only just in time, as
doubtless many of these customs will soon pass away.
It is, however, surprising to find how much has been left;
how tenaciously the English race clings to that which
habit and usage have established ; how deeply rooted they
are in the affections of the people. It is really remarkable
that at the present day, in spite of ages of education and
social enlightenment, in spite of centuries of Christian
teaching and practice, we have now amongst us many
customs which owe their origin to pagan beliefs and
the superstitions of our heathen forefathers, and have no
other *raison d'être* for their existence than the wild legends
of Scandinavian mythology.

We have still our Berkshire mummers at Christmas,
who come to us disguised in strange garb and begin their
quaint performance with the doggerel rhymes—

> I am King George, that noble champion bold,
> And with my trusty sword I won ten thousand pounds in gold ;
> 'Twas I that fought the fiery dragon, and brought him to the slaughter,
> And by these means I won the King of Egypt's daughter.[2]

Other counties have their own versions. In Staffordshire
they are known as the " Guisers," in Cornwall as the
" Geese-dancers," in Sussex as the "Tipteerers." Carol-
singers are still with us, but often instead of the old carols
they sing very badly and irreverently modern hymns,

[1] *Old English Customs Extant at the Present Time* (Methuen and Co.).
[2] The book of words is printed in *Old English Customs*, by P. H.
Ditchfield.

though in Cambridgeshire you may still hear "God bless you, merry gentlemen," and the vessel-boxes (a corruption of wassail) are still carried round in Yorkshire. At Christmas Cornish folk eat giblet-pie, and Yorkshiremen enjoy furmenty; and mistletoe and the kissing-bush are still hung in the hall; and in some remote parts of Cornwall children may be seen dancing round painted lighted candles placed in a box of sand. The devil's passing-bell tolls on Christmas Eve from the church tower at Dewsbury, and a muffled peal bewails the slaughter of the children on Holy Innocents' Day. The boar's head is still brought in triumph into the hall of Queen's College. Old women "go a-gooding" or mumping on St. Thomas's Day, and "hoodening" or horse-head mumming is practised at Walmer, and bull-hoodening prevails at Kingscote, in Gloucestershire. The ancient custom of "goodening" still obtains at Braughing, Herts. The *Hertfordshire Mercury* of December 28, 1907, states that on St. Thomas's Day (December 21) certain of the more sturdy widows of the village went round "goodening," and collected £4 14s. 6d., which was equally divided among the eighteen needy widows of the parish. In 1899 the oldest dame who took part in the ceremony was aged ninety-three, while in 1904 a widow "goodened" for the thirtieth year in succession. In the *Herts and Cambs Reporter* for December 23, 1904, is an account of "Gooding Day" at Gamlingay. It appears that in 1665 some almshouses for aged women (widows) were built there by Sir John Jacob, Knight. "On Wednesday last (St. Thomas's Day)," says this journal, "an interesting ceremony was to be seen. The old women were gathered at the central doorway . . . preparatory to a pilgrimage to collect alms at the houses of the leading inhabitants. This old custom, which has been observed for nearly three hundred years, it is safe to say, will not fall into desuetude, for it usually results in each poor widow realising a gold coin." In the north of England first-footing on New Year's Eve is common, and a dark-complexioned person is esteemed as a herald of good fortune. Wassailing exists in Lancashire, and the apple-wassailing has not quite died out on Twelfth Night. Plough Monday is still observed in Cambridgeshire, and the "plough-bullocks" drag around the parishes their ploughs and perform a weird play. The Haxey hood is still thrown at that place in Lincolnshire on the Feast of the Epiphany, and valentines are not quite forgotten by rural lovers.

Shrovetide is associated with pancakes. The pancake bell is still rung in many places, and for some occult reason it is the season for some wild football games in the streets and lanes of several towns and villages. At St. Ives on the Monday there is a grand hurling match, which resembles a Rugby football contest without the kicking of the ball, which is about the size of a cricket-ball, made of cork or light wood. At Ashbourne on Shrove-Tuesday thousands join in the game, the origin of which is lost in the mists of antiquity. As the old church clock strikes two a little speech is made, the National Anthem sung, and then some popular devotee of the game is hoisted on the shoulders of excited players and throws up the ball. "She's up," is the cry, and then the wild contest begins, which lasts often till night-fall. Several efforts have been made to stop the game, and even the judge of the Court of Queen's Bench had to decide whether it was legal to play the game in the streets. In spite of some opposition it still flourishes, and is likely to do so for many a long year. Sedgefield, Chester-le-Street, Alnwick, Dorking also have their famous football fights, which differ much from an ordinary league match. In the latter thousands look on while twenty-two men show their skill. In these old games all who wish take part in them, all are keen champions and know nothing of professionalism.

"Ycleping," or, as it is now called, clipping churches, is another Shrovetide custom, when the children join hands round the church and walk round it. It has just been revived at Painswick, in the Cotswolds, where after being performed for many hundred years it was discontinued by the late vicar. On the patron saint's day (St. Mary's) the children join hands in a ring round the church and circle round the building singing. It is the old Saxon custom of "ycleping," or naming the church on the anniversary of its original dedication.

Simnels on Mothering Sunday still exist, reminding us of Herrick's lines :—

> I'll to thee a Simnel bring,
> 'Gainst thou goes a mothering ;
> So that when she blesseth thee
> Half the blessing thou'lt give me.

Palm Sunday brings some curious customs. At Roundway Hill, and at Martinsall, near Marlborough, the people bear "palms," or branches of willow and hazel, and the boys play a curious game of knocking a ball with hockey-sticks up the hill ; and in Buckinghamshire it is called Fig Sunday, and also in Hertfordshire. Hertford, Kempton, Edlesborough, Dunstable are homes of the custom, nor is the practice of eating figs and fig-pies unknown in Bedfordshire, Northamptonshire, Oxfordshire, Wilts, and North Wales. Possibly the custom is connected with the withering of the barren fig-tree.

Good Friday brings hot-cross-buns with the well-known rhyme. Skipping on that day at Brighton is, I expect, now extinct. Sussex boys play marbles, Guildford folk climb St. Martha's Hill, and poor widows pick up sixpences from a tomb in the churchyard of St. Bartholomew the Great, London, on the same Holy Day.

Easter brings its Pace eggs, symbols of the Resurrection, and Yorkshire children roll them against one another in fields and gardens. The Biddenham cakes are distributed, and the Hallaton hare-scramble and bottle-kicking provide a rough scramble and a curious festival for Easter Monday. On St. Mark's Day the ghosts of all who will die during the year in the villages of Yorkshire pass at midnight before the waiting people, and

Hock-tide brings its quaint diversions to the little Berk-shire town of Hungerford.

The diversions of May Day are too numerous to be chronicled here, and I must refer the reader to my book for a full description of the sports that usher in the spring ; but we must not forget the remarkable Furry Dance at Helston on May 8th, and the beating of the bounds of many a township during Rogation Week. Our boys still wear oak-leaves on Royal Oak Day, and the Durham Cathedral choir sing anthems on the top of the tower in memory of the battle of Neville's Cross, fought so long ago as the year 1346.

Club-feasts and morris-dancers delight the rustics at Whitsuntide, and the wakes are well kept up in the north of England, and rush-beating at Ambleside, and hay-strewing customs in Leicestershire. The horn dance at Abbot Bromley is a remarkable survival. The fires on Midsummer Eve are still lighted in a few places in Wales, but are fast dying out. Ratby, in Leicestershire, is a home of old customs, and has an annual feast, when the toast of the immortal memory of John of Gaunt is drunk with due solemnity. Harvest customs were for-merly very numerous, but are fast dying out before the reaping-machines and agricultural depression. The " kern-baby " has been dead some years.

Bonfire night and the commemoration of the discovery of Gunpowder Plot and the burning of " guys " are still kept up merrily, but few know the origin of the festivities or concern themselves about it. Soul cakes and souling still linger on in Cheshire, and cattering and clemmening on the feasts of St. Catherine and St. Clement are still observed in East Sussex.

Very remarkable are the local customs which linger on in some of our towns and villages and are not confined to any special day in the year. Thus, at Abbots Ann, near Andover, the good people hang up effigies of arms and hands in memory of girls who died unmarried, and gloves and garlands of roses are sometimes hung for the same

purpose. The Dunmow Flitch is a well-known matri-
monial prize for happy couples who have never quarrelled
during the first year of their wedded life; while a Skim-
merton expresses popular indignation against quarrelsome
or licentious husbands and wives.

Many folk-customs linger around wells and springs,
the haunts of nymphs and sylvan deities who must be
propitiated by votive offerings and are revengeful when
neglected. Pins, nails, and rags are still offered, and the
custom of "well-dressing," shorn of its pagan associations and adapted to Christian usage, exists in all its
glory at Tissington, Youlgrave, Derby, and several other
places.

The three great events of human life—birth, marriage,
and death—have naturally drawn around them some of
the most curious beliefs. These are too numerous to be
recorded here, and I must again refer the curious reader
to my book on old-time customs. We should like to
dwell upon the most remarkable of the customs that
prevail in the City of London, in the halls of the Livery
Companies, as well as in some of the ancient boroughs
of England, but this record would require too large a
space. Bell-ringing customs attract attention. The curfew-
bell still rings in many towers; the harvest-bell, the
gleaning-bell, the pancake-bell, the "spur-peal," the
eight-hours' bell, and sundry others send out their
pleasing notice to the world. At Aldermaston land is
let by means of a lighted candle. A pin is placed through
the candle, and the last bid that is made before that pin
drops out is the occupier of the land for a year. The
Church Acre at Chedzoy is let in a similar manner, and
also at Todworth, Warton, and other places. Wiping
the shoes of those who visit a market for the first time is
practised at Brixham, and after that little ceremony they
have to "pay their footing." At St. Ives raffling for
Bibles continues, according to the will of Dr. Wilde in
1675, and in church twelve children cast dice for six
Bibles. Court, Bar, and Parliament have each their

peculiar customs which it would be interesting to note, if space permitted ; and we should like to record the curious bequests, doles, and charities which display the eccentricities of human nature and the strange tenures of land which have now fallen into disuse.

It is to be hoped that those who are in a position to preserve any existing custom in their own neighbourhood will do their utmost to prevent its decay. Popular customs are a heritage which has been bequeathed to us from a remote past, and it is our duty to hand down that heritage to future generations of English folk.

CHAPTER XIX

THE VANISHING OF ENGLISH SCENERY
AND NATURAL BEAUTY

NOT the least distressing of the losses which we have to mourn is the damage that has been done to the beauty of our English landscapes and the destruction of many scenes of sylvan loveliness. The population of our large towns continues to increase owing to the insensate folly that causes the rural exodus. People imagine that the streets of towns are paved with gold, and forsake the green fields for a crowded slum, and after many vicissitudes and much hardship wish themselves back again in their once despised village home. I was lecturing to a crowd of East End Londoners at Toynbee Hall on village life in ancient and modern times, and showed them views of the old village street, the cottages, manor-houses, water-mills, and all the charms of rural England, and after the lecture I talked with many of the men who remembered their country homes which they had left in the days of their youth, and they all wished to go back there again, if only they could find work and had not lost the power of doing it. But the rural exodus continues. Towns increase rapidly, and cottages have to be found for these teeming multitudes. Many a rural glade and stretch of woodland have to be sacrificed, and soon streets are formed and rows of unsightly cottages spring up like magic, with walls terribly thin, that can scarcely stop the keenness of the wintry blasts, so thin that each neighbour can hear your conversation, and if a man has a few words with his wife all the inhabitants of the row can hear him.

Garden cities have arisen as a remedy for this evil, carefully planned dwelling-places wherein some thought is given to beauty and picturesque surroundings, to plots for gardens, and to the comfort of the fortunate citizens. But some garden cities are garden only in name. Cheap villas surrounded by unsightly fields that have been spoilt and robbed of all beauty, with here and there unsightly heaps of rubbish and refuse, only delude themselves and other people by calling themselves garden cities. Too often there is no attempt at beauty. Cheapness and speedy construction are all that their makers strive for.

These growing cities, ever increasing, ever enclosing fresh victims in their hideous maw, work other ills. They require much food, and they need water. Water must be found and conveyed to them. This has been no easy task for many corporations. For many years the city of Liverpool drew its supply from Rivington, a range of hills near Bolton-le-Moors, where there were lakes and where they could construct others. Little harm was done there; but the city grew and the supply was insufficient. Other sources had to be found and tapped. They found one in Wales. Their eyes fell on the Lake Vyrnwy, and believed that they found what they sought. But that, too, could not supply the millions of gallons that Liverpool needed. They found that the whole vale of Llanwddyn must be embraced. A gigantic dam must be made at the lower end of the valley, and the whole vale converted into one great lake. But there were villages in the vale, rural homes and habitations, churches and chapels, and over five hundred people who lived therein and must be turned out. And now the whole valley is a lake. Homes and churches lie beneath the waves, and the graves of the "women that sleep," of the rude forefathers of the hamlet, of bairns and dear ones are overwhelmed by the pitiless waters. It is all very deplorable.

And now it seems that the same thing must take place again : but this time it is an English valley that is concerned, and the people are the country folk of North Hampshire. There is a beautiful valley not far from Kingsclere and Newbury, surrounded by lovely hills covered with woodland. In this valley in a quiet little village appropriately called Woodlands, formed about half a century ago out of the large parish of Kingsclere, there is a little hamlet named Ashford Hill, the modern church of St. Paul, Woodlands, pretty cottages with pleasant gardens, a village inn, and a dissenting chapel. The churchyard is full of graves, and a cemetery has been lately added. This pretty valley with its homes and church and chapel is a doomed valley. In a few years time if a former resident returns home from Australia or America to his native village he will find his old cottage gone from the light of the sun and buried beneath the still waters of a huge lake. It is almost certain that such will be the case with this secluded rural scene. The eyes of Londoners have turned upon the doomed valley. They need water, and water must somehow be procured. The great city has no pity. The church and the village will have to be removed. It is all very sad. As a writer in a London paper says : " Under the best of conditions it is impossible to think of such an eviction without sympathy for the grief that it must surely cause to some. The younger residents may contemplate it cheerfully enough ; but for the elder folk, who have spent lives of sunshine and shade, toil, sorrow, joy, in this peaceful vale, it must needs be that the removal will bring a regret not to be lightly uttered in words. The soul of man clings to the localities that he has known and loved ; perhaps, as in Wales, there will be some broken hearts when the water flows in upon the scenes where men and women have met and loved and wedded, where children have been born, where the beloved dead have been laid to rest."

The old forests are not safe. The Act of 1851 caused the destruction of miles of beautiful landscape. Peacock, in his story of *Gryll Grange*, makes the announcement that the New Forest is now enclosed, and that he proposes never to visit it again. Twenty-five years of ruthless devastation followed the passing of that Act. The deer disappeared. Stretches of open beechwood and green lawns broken by thickets of ancient thorn and holly vanished under the official axe. Woods and lawns were cleared and replaced by miles and miles of rectangular fir plantations. The Act of 1876 with regard to forest land came late, but it, happily, saved some spots of sylvan beauty. Under the Act of 1851 all that was ancient and delightful to the eye would have been levelled, or hidden in fir-wood. The later Act stopped this wholesale destruction. We have still some lofty woods, still some scenery that shows how England looked when it was a land of blowing woodland. The New Forest is maimed and scarred, but what is left is precious and unique. It is primeval forest land, nearly all that remains in the country. Are these treasures safe? Under the Act of 1876 managers are told to consider beauty as well as profit, and to abstain from destroying ancient trees; but much is left to the decision and to the judgment of officials, and they are not always to be depended on.

After having been threatened with demolition for a number of years, the famous Winchmore Hill Woods are at last to be hewn down and the land is to be built upon. These woods, which it was Hood's and Charles Lamb's delight to stroll in, have become the property of a syndicate, which will issue a prospectus shortly, and many of the fine old oaks, beeches, and elms already bear the splash of white which marks them for the axe. The woods have been one of the greatest attractions in the neighbourhood, and public opinion is strongly against the demolition.

One of the greatest services which the National Trust is doing for the country is the preserving of the natural beauties of our English scenery. It acquires, through the generosity of its supporters, special tracts of lovely country, and says to the speculative builder " Avaunt ! " It maintains the landscape for the benefit of the public. People can always go there and enjoy the scenery, and townsfolk can fill their lungs with fresh air, and children play on the greensward. These oases afford sanctuary to birds and beasts and butterflies, and are of immense value to botanists and entomologists. Several properties in the Lake District have come under the ægis of the Trust. Seven hundred and fifty acres around Ullswater have been purchased, including Gowbarrow Fell and Aira Force. By this, visitors to the English lakes can have unrestrained access over the heights of Gowbarrow Fell, through the glen of Aira and along a mile of Ullswater shore, and obtain some of the loveliest views in the district. It is possible to trespass in the region of the lakes. It is possible to wander over hills and through dales, but private owners do not like trespassers, and it is not pleasant to be turned back by some officious servant. Moreover, it needs much impudence and daring to traverse without leave another man's land, though it be bare and barren as a northern hill. The Trust invites you to come, and you are at peace, and know that no man will stop you if you walk over its preserves. Moreover, it holds a delectable bit of country on Lake Derwentwater, known as the Brandlehow Park Estate. It extends for about a mile along the shore of the lake and reaches up the fell-side to the unenclosed common on Catbels. It is a lovely bit of woodland scenery. Below the lake glistens in the sunlight and far away the giant hills Blencatha, Skiddaw, and Borrowdale rear their heads. It cost the Trust £7000, but no one would deem the money ill-spent. Almost the last remnant of the primeval fenland of East Anglia, called Wicken Fen, has been acquired by the Trust, and also Burwell Fen, the home of many rare insects and plants. Near London we see many bits of picturesque land that have been rescued, where the teeming population of the great city can find rest and recreation. Thus at Hindhead, where it has been said villas seem to have broken out upon the once majestic hill like a red skin eruption, the Hindhead Preservation Committee and the Trust have secured 750 acres of common land on the summit of the hill, including the Devil's Punch Bowl, a bright oasis amid the dreary desert of villas. Moreover, the Trust is waging a battle with the District Council of Hambledon in order to prevent the Hindhead Commons from being disfigured by digging for stone for mending roads, causing unsightliness and the sad disfiguring of the commons. May it succeed in its praiseworthy endeavour. At Toy's Hill, on a Kentish hillside, overlooking the Weald, some valuable land has been acquired, and part of Wandle Park, Wimbledon, containing the Merton Mill Pond and its banks, adjoining the Recreation Ground recently provided by the Wimbledon Corporation, is now in the possession of the Trust. It is intended for the quiet enjoyment of rustic scenery by the people who live in the densely populated area of mean streets of Merton and Morden, and not for the lovers of the more strenuous forms of recreation. Ide Hill and Crockham Hill, the properties of the Trust, can easily be reached by the dwellers in London streets.

We may journey in several directions and find traces of the good work of the Trust. At Barmouth a beautiful cliff known as Dinas-o-lea, Llanlleiana Head, Anglesey, the fifteen acres of cliff land at Tintagel, called Barras Head, looking on to the magnificent pile of rocks on which stand the ruins of King Arthur's Castle, and the summit of Kymin, near Monmouth, whence you can see a charming view of the Wye Valley, are all owned and protected by the Trust. Every one knows the curious appearance of Sarsen stones, often called Grey Wethers from their likeness to a flock of sheep lying down amidst the long grass of a Berkshire or Wiltshire down. These stones are often useful for building purposes and for road-mending. There is a fine collection of these curious stones, which were used in prehistoric times for building Stonehenge, at Pickle Dean and Lockeridge Dean. These are adjacent to high roads and would soon have fallen a prey to the road surveyor or local builder. Hence the authorities of this Trust stepped in ; they secured for the nation these characteristic examples of a unique geological phenomenon, and preserved for all time a curious and picturesque feature of the country traversed by the old Bath Road. All that the Trust requires is "more force to its elbow," increased funds for the preservation of the natural beauty of our English scenery, and the increased appreciation on the part of the public and of the owners of unspoilt rural scenes to extend its good work throughout the counties of England.

A curious feature of vanished or vanishing England is the decay of our canals, which here and there with their unused locks, broken towpaths, and stagnant waters covered with weeds form a pathetic and melancholy part of the landscape. If you look at the map of England you will see, besides the blue curvings that mark the rivers, other threads of blue that show the canals. Much was expected of them. They were built just before the railway era. The whole country was covered by a network of canals. Millions were spent upon their construction. For a brief space they were prosperous. Some places, like our Berkshire Newbury, became the centres of considerable traffic and had little harbours filled with barges. Barge-building was a profitable industry. Flyboats sped along the surface of the canals conveying passengers to towns or watering-places, and the company were very bright and enjoyed themselves. But all are dead highways now, strangled by steam and by the railways. The promoters of canals opposed the railways with might and main, and tried to protect their properties. Hence the railways were obliged to buy them up, and then left them lone and neglected. The change was tragic. You can, even now, travel all over the country by the means of these silent waterways.   You start from London along the Regent's Canal, which joins the Grand Junction Canal, and this spreads forth northwards and joins other canals that ramify to the Wash, to Manchester and Liverpool and Leeds.   You can go to every great town in England as far as York if you have patience and endless time.   There are four thousand miles of canals in England.   They were not well constructed ; we built them just as we do many other things, without any regular system, with no uniform depth or width or carrying capacity, or size of locks or height of bridges. Canals bearing barges of forty tons connect with those capable of bearing ninety tons.   And now most of them are derelict, with dilapidated banks, foul bottoms, and shallow horse haulage.   The bargemen have taken to other callings, but occasionally you may see a barge looking gay and bright drawn by an unconcerned horse on the towpath, with a man lazily smoking his pipe at the helm and his family of water gipsies, who pass an open-air, nomadic existence, tranquil, and entirely innocent of schooling.   He is a survival of an almost vanished race which the railways have caused to disappear.

Much destruction of beautiful scenery is, alas! inevitable.   Trade and commerce, mills and factories, must work their wicked will on the landscapes of our country. Mr. Ruskin's experiment on the painting of Turner, quoted in our opening chapter, finds its realisation in many places.   There was a time, I suppose, when the Mersey was a pure river that laved the banks carpeted with foliage and primroses on which the old Collegiate Church of Manchester reared its tower.   It is now, and has been for years, an inky-black stream or drain running between stone walls, where it does not hide its foul waters for very shame beneath an arched culvert.   There was a time when many a Yorkshire village basked in the sunlight.   Now they are great overgrown towns usually enveloped in black smoke.   The only day when you can

see the few surviving beauties of a northern manufactur-
ing town or village is Sunday, when the tall factory
chimneys cease to vomit their clouds of smoke which kills
the trees, or covers the struggling leaves with black soot.
We pay dearly for our commercial progress in this
sacrifice of Nature's beauties.

CHAPTER XX

CONCLUSION

WHATEVER method can be devised for the prevention of the vanishing of England's chief characteristics are worthy of consideration. First there must be the continued education of the English people in the appreciation of ancient buildings and other relics of antiquity. We must learn to love them, or we shall not care to preserve them. An ignorant squire or foolish landowner may destroy in a day some priceless object of antiquity which can never be replaced. Too often it is the agent who is to blame. Squires are very much in the hands of their agents, and leave much to them to decide and carry out. When consulted they do not take the trouble to inspect the threatened building, and merely confirm the suggestions of the agents. Estate agents, above all people, need education in order that the destruction of much that is precious may be averted.

The Government has done well in appointing commissions for England, Scotland, and Wales to inquire into and report on the condition of ancient monuments, but we lag behind many other countries in the task of protecting and preserving the memorials of the past.

In France national monuments of historic or artistic interest are scheduled under the direction of the Minister of Public Instruction and Fine Arts. In cases in which a monument is owned by a private individual, it usually may not be scheduled without the consent of the owner, but if his consent is withheld the State Minister is empowered to purchase compulsorily. No monument so scheduled may be destroyed or subjected to works of restoration, repair, or alteration without the consent of the Minister, nor may new buildings be annexed to it without permission from the same quarter. Generally speaking, the Minister is advised by a commission of historical monuments, consisting of leading officials connected with fine arts, public buildings, and museums. Such a commission has existed since 1837, and very considerable sums of public money have been set apart to enable it to carry on its work. In 1879 a classification of some 2500 national monuments was made, and this classification has been adopted in the present law. It includes megalithic remains, classical remains, and medieval, Renaissance, and modern buildings and ruins.[1]

We do not suggest that in England we should imitate the very drastic restorations to which some of the French abbeys and historic buildings are subjected. The authorities have erred greatly in destroying so much original work and their restorations, as in the case of Mont St. Michel, have been practically a rebuilding.

The Belgian people appear to have realized for a very long time the importance of preserving their historic and artistic treasures. By a royal decree of 1824 bodies in charge of church temporalities are reminded that they are managers merely, and while they are urged to undertake in good time the simple repairs that are needed for the preservation of the buildings in their charge, they are strictly forbidden to demolish any ecclesiastical building without authority from the Ministry which deals with the subject of the fine arts. By the same decree they are likewise forbidden to alienate works of art or historical monuments placed in churches. Nine years later, in 1835, in view of the importance of assuring the preservation of all national monuments remarkable for their antiquity, their association, or their artistic value, another

---

[1] A paper read by Mr. Nigel Bond, Secretary of the National Trust, at a meeting of the Dorset Natural History and Antiquarian Field Club, to which paper the writer is indebted for the subsequent account of the proceedings of foreign governments with regard to the preservation of their ancient monuments.

decree was issued constituting a Royal Commission for the purpose of advising as to the repairs required by such monuments. Nearly 200,000 francs are annually voted for expenditure for these purposes. The strict application of these precautionary measures has allowed a number of monuments of the highest interest in their relation to art and archæology to be protected and defended, but it does not appear that the Government controls in any way those monuments which are in the hands of private persons.[1]

In Holland public money to the extent of five or six thousand pounds a year is spent on preserving and maintaining national monuments and buildings of antiquarian and architectural interest. In Germany steps are being taken which we might follow with advantage in this country, to control and limit the disfigurement of landscapes by advertisement hoardings.

A passage from the ministerial order of 1884 with reference to the restoration of churches may be justly quoted :—

"If the restoration of a public building is to be completely successful, it is absolutely essential that the person who directs it should combine with an enlightened æsthetic sense an artistic capacity in a high degree, and, moreover, be deeply imbued with feelings of veneration for all that has come down to us from ancient times. If a restoration is carried out without any real comprehension of the laws of architecture, the result can only be a production of common and dreary artificiality, recognizable perhaps as belonging to one of the architectural styles, but wanting the stamp of true art, and, therefore, incapable of awakening the enthusiasm of the spectator."

And again :—

"In consequence of the removal or disfigurement of monuments which have been erected during the course of centuries—monuments which served, as it were, as documents of the historical development of past periods of culture, which have, moreover, a double interest and value if left undisturbed on the spot where they were

[1] *Ibid.*

originally erected—the sympathy of congregations with the history of their church is diminished, and, a still more lamentable consequence, a number of objects of priceless artistic value destroyed or squandered, whereby the property of the church suffers a serious loss."

How much richer might we be here in England if only our central authorities had in the past circulated these admirable doctrines !

Very wisely has the Danish Government prohibited the removal of stones from monuments of historic interest for utilitarian purposes, such as is causing the rapid disappearance of the remains on Dartmoor in this country ; and the Greeks have stringent regulations to ensure the preservation of antiquities, which are regarded as national property, and may on no account be damaged either by owner or lessee. It has actually been found necessary to forbid the construction of limekilns nearer than two miles from any ancient ruins, in order to remove the temptation for the filching of stones. In Italy there are stringent laws for the protection of historical and ancient monuments. Road-mending is a cause of much destruction of antiquarian objects in all countries, even in Italy, where the law has been invoked to protect ancient monuments from the highway authorities.

We need not record the legal enactments of other Governments, so admirably summarized by Mr. Bond in his paper read before the Dorset Natural History and Antiquarian Field Club. We see what other countries much poorer than our own are doing to protect their national treasures, and though the English Government has been slow in realizing the importance of the ancient monuments of this country, we believe that it is inclined to move in the right direction, and to do its utmost to preserve those that have hitherto escaped the attacks of the iconoclasts, and the heedlessness and stupidity of the Gallios "who care for none of these things."

When an old building is hopelessly dilapidated, what methods can be devised for its restoration and preservation? To pull it down and rebuild it is to destroy its historical associations and to make it practically a new structure. Happily science has recently discovered a new method for the preserving of these old buildings without destroying them, and this good angel is the grouting machine, the invention of Mr. James Great-head, which has been the means of preventing much of vanishing England. Grout, we understand, is a mixture of cement, sand, and water, and the process of grouting was probably not unknown to the Romans. But the grouting machine is a modern invention, and it has only been applied to ancient buildings during the last six or seven years.[1] It is unnecessary to describe its mechanism, but its admirable results may be summarized. Suppose an old building shows alarming cracks. By compressed air you blow out the old decayed mortar, and then damp-ing the masonry by the injection of water, you insert the nozzle of the machine and force the grout into the cracks and cavities, and soon the whole mass of decayed masonry is cemented together and is as sound as ever it was. This method has been successfully applied to Winchester Cathedral, the old walls of Chester, and to various churches and towers. It in no way destroys the charac-teristics and features of the building, the weatherworn surfaces of the old stones, their cracks and deformations, and even the moss and lichen which time has planted on them need not be disturbed. Pointing is of no avail to preserve a building, as it only enters an inch or two in depth. Underpinning is dangerous if the building be badly cracked, and may cause collapse. But if you shore the structure with timber, and then weld its stones to-gether by applying the grouting machine, you turn the whole mass of masonry into a monolith, and can then strengthen the foundations in any way that may be found necessary. The following story of the saving of an old church, as told by Mr. Fox, proclaims the merits of this

[1] A full account of this useful invention was given in the *Times* Engineer-ing Supplement, March 18th, 1908, by Mr. Francis Fox, M.Inst.C.E.

scientific invention better than any description can possibly do :—

"The ancient church of Corhampton, near Bishops Waltham, in Hampshire, is an instance. This Saxon church, 1300 years old, was in a sadly dilapidated condition. In the west gable there were large cracks, one from the ridge to the ground, another nearer the side wall, both wide enough for a man's arm to enter ; whilst at the northwest angle the Saxon work threatened to fall bodily off. The mortar of the walls had perished through age, and the ivy had penetrated into the interior of the church in every direction. It would have been unsafe to attempt any examination of the foundations for fear of bringing down the whole fabric; consequently the grouting machine was applied all over the building. The grout escaped at every point, and it occupied the attention of the masons both inside and outside to stop it promptly by plastering clay on to the openings from which it was running.

"After the operation had been completed and the clay was removed, the interior was found to be completely filled with cement set very hard ; and sufficient depth having been left for fixing the flint work outside and tiling inside, the result was that no trace of the crack was visible, and the walls were stronger and better than they had ever been before. Subsequent steps were then taken to examine and, where necessary, to underpin the walls, and the church is saved, as the vicar, the Rev. H. Churton, said, ' all without moving one of the Saxon " long and short " stones.' "

In our chapter on the delightful and picturesque old bridges that form such beautiful features of our English landscapes, we deplored the destruction now going on owing to the heavy traction-engines which some of them have to bear and the rush and vibration of motor-cars which cause the decay of the mortar and injure their stability. Many of these old bridges, once only wide enough for pack-horses to cross, then widened for the accommodation of coaches, beautiful and graceful in every way, across which Cavaliers rode to fight the Roundheads, and were alive with traffic in the old coaching days, have been pulled down and replaced by the

hideous iron-girder arrangements which now disfigure so
many of our streams and rivers. In future, owing to this
wonderful invention of the grouting machine, these old
bridges can be saved and made strong enough to last
another five hundred years. Mr. Fox tells us that an
old Westmoreland bridge in a very bad condition has
been so preserved, and that the celebrated " Auld Brig
o' Ayr " has been saved from destruction by this means.
A wider knowledge of the beneficial effects of this wonderful machine would be of invaluable service to the country,
and prevent the passing away of much that in these pages
we have mourned. By this means we may be able to
preserve our old and decaying buildings for many centuries, and hand down to posterity what Ruskin called
the great entail of beauty bequeathed to us.

Vanishing England has a sad and melancholy sound.
Nevertheless, the examples we have given of the historic
buildings, and the beauties of our towns and villages,
prove that all has not yet disappeared which appeals to
the heart and intellect of the educated Englishman. And
oftentimes the poor and unlearned appreciate the relics
that remain with quite as much keenness as their richer
neighbours. A world without beauty is a world without
hope. To check vandalism, to stay the hand of the
iconoclast and destroyer, to prevent the invasion and
conquest of the beauties bequeathed to us by our forefathers by the reckless and ever-engrossing commercial
and utilitarian spirit of the age, are some of the objects
of our book, which may be useful in helping to preserve
some of the links that connect our own times with the
England of the past, and in increasing the appreciation
of the treasures that remain by the Englishmen of
to-day.

INDEX